Joint Workshop on Bibliometric-enhanced Information Retrieval and Natural Language Processing for Digital Libraries (BIRNDL 2016)

Held at Joint Conference on Digital Libraries (JCDL 2016)

New Brunswick, New Jersey, USA
23 June 2016

Editors:

Philipp Mayr   **Guillaume Cabanac**
Ingo Frommholz   **Dietmar Wolfram**

ISBN: 978-1-5108-2511-6

TABLE OF CONTENTS

Editorial for the Joint Workshop on Bibliometric-enhanced Information Retrieval and Natural Language Processing for Digital Libraries (BIRNDL) at JCDL 2016

Philipp Mayr[1], Ingo Frommholz[2], Guillaume Cabanac[3], and Dietmar Wolfram[4]

[1] GESIS - Leibniz-Institute for the Social Sciences, Cologne, Germany,
philipp.mayr@gesis.org
[2] Institute for Research in Applicable Computing, University of Bedfordshire,
Luton, UK,
ingo.frommholz@beds.ac.uk
[3] University of Toulouse, Computer Science Department, IRIT UMR 5505, France
guillaume.cabanac@univ-tlse3.fr
[4] School of Information Studies, University of Wisconsin-Milwaukee, USA
dwolfram@uwm.edu

1 Introduction

After the success of two parent workshops series – the 1st NLPIR4DL workshop in 2009, and the series of three Bibliometric-enhanced Information Retrieval (BIR) workshops in 2014, 2015 and 2016 – BIRNDL[5] at JCDL 2016 [1] will investigate how natural language processing, information retrieval, scientometric and recommendation techniques can advance the state-of-the-art in scholarly document understanding, analysis and retrieval at scale. Researchers are in need of assistive technologies to track developments in an area, identify the approaches used to solve a research problem over time and summarize research trends. Digital libraries require semantic search, question-answering as well as automated recommendation and reviewing systems to manage and retrieve answers from scholarly databases. Full document text analysis can help to design semantic search, translation and summarization systems; citation and social network analyses can help digital libraries to visualize scientific trends, bibliometrics and relationships and influences of works and authors. These approaches can be supplemented with the metadata supplied by digital libraries, such as usage data.

This workshop will be relevant to scholars in several fields of computer science, information science and computational linguistics; it will also be of importance for all stakeholders in the publication pipeline: implementers, publishers and policymakers – with this workshop we hope to bring a number of these contributors together. Today's publishers continue to seek new ways to be relevant to their consumers, in disseminating the right published works to their audience.

---

[5] http://wing.comp.nus.edu.sg/birndl-jcdl2016/

Formal citation metrics are increasingly a factor in decision-making by universities and funding bodies worldwide, making the need for research in such topics more pressing.

The BIRNDL event was split into two parts: the regular research paper track and the CL-SciSumm Shared Task system track.

2 Overview of the papers

The workshop featured one keynote talk, three paper sessions and one poster and demo interactive session. The BIRNDL organizers have accepted 5 long and 4 short papers for presentation in the research paper track. The CL-SciSumm organizers have accepted 9 system papers in the CL-SciSumm track. All papers in both tracks are included in the proceedings. The following briefly outlines the keynote and three paper sessions. The system papers in the CL-SciSumm track are outline in an overview paper [2].

2.1 Keynote

Dietmar Wolfram provided the keynote address on "Bibliometrics, Information Retrieval and Natural Language Processing: Natural Synergies to Support Digital Library Research"[3]. Until recently, methods developed for IR and bibliometrics that can be mutually beneficial have not been widely explored. This is changing as evidenced by recent themed meetings that have brought together researchers with interests that bridge both areas. Similarly, applications of language-based methods have provided new tools for research in bibliometrics and IR. The presenter discussed examples of the synergies that exist at the intersections of these three areas, not only for IR system design and evaluation, but also to provide insights into the structure of disciplines and their research communities.

2.2 Session 1

In their article "Multiple In-text Reference Phenomenon", Bertin and Atanassova studied the distribution of multiple in-text references (MIR), which are based on sentences with more than one reference [4]. A corpus of 80,000 PLOS papers was used for the analysis and references were counted based on the publications' IMRaD structure. The results revealed, for instance, that 41% of sentences with citations contain MIRs, with more than half of them in the introduction. Potential applications of this study comprised works on clustering, co-citation networks and summarization.

Citations to retracted paper were the focus of the contribution "Post Retraction Citations in Context" by Halevi and Bar-Ilan [5]. Citations to retracted articles might put the credibility of scientific work in jeopardy, hence it is a field worth studying. The authors discuss 5 case studies of retracted papers and the negative, positive and neutral citations they received after retraction. The authors expressed their concern about the fact that retracted articles still attract citations, and provide some recommendation for publishers.

In his paper "Incorporating Satellite Documents into Co-citation Networks for Scientific Paper Searches", Masaki Eto examined the use of enlarged co-citation networks to improve IR search performance for documents from the Open Access Subset of PubMed Central [6]. Satellite documents to expand the network of linkages beyond direct co-citations were identified based on search terms appearing in documents co-cited with a seed document. Results of the study revealed that the proposed method provided better search performance than a baseline approach that did not incorporate the enlarged network.

To master the huge amount of scientific literature produced nowadays and make sense of the rich pool of knowledge they provide, Ronzano et *al.* introduced the Scientific Knowledge Miner project [7]. Based on a previous text mining project, SKM aims at extending the existing Dr. Inventor Scientific Text Mining Framework, and offers services like summarization and citation recommendation.

2.3   Session 2

Ha Jin Kim, Juyoung An, Yoo Kyung Jeong and Min Song presented the results of their research on "Exploring the Leading Authors and Journals in Major Topics by Citation Sentences and Topic Modeling" [8]. The authors employed an Author-Journal-Topic (AJT) model to identify leading journals and authors in the area of Oncology along with major topics that are shared among researchers. A key finding was that influential authors and journals identified using topic modeling did not necessarily correspond to those identified using citation-based measures. The authors concluded that the AJT model may be used to identify latent meaning in citation sentences.

Aravind Sesagiri Raamkumar, Schubert Foo, and Natalie Pang tackled a compelling question every scientist wonders while writing: "What papers should I cite from my reading list? User evaluation of a manuscript preparatory assistive task" [9]. They introduced techniques for shortlisting papers from a personal bibliography and discussed their effectiveness based on user evaluations. A panel of 116 users — balanced between students and staff members — rated the recommendations according to a variety of criteria, such as relevance, usefulness, importance, and certainty. Their positive feedback stresses the usefulness and relevance of this paper recommendation contribution.

2.4   Session 3

Jevin West and Jason Portenoy focusedon a largely ignored facet of scholarly papers – the equations [10], in their paper, "Delineating Fields Using Mathematical Jargon". They extracted mathematical symbols from Latex source files in the arXiv repository, performed an analysis of the distribution of these symbols across different fields and calculated the "jargon distance" between fields. The main research goal of their paper was to find ways to utilize equations and formal notation in scholarly recommendation.

Joseph Mariani, Gil Francopoulo, and Patrick Paroubek discussed "A study of reuse and plagiarism in speech and natural language processing papers" [11]. They designed an algorithm based on n-gram comparisons to detect (self-)reuse and (self-)plagiarism. It was tested on the NLP4NLP dataset comprising about 65k NLP papers published during the past five decades. Results stress frequent self-plagiarism while uncommon plagiarism in the scientific literature of NLP.

Philipp Mayr presented a case study "How do practitioners, PhD students and postdocs in the social sciences assess topic-specific recommendations?" where different types of researchers in the social sciences assessed the relevance of search term, author name and journal name recommendations according to their research topics [12]. His results showed that simple bibliometric-enhanced recommendation services can be useful where they are integrated in an interactive retrieval task.

2.5 CL-SciSumm Shared Task

As part of this workshop, our colleagues at the National University of Singapore organized the CL-SciSumm Shared Task 2016[6] – a shared task on scientific paper summarization in the Computational Linguistics domain. This proceedings includes an outline of their Shared Task, as well as detailed system reports from the ten participating systems who completed the Task [2].

3 Outlook

This workshop is the first step to foster a reflection on the interdisciplinarity and the benefits that the disciplines Bibliometrics, IR and NLP can drive from it in a digital libraries context. In the future we plan follow-up workshops at IR, NLP and Digital Libraries venues. Furthermore we are working with the International Journal on Digital Libraries to offer a special issue on topics discussed at BIRNDL, for extended versions of BIRNDL workshop papers, shared task descriptions, as well as a general call for submissions.[7]

4 Acknowledgments

We are indebted to the referees who contributed to the review process: Colin Batchelor, Joeran Beel, Patrice Bellot, Marc Bertin, Guillaume Cabanac, Cornelia Caragea, Zeljko Carevic, Muthu Kumar Chandrasekaran, Jason S. Chang, Ingo Frommholz, Lee Giles, Bela Gipp, Daniel Hienert, Rahul Jha, Min-Yen Kan, Noriko Kando, Roman Kern, Claus-Peter Klas, Cyril Labbé, Birger Larsen, Elizabeth Liddy, Stasa Milojevic, Prasenjit Mitra, Marie-Francine Moens, Peter Mutschke, Doug Oard, Cécile Paris, Philipp Schaer, Andrea Scharnhorst, Henry Small, Simone Teufel, Mike Thelwall, Alex Wade, and Dietmar Wolfram.

---

[6] http://wing.comp.nus.edu.sg/cl-scisumm2016/

[7] See information at http://wing.comp.nus.edu.sg/birndl-jcdl2016.

References

1. Cabanac, G., Chandrasekaran, M.K., Frommholz, I., Jaidka, K., Kan, M.Y., Mayr, P., Wolfram, D.: Joint Workshop on Bibliometric-enhanced Information Retrieval and Natural Language Processing for Digital Libraries (BIRNDL 2016). In: JCDL '16: Proceedings of the 16th ACM/IEEE-CS on Joint Conference on Digital Libraries, ACM New York, NY, USA (2016) 299–300
2. Jaidka, K., Chandrasekaran, M.K., Rustagi, S., Kan, M.Y.: Overview of the CL-SciSumm 2016 Shared Task. In: Proc. of the Joint Workshop on Bibliometric-enhanced Information Retrieval and Natural Language Processing for Digital Libraries (BIRNDL2016). (2016)
3. Wolfram, D.: Bibliometrics, Information Retrieval and Natural Language Processing: Natural Synergies to Support Digital Library Research. In: Proc. of the Joint Workshop on Bibliometric-enhanced Information Retrieval and Natural Language Processing for Digital Libraries (BIRNDL2016). (2016) 6–13
4. Bertin, M., Atanassova, I.: Multiple In-text Reference Aggregation Phenomenon. In: Proc. of the Joint Workshop on Bibliometric-enhanced Information Retrieval and Natural Language Processing for Digital Libraries (BIRNDL2016). (2016) 14–22
5. Halevi, G., Bar-Ilan, J.: Post Retraction Citations in Context. In: Proc. of the Joint Workshop on Bibliometric-enhanced Information Retrieval and Natural Language Processing for Digital Libraries (BIRNDL2016). (2016) 23–29
6. Eto, M.: Incorporating Satellite Documents into Co-citation Networks for Scientific Paper Searches. In: Proc. of the Joint Workshop on Bibliometric-enhanced Information Retrieval and Natural Language Processing for Digital Libraries (BIRNDL2016). (2016) 30–35
7. Ronzano, F., Freire, A., Saez-Trumper, D., Saggion, H.: Making Sense of Massive Amounts of Scientific Publications: the Scientific Knowledge Miner Project. In: Proc. of the Joint Workshop on Bibliometric-enhanced Information Retrieval and Natural Language Processing for Digital Libraries (BIRNDL2016). (2016) 36–41
8. Kim, H.J., An, J., Jeong, Y.K., Song, M.: Exploring the leading authors and journals in major topics by citation sentences and topic modeling. In: Proc. of the Joint Workshop on Bibliometric-enhanced Information Retrieval and Natural Language Processing for Digital Libraries (BIRNDL2016). (2016) 42–50
9. Raamkumar, A.S., Foo, S., Pang, N.: What papers should I cite from my reading list? User evaluation of a manuscript preparatory assistive task. In: Proc. of the Joint Workshop on Bibliometric-enhanced Information Retrieval and Natural Language Processing for Digital Libraries (BIRNDL2016). (2016) 51–62
10. West, J., Portenoy, J.: Delineating Fields Using Mathematical Jargon. In: Proc. of the Joint Workshop on Bibliometric-enhanced Information Retrieval and Natural Language Processing for Digital Libraries (BIRNDL2016). (2016) 63–71
11. Mariani, J., Francopoulo, G., Paroubek, P.: A study of reuse and plagiarism in speech and natural language processing papers. In: Proc. of the Joint Workshop on Bibliometric-enhanced Information Retrieval and Natural Language Processing for Digital Libraries (BIRNDL2016). (2016) 72–83
12. Mayr, P.: How do practitioners, PhD students and postdocs in the social sciences assess topic-specific recommendations? In: Proc. of the Joint Workshop on Bibliometric-enhanced Information Retrieval and Natural Language Processing for Digital Libraries (BIRNDL2016). (2016) 84–92

Bibliometrics, Information Retrieval and Natural Language Processing:
Natural Synergies to Support Digital Library Research

Dietmar Wolfram[1]

[1]School of Information Studies, University of Wisconsin-Milwaukee
P.O. Box 413, Milwaukee, WI U.S.A. 53201
dwolfram@uwm.edu

Abstract Historically, researchers have not fully capitalized on the potential synergies that exist between bibliometrics and information retrieval (IR). Knowledge of regularities in information production and use, as well as citation relationships in bibliographic databases that are studied in bibliometrics, can benefit IR system design and evaluation. Similarly, techniques developed for IR and database technology have made the investigation of large-scale bibliometric phenomena feasible. Both fields of study have also benefitted directly from developments in natural language processing (NLP), which have provided new tools and techniques to explore research problems in bibliometrics and IR. Digital libraries, with their full text, multimedia content, along with searching and browsing capabilities, represent ideal environments in which to investigate the mutually beneficial relationships that can be forged among bibliometrics, IR and NLP. This brief presentation highlights the symbiotic relationship that exists among bibliometrics, IR and NLP.

Keywords: bibliometrics, information retrieval, digital libraries, natural language processing

1 Introduction

Both information retrieval (IR) and bibliometrics have long histories as distinct areas of investigation in information science. IR has focused on the storage, representation and retrieval of documents (text or other media) from the system and user perspectives. Bibliometrics and its allied areas (informetrics, scientometrics, webmetrics, or simply "metrics") have focused on discovering and understanding regularities that exist in the way information is produced and used--but this simple definition belies the breadth of research undertaken. Units of analysis may be words, metadata fields, publications, authors, journals, research groups, institutions, sub-fields, disciplines or geographic regions. Applications of the study of these regularities and underlying processes extend to equally diverse areas such as science policy, subject indexing and IR system design, including digital libraries (DLs).

The documentary contents of bibliographic IR systems and their associated indexes provide much of the data that metrics researchers rely on today to conduct their research. Conversely, many of the processes within IR are directly informed by metrics research. Surprisingly, there has been little overlap in the research agendas of these two areas of study over the history of information science. This is changing with the growing recognition of the common interests and the tools and techniques used by IR and metrics researchers that can help to advance the research agendas of each field [1]. The recent international BIR workshops [2,3,4] have brought together researchers with combined interests in bibliometrics and IR. The BIR research presentations demonstrate the potential synergies that exist between these two areas. With large, full text databases now commonplace, both IR and bibliometrics have also benefitted from developments in natural language processing (NLP) and computational linguistics, where text-based techniques have improved document retrieval and the ability to explore relationships among entities of interest in metrics research.

In a sense, digital libraries represent an ideal environment in which to study the intersection of IR, bibliometrics and NLP, whether the DLs consist of repositories of formal publications or heterogeneous collections of multimedia documents. With content representation and search functionality found in more traditional IR environments, hyperlinks that mimic relationships similar to those found in citation analysis, and full text contents that lend themselves to NLP analysis. This brief overview outlines how developments in IR and bibliometrics, along with language-based methods, have helped to advance research in both areas. These intersections are most evident in bibliographic databases, but also extend to more heterogeneous digital libraries.

2   Information Retrieval Research

IR research has focused on the design of more efficient and effective systems to match documents to queries to meet the information needs of users. Early IR research was more system-centered, but user-centered approaches are now employed alongside system-centered approaches in the design and evaluation of IR systems. Bibliometrics provides useful methods for the analysis of both system content and system usage, to better understand system processes and user dynamics. In essence, IR processes represent forms of information production and use [5], where observed patterns follow classic power law distributions or possibly unimodal distributions (e.g., lognormal or Poisson-like). Furthermore, metric studies of scientific communication can provide frameworks to assist in the design of IR systems.

Aspects of IR system content that lend themselves to bibliometric modeling include index term frequency distributions, indexing exhaustivity or term assignment, term co-occurrence frequency distributions, database and index growth, and more recently, aspects of web-based IR such as frequency distributions of inlinks/outlinks and document persistence [6]. Applications of bibliometric modeling to IR systems have included the development of simulations to model IR system processes to better understand system interactions. These models also can be used to observe retrieval efficiency under different situations to identify preferred file structures or for space planning [7,8].

User interactions with IR systems as recorded by transaction logs may be similarly modeled. Characteristics that can be modeled include search terms used per query, frequency distributions of query terms, query term co-occurrence, query frequency distributions, search session length based on queries or other actions, user search and browsing regularities, and site/document visitation frequency. Search and browsing patterns may be modeled using network analysis methods, similar to those applied in citation analysis, to identify issues with interface use [9], or clustering techniques may be applied to identify larger scale search session patterns [10].

Beyond mathematical modeling of specific bibliometric characteristics of IR systems, higher level aspects of science models also can inform the search and retrieval process of scientific literature. Mutschke and Mayr [11], for instance, recognize this important observation and demonstrate that retrieval performance can benefit by ranking results based on our understanding of models of science.

Citation-based connections between bibliographic records serve as a readily exploitable data source for expanding searching and browsing options for users. These ideas have been implemented in experimental systems over the past several decades such as I^3R [12] and BIRS [13], with the latter also supporting query expansion through visualizations of relationships among searchable entities. The importance of citation linkages is also recognized by commercial database vendors such as

EBSCO and ProQuest, which now provide active hyperlinks to references included in full text articles and to citing articles, where available.

For much of the history of IR, the research focus was on the representation and retrieval of document surrogates with limited natural language. Representation and retrieval were based on metadata fields, keywords or controlled vocabularies. Models to support query and document matching were based on bag-of-words approaches that treated terms independently of one another. Context and semantics played no role in determining the aboutness of documents. At the same time, computational challenges increased as the size of databases grew. IR models such as the vector space model became more computationally expensive due to the high dimensionality associated with representing documents and processing document-query matching.

IR research has been more responsive to taking advantage of advanced NLP techniques to provide a more natural search environment for users and to extend retrieval evaluation beyond simple term independence models. Dimensionality reduction techniques that lower the computational overhead associated with IR processing have become commonplace since early approaches based on latent semantic analysis were introduced over 25 years ago. Successors based on language modeling [14], including topic modeling [15], have provided novel ways to tackle information search and retrieval. The applications have more recently included the recommendation of scientific articles [16] and the identification of search terms [17]. Language-based techniques have also been used to identify additional index terms for documents based on language surrounding citations appearing in citing documents [18].

3   Bibliometrics Research

The relationship between IR and bibliometrics research can be considered in some ways symbiotic [19]. As noted above, methods used in metrics research have informed IR research. Conversely, tools and techniques developed to support IR research have been adapted to support metrics research. An exemplar is the development and application of PageRank [20] used by Google to rank webpages. It was directly influenced by citation analysis methods used in bibliometrics research. The developers recognized the parallels between citations and webpage inlinks. The effectiveness of PageRank is evident in Google's longstanding success as a search engine. More recently, PageRank-based approaches have been reapplied to citation analysis research problems [21]. Other similar network-based approaches, such as Eigenfactor (URL: `http://www.eigenfactor.org`), provide additional ways to rank journals or support methods to rank or recommend articles [22]. Furthermore, the h-index, initially developed to measure author impact, has been demonstrated to have application for the ranking of webpages, similar to PageRank, but with less computational overhead [23].

Citation analysis has been a core area of bibliometrics research for over 50 years. Citation relationships in the form of direct citations, co-citations or bibliographic coupling create a network of linkages among documents, authors, and publication venues that allows one to visualize the intellectual structure of a field [24], or all of science [25]. Similarly, co-authorship-based studies provide another type of linkage that allows researchers to gain deeper insights into the dynamics of research communities [26]. One limitation inherent in citation-based studies is that relationships among entities of interest only exist if the linkages exist. The lack of direct citation, co-citation, bibliographic coupling or co-authorship should not preclude the possibility of relationships.

This situation can be addressed using approaches that integrate the vocabulary used by the entities of interest, usually employing keyword or controlled vocabulary co-occurrence, which takes bibliometric studies more into the realm of IR research. Still, there are concerns with keyword-based approaches in bibliometrics research that mirror the same bag-of-words issues found in IR research. The assumption of independence of vocabulary in bibliographic entities, whether as keywords or subject terms, creates the same issues observed earlier in IR studies. The ability to work with full text and natural language can improve these analyses. More recent research has moved beyond simple co-occurrence to identify relationships among entities of interest. Of particular note has been the application of topic modeling techniques, such as Latent Dirichlet Analysis (LDA) [27], to bibliographic records to identify relationships among bibliometric entities of interest, for instance, authors [28,29], that may not be reflected through citation or collaboration. Tang et al. [30] have developed a searchable system initially called ArnetMiner (now AMiner, URL: `http://aminer.org`) that profiles researchers based on publication content and supports expertise search.

4   Conclusion

The application of bibliometric methods for IR research and vice versa has evolved over the past forty years, from bibliometric modeling of IR system processes to the exploitation of citation relationships to provide extended browsing capabilities to identify potentially relevant documents based on citation linkages. More recently, the adoption of language-based methods from NLP and computational linguistics has benefitted both IR and bibliometrics research. Applications of language-based approaches are still relatively new in bibliometric contexts. Link-based analysis (citations, co-authorship, hyperlinks) in combination with textual analysis can capitalize on the strengths of both approaches [31]. The analysis of full text collections--whether bibliographic databases or heterogeneous, multimedia digital libraries--offers many opportunities for further study. The applications of citation-based methods and emerging language-based methods are evident in the range of presentations given at the BIRNDL workshop, which include the use of citation methods, text mining and topic modeling to enhance retrieval in full text or digital library environments, scholarly communication and our understanding of disciplinary boundaries.

5   References

1. Mayr, P., Scharnhorst, A.: Scientometrics and Information Retrieval: Weak-links Revitalized. Scientometrics 102, 2193–2199 (2015)

2. Mayr, P., Scharnhorst, A., Larsen, B., Schaer, P., Mutschke, P.: Bibliometric-enhanced Information retrieval. In Advances in Information Retrieval (pp. 798-801). Springer International Publishing (2014)

3. Mayr, P., Frommholz, I., Scharnhorst, A., Mutschke, P.: Bibliometric-enhanced Information Retrieval: 2nd International BIR Workshop. In Advances in Information Retrieval (pp. 845-848). Springer International Publishing (2015)

4. Mayr, P., Frommholz, I., Cabanac, G.: Editorial for the 3rd Bibliometric-Enhanced Information Retrieval Workshop at ECIR 2016 (2016)

5. Egghe, L.: Power Laws in the Information Production Process: Lotkaian Informetrics. Elsevier (2005)

6. Wolfram, D.: Applied Informetrics for Information Retrieval Research. Libraries Unlimited (2003)

7. Wolfram, D.: Applying Informetric Characteristics of Databases to IR System File Design, Part I: Informetric Models. Information Processing and Management, 28(1), 121-133 (1992)

8. Wolfram, D.: Applying Informetric Characteristics of Databases to IR System Design, Part II: Simulation Comparisons. Information Processing and Management, 28(1), 135-151 (1992)

9. Han, H.J., Joo, S., Wolfram, D.: Using Transaction Logs to Better Understand User Search Session Patterns in an Image-Based Digital Library. Journal of the Korean Biblia Society for Library and Information Science. 25(1), 19-37 (2014)

10. Wolfram, D., Wang, P., Zhang, J.: Identifying Web Search Session Patterns Using Cluster Analysis: A Comparison of Three Search Environments. Journal of the American Society for Information Science and Technology, 60(5), 896-910 (2009)

11. Mutschke, P., Mayr, P.: Science Models for Search: A Study on Combining Scholarly Information Retrieval and Scientometrics. Scientometrics, 102, 2323-2345 (2015)

12. Croft, W.B., Thompson, R.H.: I R: A New Approach to the Design of Document Retrieval Systems. Journal of the American Society for Information Science, 38(6), 389-404 (1987)

13. Ding, Y., Chowdhury, G. G., Foo, S., Qian, W. Bibliometric information retrieval system (BIRS): A web search interface utilizing bibliometric research results. Journal of the American Society for Information Science, 51(13), 1190-1204 (2000)

14. Ponte, J.M., Croft, W.B.: A Language Modeling Approach to Information Retrieval. In Proceedings of the 21st annual international ACM SIGIR Conference on Research and Development in Information Retrieval (pp. 275-281). ACM (1998)

15. Wei, X., Croft, W. B.: LDA-based Document Models for Ad-Hoc Retrieval. In Proceedings of the 29th Annual International ACM SIGIR Conference on Research and Development in Information Retrieval (pp. 178-185). ACM (2006)

16. Wang, C., Blei, D.M.: Collaborative Topic Modeling For Recommending Scientific Articles. In Proceedings of the 17th ACM SIGKDD International Conference on Knowledge Discovery and Data Mining (pp. 448-456). ACM (2011)

17. Koopman, R., Wang, S., Scharnhorst, A., Englebienne, G.: Ariadne's Thread: Interactive Navigation in a World of Networked Information. In Proceedings of the 33rd Annual ACM Conference Extended Abstracts on Human Factors in Computing Systems (pp. 1833-1838). ACM (2015)

18. Ritchie, A., Robertson, S., Teufel, S.: Comparing Citation Contexts for Information Retrieval. In Proceedings of the 17th ACM conference on Information and knowledge management (pp. 213-222). ACM (2008)

19. Wolfram, D.: The Symbiotic Relationship between Information Retrieval and Informetrics. Scientometrics, 102, 2201-2214 (2015)

20. Page, L., Brin, S., Motwani, R., Winograd, T.: The PageRank Citation Ranking: Bringing Order to the Web. http://ilpubs.stanford.edu:8090/422/1/1999-66.pdf (1999)

21. Waltman, L., Yan, E.: PageRank-related Methods for Analyzing Citation Networks. In Y. Ding, R. Rousseau and D. Wolfram (Eds.). Measuring Scholarly Impact. (pp. 83-100). Springer (2014)

22. West, J. D., Wesley-Smith, I., Bergstrom, C. T.: A Recommendation System Based on Hierarchical Clustering of an Article-level Citation Network. IEEE Transactions on Big Data (Forthcoming)

23. Bar-Ilan, J., Levene, M.: The hw-rank: An h-index Variant for Ranking Web Pages, Scientometrics, 102, 2247–2253 (2015)

24. White, H.D., McCain, K.W.: Visualizing a Discipline: An Author Co-Citation Analysis of Information Science, 1972-1995. Journal of the American Society for Information Science, 49, 327-355 (1998)

25. Boyack, K.W., Klavans, R., Börner, K.: Mapping the Backbone of Science. Scientometrics, 64, 351-374 (2005)

26. Glänzel, W., Schubert, A.: Analysing Scientific Networks through Co-Authorship. In Handbook of Quantitative Science and Technology Research (pp. 257-276). Springer Netherlands (2004)

27. Blei, D.M., Ng, A.Y., & Jordan, M.J.: Latent Dirichlet allocation. Journal of Machine Learning Research, 3, 993–1022 (2003)

28. Rosen-Zvi, M., Griffiths, T., Steyvers, M., Smyth, P.: The Author-topic Model for Authors and Documents. In Proceedings of the 20th Conference on Uncertainty in Artificial Intelligence (pp. 487-494). AUAI Press (2004)

29. Lu, K., Wolfram, D.: Measuring Author Research Relatedness: A Comparison of Word-Based, Topic-Based and Author Co-Citation Approaches. Journal of the American Society for Information Science and Technology, 63, 1973-1986 (2012)

30. Tang, J., Zhang, J., Yao, L., Li, J., Zhang, L., Su, Z.: ArnetMiner: Extraction and Mining of Academic Social Networks. In Proceedings of the 14th ACM SIGKDD International Conference on Knowledge Discovery and Data Mining (pp. 990-998). ACM (2008)

31. Zitt, M.: Meso-level Retrieval: IR-bibliometrics Interplay And Hybrid Citation-Words Methods In Scientific Fields Delineation, Scientometrics, 102, 2223–2245 (2015)

Multiple In-text Reference Phenomenon

Marc Bertin[1] and Iana Atanassova[2]

[1] Centre Interuniversitaire de Rercherche sur la Science et la Technologie (CIRST),
Université du Québec à Montréal (UQAM), Canada,
`bertin.marc@gmail.com`
[2] Centre Tesnière, University of Franche-Comté, France,
`iana.atanassova@univ-fcomte.fr`

Abstract. In this paper we consider sentences that contain Multiple In-text References (MIR) and their position in the rhetorical structure of articles. We carry out the analysis of MIR in a large scale dataset of about 80,000 research articles published by the Public Library of Science in 7 journals. We analyze two major characteristics of MIR: their positions in the IMRaD structure of articles, and the number of in-text references that make up a MIR in the different journals. We show that MIR are rather frequent in all sections of the rhetorical structure. In the Introduction section, sentences containing MIR account for more than half of the sentences with references.

Keywords: Multiple In-text References, Bibliometrics, Citation Analysis, In-text References, Content Citation Analysis, IMRaD structure

1 Introduction

In a scientific article, the frequency of in-text references is highly dependent on the rhetorical structure. For example Bertin et al. [2] study the differences between the four sections of the IMRaD (Introduction, Methods, Results and Discussion) structure in terms of the density of citations.

The phenomenon of multiple in-text references in scientific papers has not yet been studied. In recent works on the rhetorical structure of articles [1–3], the studies are based on the presence of in-text references in sentences but their number in a single sentence is not taken into consideration. Several works exist on a related problem which is the proximity of co-citations in texts [5]. Liu and Chen [9, 10] propose a four level co-citation proximity scheme for the levels of article, section, paragraph and sentence.

Our approach allows to identifies multiple in-text references. In general, the presence of more than one in-text references in the same sentence gives us information about a relative proximity between the works that are cited. Previous studies on in-text references take into account word windows or sentences to study citation contexts. However, some recent works show the importance and the difficulty in identifying citation blocks that are spans of citations that may encompass one or more sentences [7]. Another related question, the recurrence of in-text references or re-citations, has been the object of several studies [6, 15].

We focus on text spans in articles that contain more than one in-text references that appear very close to each other. We consider sentences as a basic textual unit, and we examine sentences containing more than one in-text reference. We call this phenomenon *Multiple In-text References (MIR)*. For example, the following sentence contains a MIR composed of 4 references, where 3 of the references appear in the range *"[74–76]"*:

> *"Indeed, it has long been proposed on thermodynamic grounds that transcription factors would bind at low, nonfunctional levels throughout the genome either via sequence-independent [74–76] or sequence-specific DNA binding [32]."*[3]

In this paper, we present the results on the behavior of MIR and their positions in the IMRaD structure that we obtain by processing a large scale corpus of about 80,000 research articles. The key idea involves identifying the number of in-text references at the level of the sentence. We analyze two major characteristics of MIR. The first one is their positions in the IMRaD structure, and the second one is the number of in-text references that make up a MIR.

2 Method

To address the problem of the identification of MIR and their positions in the rhetorical structure of articles, we have processed a large-scale corpus of articles that follow the IMRaD structure. In fact, during the last decades, IMRaD has imposed itself as a standard rhetorical framework for scientific articles in the experimental sciences.

The objective of our study is to determine the locations where MIR are most likely to appear in the rhetorical structure of scientific articles. We also study the number of in-text references in the sentences.

2.1 Dataset

To perform this study we have analyzed a dataset of seven peer-reviewed academic journals published in Open Access by the Public Library of Science (PLOS). Six of the journals are domain-specific (*PLOS Biology, PLOS Computational Biology, PLOS Genetics, PLOS Medicine, PLOS Neglected Tropical Diseases*) and the 7th is *PLOS ONE*, which is a general journal that covers all fields of science and social sciences. We have processed the entire dataset of about 80,000 research articles in full text published up to September 2013.

The dataset is in the XML JATS format, where the body of the articles consists of sections and paragraphs that are identified as distinct XML elements. The in-text references are also, for the most part, present as XML elements and linked to the corresponding elements in the bibliography of the article.

---

[3] PLOS Biology, 2008, DOI: 10.1371/journal.pbio.0060027.

2.2 Identification of the IMRaD Structure

To identify the IMRaD structure of articles, we have analyzed all section titles and categorized the sections. All seven journals use similar publication models, where authors are explicitly encouraged to use the IMRaD structure. As a result, more than 97% of the research articles in the corpus contain the four main section types (Introduction, Methods, Results and Discussion), although not always in the same order. While the relative position of a section may have an influence on the number of references found in the section, e.g. a Discussion section that appears immediately after an Introduction section may have more references than a Discussion section that appears at the end of the article, the order in which the sections appear in an article has not been taken into consideration for this study. The detailed results of the analysis of the IMRaD structure for this corpus are presented by Bertin et al. [2].

2.3 Identification and Processing of MIR

In order to identify sentences containing MIR, we need to perform the following steps:

1. Segment all paragraphs into sentences;
2. Identify all in-text references;
3. Consider the number of in-text references in each sentence.

The first step was done by analyzing the punctuation and capitalization of the text in order to identify sentence ends. Our corpus contains a total of 15,852,120 sentences, out of which 3,528,514 (around 22%) contain in-text references.

The second step may seem trivial given that the in-text references are present as elements in the XML tree of the article. In the case of MIR however, this is not always true. When in-text references are in a numeric form, reference ranges are often present in sentences containing MIR. For example, we can consider the following sentence in the corpus with XML markup:

> *"A number of recent studies have used a modification of the picture viewing procedure by substituting pleasant pictures with photographs of loved, familiar faces* <xref ref-type="bibr" rid="pone.0041631-Bartels1">*[16]*</xref> – <xref ref-type="bibr" rid="pone.0041631-Xu2">*[24]*</xref>*."*[4]

The in-text references in this sentence *"[16]–[24]"* are identified as two *xref* elements that point to the corresponding bibliography items. In reality, the sentence contains 9 different citations: all the works from [16] to [24] are cited; and 7 of these citations are not present in the XML markup. In such cases, we call *implicit in-text references* those in-text references that are part of a range but that are not mentioned by their numbers in the sentence.

In order to identify correctly MIR and their number in sentences it is important to detect in-text reference ranges and implicit references. To do this, we

---

[4] PLOS ONE, 2012, DOI: 10.1371/journal.pone.0041631.

first examine the context of each *xref* element and identify all possible ranges. Then, we generate the list of implicit references and the links between these references and the bibliography items. A similar method for the processing of in-text reference ranges was used by Bertin et al. [1].

The occurrences of in-text reference ranges are rather numerous in our corpus. We found out that reference ranges are present in 19.19% of all sentences containing MIR and implicit in-text references account for 12.38% of the MIR.

3   Results

We first observe the presence of MIR in the four section types of the IMRaD structure and then we examine the number of the MIR according to the different journals.

3.1   Use of MIR in the IMRaD Structure

Table 1 presents the percentage of sentences containing Multiple In-text References (MIR) among all sentences with in-text references in the four section types of the IMRaD Structure (I-M-R-D). We observe that MIR are present for the most part in the Introduction section where more than half of the sentences with in-text references contain MIR (52.78%). This result is consistent with the observation that the Introduction section often includes a state of the art with a literature review in which MIR are most likely to appear. As for the Methods and Results sections, they have around 25% and 35% of MIR respectively.

	I	M	R	D	Total
Sentences with MIR	52.78%	25.05%	35.59%	42.65%	*41.43%*
Sentences without MIR	47.22%	74.95%	64.41%	57.35%	*58.57%*

Table 1: MIR in the IMRaD Structure

The results in this table for the four different section types are not unexpected. In fact, the relative quantity of MIR in the sections follows the overall distribution of references in the IMRaD structure, shown in Bertin et al. [2], where the Methods section contains the smallest number of in-text references, followed by the Results section. The Introduction section, which is also the shortest one on average, contains the highest number of citations.

Table 1 shows also that MIR appear very often: in around 41% of all sentences containing in-text references. This means that in a scientific article, the largest number of in-text references appear in groups of several references situated closely in the textual space, i.e. in the same sentence.

Number of in-text references in MIR	I	M	R	D
2	21.74%	15.67%	19.49%	20.74%
3	11.63%	4.43%	7.31%	9.34%
4	6.25%	1.53%	3.05%	4.36%
5	3.45%	0.68%	1.39%	2.12%
6	2.04%	0.34%	0.70%	1.13%
7	1.22%	0.17%	0.39%	0.64%
8	0.77%	0.10%	0.23%	0.36%
9	0.48%	0.06%	0.14%	0.21%
10	0.32%	0.05%	0.10%	0.13%
11	0.22%	0.03%	0.07%	0.08%
12	0.15%	0.02%	0.05%	0.06%
13	0.10%	0.02%	0.04%	0.04%
14	0.08%	0.01%	0.03%	0.03%
15	0.05%	0.01%	0.03%	0.02%

Table 2: Percentage of sentences with MIR in the IMRaD structure

Table 2 presents the percentage of sentences with MIR of different sizes among all sentences containing citations in each of the four section types. Considering the MIR with 2 elements, we observe that there is little difference between the sections Introduction, Results and Discussion. Then, the differences between the sections increase with the number of in-text references. This means that, while MIR with 2 elements appear almost homogeneously in an article, the MIR with higher number of elements are more and more exclusively reserved to the Introduction section. This phenomenon again, is explained by the presence of the state of the art in the Introduction with a very high concentration of in-text references.

3.2 MIR in the PLOS Journals

Figure 1 presents the relative number of sentences with MIR in each of the journals. The horizontal axis gives the number of in-text references in the same sentence in a logarithmic scale. The vertical axis gives the average number of sentences per article containing MIR in a logarithmic scale.

We observe some differences between the journals in the use of very large MIR (number of elements 20 and above). In fact, the journal PLOS Medicine stands out because it uses MIR with relatively high number of elements.

Table 3 presents the average and the maximal number of elements in MIR observed in the 7 journals. PLOS Medicine has the highest average number of elements in MIR. In fact, articles in this journal tend to be short, but with a very high number of references and many of them appearing in the same sentence. PLOS ONE and PLOS Medicine have very high maximal number of elements in MIR. However, as we can see on figure 1, MIR with a high number of elements in PLOS ONE tend to be less frequent than those in PLOS Medicine.

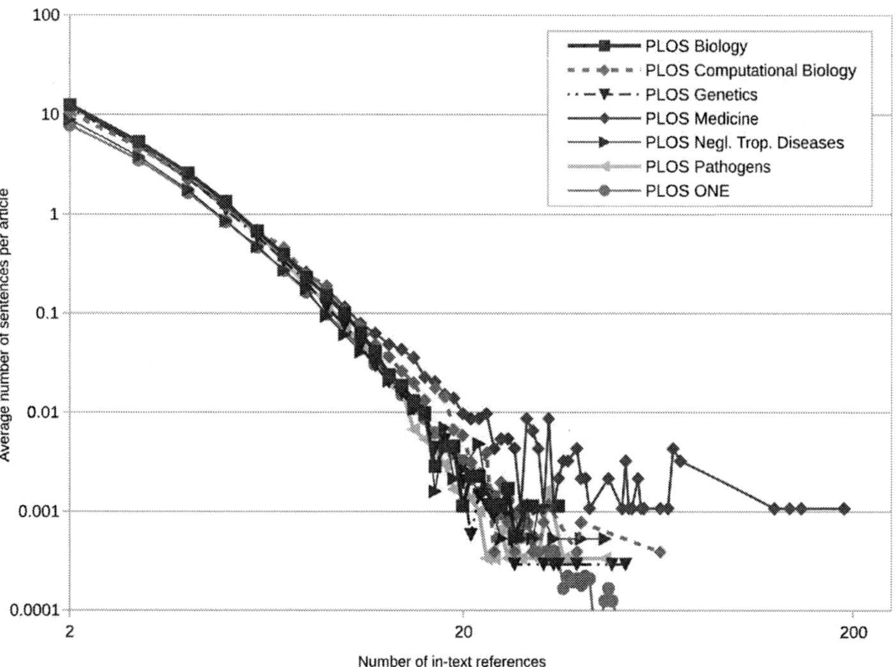

Fig. 1: MIR in the 7 PLOS Journals

Some examples of sentences containing MIR with very high number of In-text References are presented in table 4. In fact, these examples are extracted from articles in the medical domain that are of a specific type: systematic reviews. This kind of articles has for objective to sum up the best available research on a specific topic by collecting and synthesizing the results of other studies that fit pre-specified eligibility criteria. For this reason, we find in these articles sentences that cite a large number of other works. Moreover, as we can see on table 4, these sentences are not necessarily in the Introduction section but appear quite often in the Results and Methods sections.

4   Discussion and Conclusion

We have proposed a study of Multiple In-text References (MIR) in respect of their positions in the rhetorical structure of articles. This study shows the following key points:

- MIR are rather frequent in all sections of articles: 41% of the sentences with citations contain MIR;
- In the Introduction section MIR account for more than half of the sentences containing citations;

Journal	Ave. number of elements in MIR	Standard deviation	Maximal number of elements in MIR
PLOS Biology	3.0496	1.7780	35
PLOS Computational Biology	3.2183	2.0938	64
PLOS Genetics	3.0087	1.7358	52
PLOS Medicine	3.3246	3.8083	190
PLOS Negl. Tropical Diseases	3.0493	1.8583	46
PLOS Pathogens	2.9807	1.6720	46
PLOS ONE	3.1284	2.1384	288

Table 3: MIR in the 7 PLOS Journals: number of elements

Journal	Section	Sentence
PLOS Medicine	R	*The systematic review identified 188 studies that provided prevalence estimates [18,29,36–223].*
PLOS Medicine	M	*Data for calculation of the number of snakebite envenomings were obtained for 46 countries [9–60] while data for calculation of the number of deaths due to snakebite were obtained for 22 countries [9–11,18, 31,47,49,51,56,58–72] by this process.*
PLOS ONE	R	*As a result, 221 unique genes and 4 protein complexes (DNA-PK, HSP70, MRN(95), RAS) were identified from around 200 papers that studied radiation response-related biomarkers [4], [14]–[185].*
PLOS ONE	M	*Details of each study [11]–[113] were entered into a database by one investigator with a 100% re-check.*

Table 4: Examples of sentences with high number of in-text references

- The MIR with two elements are the most homogeneous: they appear quite often in the Introduction, Results and Discussion sections (about 20% of sentences with citations) and in about 15% of sentences with citations in the Methods section;
- There exist sentences with very high number of in-text citations (more than 100). Such sentences are specific to the domain of medicine and the systematic review article type.

In this study, the notion of MIR raises the question of the importance and role of MIR in scientific articles. We show the behavior and location of sentences that contain MIR. The implications of this study are relevant from the perspective of networks as bibliographic coupling [8], clustering [14] and co-citation [13], but also for the analysis of the functions of citations. Furthermore, many applications can benefit from the differentiation between single and multiple references such as automatic summarization [4, 12] or automatic generation of surveys [11]. More generally, the distribution of MIR along the text progression has important implications for understanding the contexts of citations. For example, we can consider the following sentence:

> *"Previous attempts to apply functional genomics methods to address these questions used various approaches, including **DNA microarrays** (Hayward et al. 2000; Ben Mamoun et al. 2001; Le Roch et al. 2002), **serial analysis of gene expression** (Patankar et al. 2001), and **mass spectrometry** (Florens et al. 2002; Lasonder et al. 2002) on a limited number of samples from different developmental stages."*[5]

In this sentence, there are 3 groups of in-text references and each group is characterized by a noun group that identifies topics related to the in-text references. The automatic identification of these topics will allow to assign them to each of the references.

This example shows that work at the level of sentences is not enough if we want to obtain fine and accurate results for content citation analysis. The observations of this study suggest the presence of MIR implies the existence of features such as topics, keywords, methods, etc. that are common to all works cited in the MIR group. This means that by examining the text content of such sentences one can obtain information on the topics that are shared by the group of cited works.

5 Acknowledgments

We thank Benoit Macaluso of the Observatoire des Sciences et des Technologies (OST), Montreal, Canada, for harvesting and providing the PLOS data set.

References

1. Bertin, M., Atanassova, I., Larivière, V., Gingras, Y.: The distribution of references in scientific papers: an analysis of the imrad structure. In: 14th International Society of Scientometrics and Informatics Conference. International Society for Scientometrics and Infometrics, Vienna, Austria (July 15-19 2013)
2. Bertin, M., Atanassova, I., Larivire, V., Gingras, Y.: The invariant distribution of references in scientific papers. Journal of the Association for Information Science and Technology 67(1), 164177 (January 2016)
3. Ding, Y., Liu, X., Guo, C., Cronin, B.: The distribution of references across texts: Some implications for citation analysis. Journal of Informetrics 7(3), 583–592 (2013)
4. Elkiss, A., Shen, S., Fader, A., Erkan, G., States, D., Radev, D.: Blind men and elephants: What do citation summaries tell us about a research article? Journal of the American Society for Information Science and Technology 59(1), 51–62 (2008)

---

[5] PLOS Biology, 2003, DOI: 10.1371/journal.pbio.0000005.

5. Gipp, B., Beel, J.: Citation Proximity Analysis (CPA) A new approach for identifying related work based on Co-Citation Analysis. In: Larsen, B., Leta, J. (eds.) 12th International Conference on Scientometrics and Informetrics. vol. 2, pp. 571–575. International Society for Scientometrics and Informetrics, Rio de Janeiro, Brazil (July 14-17 2009)

6. Hu, Z., Chen, C., Liu, Z.: The recurrence of citations within a scientific article. In: Salah, A., Tonta, A., Akdag Salah, C., Sugimoto, U.A. (eds.) 15th International Society of Scientometrics and Informetrics Conference. International Society for Scientometrics and Infometrics, Bogazii University Printhouse, Istanbul, Turkey (June 29 to July 3 2015)

7. Kaplan, D., Tokunaga, T., Teufel, S.: Citation block determination using textual coherence. Journal of Information Processing 24(3), 540–553 (May 2016)

8. Kessler, M.M.: Bibliographic coupling between scientific papers. American documentation 14(1), 10–25 (1963)

9. Liu, S., Chen, C.: The proximity of co-citation. Scientometrics 91(2), 495–511 (2011)

10. Liu, S., Chen, C.: The Effects of Co-citation Proximity on Co-citation Analysis. In: 13th Conference of the International Society for Scientometrics and Informetrics. vol. 1 and 2, pp. 474–484. International Society for Scientometrics and Infometrics, Durban, South Africa (July 4-7 2011)

11. Mohammad, S., Dorr, B., Egan, M., Hassan, A., Muthukrishan, P., Qazvinian, V., Radev, D., Zajic, D.: Using citations to generate surveys of scientific paradigms. In: Proceedings of Human Language Technologies: The 2009 Annual Conference of the North American Chapter of the Association for Computational Linguistics. pp. 584–592. Association for Computational Linguistics, Boulder, Colorado, USA (May 31 to June 5 2009)

12. Qazvinian, V., Radev, D.R.: Scientific paper summarization using citation summary networks. In: Proceedings of the 22nd International Conference on Computational Linguistics. vol. 1, pp. 689–696. Association for Computational Linguistics, Manchester, UK (Aug 18-22 2008)

13. Small, H.: Co-citation in the scientific literature: A new measure of the relationship between two documents. Journal of the American Society for information Science 24(4), 265–269 (1973)

14. Small, H., Sweeney, E., Greenlee, E.: Clustering the science citation index using co-citations. ii. mapping science. Scientometrics 8(5-6), 321–340 (1985)

15. Zhao, D., Strotmann, A.: Re-citation analysis: Promising for research evaluation, knowledge network analysis, knowledge representation and information retrieval? In: 15th International Society of Scientometrics and Informatics Conference. pp. 1061–1065. International Society for Scientometrics and Infometrics, Bogazii University Printhouse, Istanbul, Turkey (June 29 to July 3 2015)

Post Retraction Citations in Context

Gali Halevi[1] and Judit Bar-Ilan[2]

[1]Icahn School of Medicine at Mount Sinai, New York, NY, USA
gali.halevi@mssm.edu
[2]Department of Information Science, Bar-Ilan University, Ramat Gan, Israel
Judit.Bar-Ilan@biu.ac.il

Abstract. In this paper we explore post retraction citations to retracted papers. The reasons for retractions in our sample were data manipulation, small sample size, scientific misconduct, and duplicate publication by the authors. We found, that the huge majority of the citations are positive, and the citing papers usually fail to mention that the cited article was retracted. Retracted articles are freely available at the publishers' site, which is probably a catalyst for receiving more citations.

1   Introduction

Studies on retracted articles show that the amount of retracted articles has increased in relative measure to the overall increase in scientific publications [1, 2]. Although retracting articles helps purge the scientific literature of erroneous or unethical research, citations to such research present a real challenge. Citing articles that were retracted especially due to plagiarism, data falsification or any other unethical practices interferes with the process of eliminating such studies form the literature and research. There are two types of retraction citations; citations that a retracted article received prior to its retraction and citations that are received post retraction and despite retraction notices [3, 4]. Both types of citations put the scientific process in jeopardy, especially when they are cited as legitimate references to previous work. Some studies on retracted articles have shown that retracted articles that received a high number of citations pre-retraction are more likely to occur additional citations post-retraction [4, 5]. A good example is described in a study by [6] who studied the case of Scott S. Reuben who was convicted of fabricating data in 25 of his studies which resulted in mass retractions of his articles. The authors of the study have shown that the popularity of Reuben's articles did not diminish post-retraction even 5 years after the retractions have been made. Another phenomenon that was identified in the literature is of authors' self-citing their retracted articles and thus contributing to the perception that their retracted work is valid [7].

In this study we sought out to find the context around post-retraction citations with the main purpose of finding out whether they are negatively, positively or neutrally mentioned. In this case study we present a sample of five retracted articles that have post-retraction citations tracked in 2015 and 2016.

2   Data collection

ScienceDirect, Elsevier's full text database was accessed in October 2014. The database was queried for the term "RETRACTED" in the article title and its retraction notice. In ScienceDirect, each retracted article is preceded with the word "RETRACTED". In addition, each Elsevier journal incorporates a retraction notice which explains who retracted article and the reason for retraction. This allowed us to manually code each article in our dataset with an additional field "retracted by" that represented the person/s requesting the retraction.

A total of 1,203 results retrieved from which 988 were retracted articles. The results excluded were retraction notices, duplicates and papers whose original titles included the word "retracted".

For this study we selected the five top articles that were cited most (more than 20 times) since 2015. This way we made sure that the papers all cite retracted articles (since they were all retracted before October 2014). The reason for this decision is that the retraction date of many of the retracted articles is unknown. For each article we extracted the citing documents and analyzed the ones appearing in 2015 and 2016. Overall, we analyzed located 125 citing documents and analyzed 109 of them; 16 documents were unavailable to us mostly because they appear in books to which we did not have access. Each citing document was inspected to identify the precise mention of the retracted article within the text. Each mention was categorized as follows:

- *Positive:* A positive citation indicates that the retracted article was cited as legitimate prior work and its findings used to corroborate the author/s current study.
- *Negative:* A negative citations indicates that the authors mentioned the retracted article as such and its findings as inappropriate.
- *Neutral:* A neutral citation indicates that the retracted article was mentioned as a publication that appears in the literature and does not include judgement on its validity.

3   Findings

3.1   Case study 1: Donmez, G., Wang, D., Cohen, D. E., & Guarente, L. (2010). RETRACTED: SIRT1 Suppresses β-Amyloid Production by Activating the α-Secretase Gene ADAM10. *Cell*, 142(2), 320-332.

This article was published in 2010 in Cell and retracted in 2014 due to irregularities in graphs and data misrepresentation in the images. Although the graphs and images did not have any bearing on the validity of the results, according to the retraction notice, the editors stated that "...the level of care in figure preparation in Donmez et al. falls well below the standard that we expect, and we are therefore retracting the paper".

We conducted an individual content analysis of the most recent 36 citations which were tracked in 2015 and 2016. We were able to analyze 32 citing articles in context. Our results show that the citations are mostly positive (see Fig. 1). One negative mention was found in a letter to the editor of Journal of Korean Medical Science written "giving the above article as an example of how altered graphics are causing bias in the biomedical field and result in numerous articles being retracted" [8].

In this case, the editor indicated that the actual results of the study were valid, and this could be the reason for the continuous citations of the article. In one other case, although the article was cited positively in the paper, in the reference list it was noted that the article was retracted.

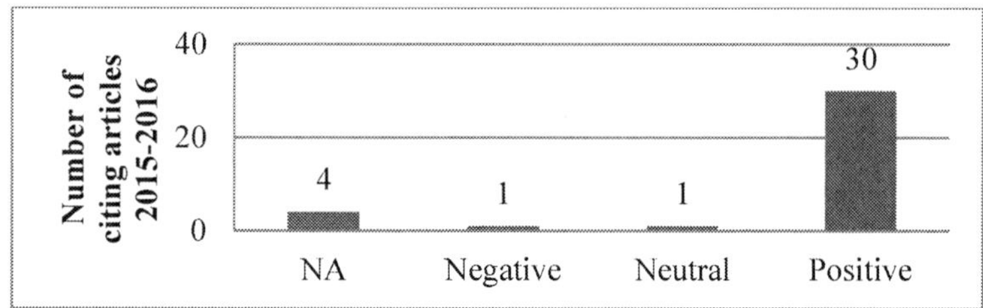

Fig. 1. Citations in context for the Donmez et al. article

3.2 Case 2: Séralini, G. E., Clair, E., Mesnage, R., Gress, S., Defarge, N., Malatesta, M., & De Vendômois, J. S. (2012). RETRACTED: Long term toxicity of a Roundup herbicide and a Roundup-tolerant genetically modified maize. *Food and chemical toxicology*, 50(11), 4221-4231.

This article, published in 2012 was the subject of a debate surrounding the validity of the findings, use of animals and even accusations of fraud. Its publication and retraction process have resulted in the "Séralini affair" which became a big media news item. The article described a 2-year study of rats which were fed genetically modified (GM) crops and showed increased tumors. The study, which was also scrutinized by government agencies, received major media attention that resulted in the creation of a social movement against GM food. The demand to label of all GM foods is still underway. Despite the accusation of fraud and fabrication of results, the editors found no such evidence to that effect. However, the article was retracted because of the "low number of animals" used in this study which lead to the conclusion that "no definitive conclusions can be reached with this small sample size".

This article was cited 109 times since its publication in 2012 with 23 citations tracked after its retraction (2015-2016) out of which 18 citing articles were accessible to us. As can be seen in Fig. 2 post-retraction citations are divided. Although more citations are seen to be negative, the positive and neutral ones are also present. The negative citations mostly point to the media frenzy around the results. Positive mentions appear in similar studies which claim that concerns raised by the GM study are valid and the dangers of GM foods to humans should be studied further.

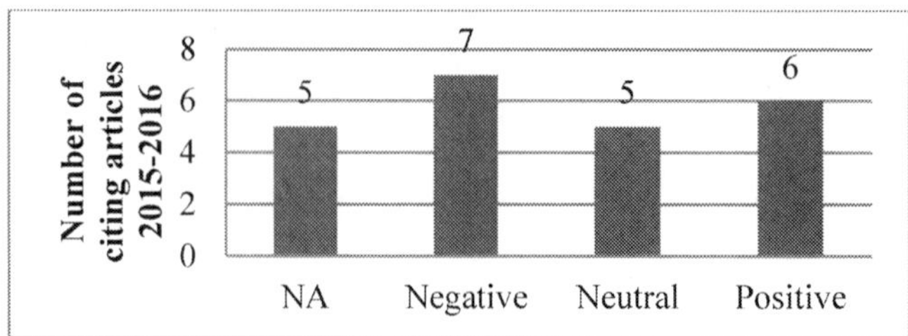

Fig. 2. Citations in context for the Séralini et al. article

The study was republished in 2014 by Environmental Sciences Europe [9]. The republication of the study stirred another controversial discussion in the scientific community with several scientists writing letters expressing their concerns regarding the appearance of the same study in another journal [10].

The republished article received 17 citations in 2015 and 2016. The vast majority of them being positive mentions (see Fig. 3). In addition, some criticism towards the peer-review practices of the retracting editors were also detected [10]. The one negative mention of the re-published article was criticism towards the media frenzy around the topic and the inability of the scientific community to refute invalid results. The authors state that "Although scientists have investigated each GMO crisis and reached scientific and rational conclusions, they have less ability to disseminate information than the media, so the public is not promptly informed of their rational and objective viewpoints as experts" [11, p.134].

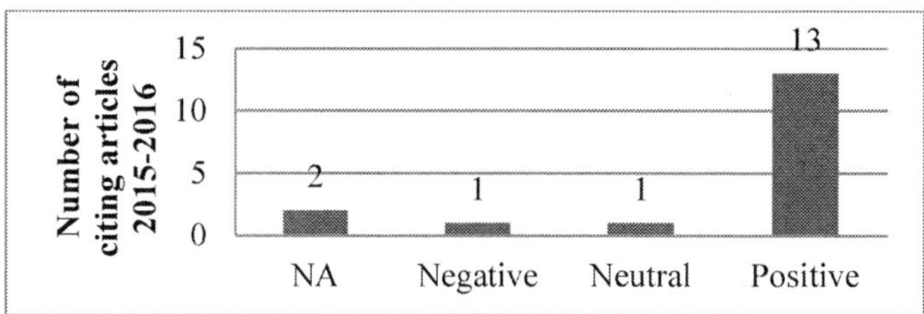

Fig. 3. Citations in context for the republished Séralini et al. article

3.3 Case 3: Mukherjee, S., Lekli, I., Gurusamy, N., Bertelli, A. A., & Das, D. K. (2009). RETRACTED: Expression of the longevity proteins by both red and white wines and their cardioprotective components, resveratrol, tyrosol, and hydroxytyrosol. *Free Radical Biology and Medicine*, 46(5), 573-578.

The leading author of the paper, Dipak Das and his lab at the University of Connecticut Health Sciences Center were the subject of an ethical investigation by the university. The results of the university's investigation led to the retraction of all of Dr. Das' papers due to scientific misconduct and data manipulation. This particular paper was investigated by the journal's ethics committee along with an additional paper that appeared in the same journal. The retraction notice states that the journal's ethics committee "analyzed the data presented, and then further concluded that …. on re-examination of these two FRBM (Free Radical Biology and Medicine) papers that they contain clear evidence of obvious cutting, pasting and manipulation of data in experimental blots." The article, which was retracted in 2012, received 85 citations since its publication in 2009, 21 of which occurred in 2015 through March 2016. All 17 citing accessible citing articles referred to the article's findings as legitimate. For example, "Plants containing resveratrol, a potent antioxidant, has been used widely in the treatment of various ailments" [12 p.1286] or "Recent studies have also shown that red wine upregulates the protein expression of sirtuin "[13, p.1213].

3.4 Case 4: Walumbwa, F. O., Wang, P., Wang, H., Schaubroeck, J., & Avolio, B. J. (2010). RETRACTED Psychological processes linking authentic leadership to follower behaviors. *The Leadership Quarterly*, 21(5), 901-914.

This article was retracted in 2014 due to serious data manipulation and falsification. In the retraction notice of this article, the editors of the journal went to great lengths to examine and re-examine the statistical claims made by the authors using the services of three separate methodologists. Following the methodologists' findings of irregularities in the reported data and falsification of results, and the authors' lack of proper response to their findings, the article was retracted from the journal. However, the article continued to be cited despite the lengthy and detailed retraction notice.

A close examination of the post retraction citations (2015- March 2016 – 24 citations of which 23 were analyzed) shows that all citations were positive citations, meaning that the citing authors used findings from this article to support their findings. The subject of "authentic leadership" is popular in management studies and has seen a surge in publications since 2012. This could explain the overall positive citations of the article.

3.5 Case 5: Li, C., Tao, X. M., & Choy, C. L. (1999). RETRACTED: On the microstructure of three-dimensional braided preforms. *Composites Science and Technology*, 59(3), 391-404.

This article, published in 1999 was retracted due to an identical version which was published 2 years earlier. In the retraction notice the editors state that "The article duplicates significant parts of a paper that had already appeared in [J China Textil Univ, 1997, 14(3), 8-13]". The authors in this case re-used data they already published on and re-published it in a different journal. However, this article has been cited even in recent years despite being retracted for many years. A content analysis of the 18 out of the 21 recently citing articles from 2015 and 2016 shows that this article is being referred to mostly in positive context or mentioned as a legitimate piece in the literature. Here too, there is one paper that cites the article positively in the text, but in the references it appears as retracted.

4   Discussion and Conclusions

As can be seen from the examples above, retracted articles continue to be cited years after retraction and despite retraction notices being posted on publishers' platforms.

In some cases, the continuous citations rates could be the result of general interest by the public or media. For example, the Séralini article evoked an ongoing public debate regarding the safety of GM foods which resulted in a call to label all such food. This could explain the continuing interest in the study and its citations. The article was also republished and thus continues to be cited despite of the fact that the authors did not modify it. In the case of the Mukherjee article, again, public interest could explain its continuing citations. Resveratrol was hailed by the media as an important supplement that could ensure longevity and good health and is an off the counter supplement available in vitamin shops. Finally, the Walumbwa article which describes 'authentic leadership' and followers' dynamic is also a topic of media and business management interest. With numerous management books published on this topic it has been accepted as a management style encouraged by corporations.

In other cases, the reason for retraction does not deter others from citing the article. For example, the Donmez article (case study 1 above) was retracted because of poor graphing and data representation. However, the editors do state in the retraction notice that these faults do not apply to the results of the study, even though on PubPeer [14] there was an extensive discussion on problems with the article. The editors' approval of the results could be the reason for the continuing citations to the article. The Li article, as another example, re-used data and thus violated the originality rule of scientific publishing. However, the data itself was not refuted by the editors and the article that was published first seems to be inaccessible.

Regardless of the reasons speculated for the post-retractions citations, the fact that invalid and falsified research is continuing to appear as valid research is concerning. We recommend that publishers use reference checks to all submitted articles to detect citations of retracted articles and remove them or at least request an explanation from the authors for citing a retracted paper in a positive or neutral manner. This explanation should clearly appear in the paper. In addition, we would recommend the deletion of retracted articles from publishers' websites. Currently, at least for the major publishers: Elsevier, Springer Nature and Wiley, but possibly a general practice, retracted articles are not only available on the publishers' site, but they are freely available, without the need for a subscription or for a one-time payment. While leaving a retraction notice, the article itself should not appear on platforms such as ScienceDirect or others. Although versions of these articles may appear elsewhere, the journal websites should not carry these versions and make it difficult for authors to download, read and consequently cite retracted articles.

5   Acknowledgement

The first author was supported by EU COST Actions PEERE (TD1306) and KnowEscape (TD1210).

References

1. Cokol, M., Ozbay, F., & Rodriguez-Esteban, R. (2008). Retraction rates are on the rise. EMBO Reports, 9(1), 2–2. http://doi.org/10.1038/sj.embor.7401143vements. Science and engineering ethics, 1-10.
2. Marcus, A., & Oransky, I. (2014). What studies of retractions tell us? Journal of Microbiology & Biology Education, 15(2), 151.
3. Unger, K., & Couzin, J. (2006). Even retracted papers endure. Science, 312(5770), 40-41.
4. Campanario, J. M. (2000). Fraud: retracted articles are still being cited. *Nature, 408*(6810), 288-288.
5. Redman, B. K., Yarandi, H. N., & Merz, J. F. (2008). Empirical developments in retraction. *Journal of Medical Ethics, 34*(11), 807-809.
6. Bornemann-Cimenti, H., Szilagyi, I. S., & Sandner-Kiesling, A. (2015). Perpetuation of retracted publications using the example of the Scott S. Reuben Case: Incidences, reasons and possible improvements. DOI 10.1007/s11948-015-9680-y
7. Madlock-Brown, C. R., & Eichmann, D. (2015). The (lack of) impact of retraction on citation networks. Science and Engineering Ethics, 21(1), 127-137.
8. Seifirad, S., Haghpanah, V., Wang, S. Y., Chan, W. P., Shin, H. K., Choi, C. W., ... & Hwang, J. H. (2015). Clothes don't make the man: Well-favored figures are game-changers in the biomedical publication. Journal of Korean Medical Science, 30, 1713.
9. Séralini, G. E., Clair, E., Mesnage, R., Gress, S., Defarge, N., Malatesta, M., ... & de Vendômois, J. S. (2014). Republished study: long-term toxicity of a Roundup herbicide and a Roundup-tolerant genetically modified maize. Environmental Sciences Europe, 26(1), 1-14.
10. Loening, U. E. (2015). A challenge to scientific integrity: A critique of the critics of the GMO rat study conducted by Gilles-Eric Séralini et al. (2012). Environmental Sciences Europe, 27(1) doi:10.1186/s12302-015-0048-3
11. Xia, J., Song, P., Xu, L., & Tang, W. (2015). Retraction of a study on genetically modified corn: Expert investigations should speak louder during controversies over safety. BioScience Trends, 9(2), 134-137. doi:10.5582/bst.2015.01047
12. Pangeni, R., Sahni, J. K., Ali, J., Sharma, S., & Baboota, S. (2014). Resveratrol: review on therapeutic potential and recent advances in drug delivery. Expert opinion on drug delivery, 11(8), 1285-1298.
13. Romain, C., Bresciani, L., Gaillet, S., Feillet-Coudray, C., Calani, L … Rouanet, J-M. (2014). Moderate chronic administration of Vineatrol-enriched red wines improves metabolic, oxidative, and inflammatory markers in hamsters fed a high-fat diet. Molecular Nutrition & Food Research. 58(5), 1212-1215.
14. PubPeer (2013). SIRT1 suppresses beta-amyloid production by activating the alpha-secretase gene ADAM10. Retrieved from https://pubpeer.com/publications/20655472

Incorporating Satellite Documents into Co-citation Networks for Scientific Paper Searches

Masaki Eto

Gakushuin Women's College
Tokyo, Japan
masaki.eto@gakushuin.ac.jp

Abstract. To improve the search performance of retrieval methods using co-citation linkages, this study proposes a technique to enlarge a co-citation network by incorporating satellite documents. This technique specifies satellite documents via full-text searches for terms obtained from documents having co-citation linkages with a seed document; the appropriateness of each co-citation linkage is checked by using the strength of the co-citation context based on the results of parsing documents that cite the seed document. This study evaluates search performance using the proposed technique with IR experiments. Specifically, the random walk with restart algorithm, which can compute similarities between the seed document and each document in the network, is applied to the enlarged and initial networks. Scores of the normalized discounted cumulative gain (nDCG@K) were then compared. The results indicate that the search performance of the retrieval methods using the enlarged network outperforms those of a baseline method using the initial network.

Keywords: Co-citation, Context, TF-IDF, Random walk with restart

1   INTRODUCTION

In the field of scientific paper searches, citations are often used to measure implicit relationships between documents. One approach to improve the search performance of retrieval methods using citation linkages is to enlarge the citation networks by incorporating additional information. In the case of a network created using direct citation linkages, i.e., the linkages between the citing and cited documents, techniques to enlarge the network of citations on the basis of additional information, such as citing text [1] or user profiles [2], have been reported.

This study enlarges the networks connected by co-citations. A co-citation is defined as a linkage between a pair of documents concurrently cited by a third document. In the simplest retrieval method using co-citation, documents having a co-citation relationship with a given seed document that are known to be relevant are presented to the user under the assumption that documents co-cited with such a seed document tend to be topically similar to the seed document. Co-citation networks have been used in bibliometrics and can also be applied to scientific paper searches (e.g., [3]).

This study proposes a technique to enlarge the co-citation network by adding word-based linkages. When documents are detected by the co-citation linkage, it is possible to obtain more appropriate search terms from the document; such terms may not have been included in the original seed document. A set of new search terms may yield additional relevant documents that were not identified simply by the co-citation linkages or the user's original representation of his or her information needs. This study defines satellite documents as documents that are specified via full-text searches for new search terms. The purpose of the proposed technique is to incorporate these satellite documents into the initial network of documents, which is already connected by co-citation linkages.

In addition, the proposed technique attempts to reduce noise satellite documents incorporated into the initial co-citation network using the co-citation context. Some studies (e.g., [3] and [4]) have reported that using the contexts of co-citations has positive effects for reducing noise documents when co-citation networks are enlarged by additional co-citation linkages; therefore, it is feasible to use co-citation contexts when enlarging co-citation networks by adding word-based linkages.

This study empirically evaluates the search performance of retrieval methods using the proposed technique with IR experiments. Specifically, the random walk with restart (RWR) algorithm [5], which can compute similarities between the seed document and each document in the network, is applied to enlarged networks and initial networks, and the results are compared by computing scores of the cutoff version of the normalized discounted cumulative gain (nDCG@K).

2   PROPOSED TECHNIQUE

2.1   Specifying satellite documents

Figure 1 shows an initial network comprising document nodes connected by undirected co-citation linkages. In this network, a search query is a seed document that is known to be relevant to the information needs of a user. The weight of the edge, w, i.e., the strength of the co-citation linkage, is computed as

$$w\,(d_1, d_2) = \text{cociting}\,(d_1, d_2). \tag{1}$$

Here, d_1 and d_2 are co-cited documents and $\text{cociting}(d_1, d_2)$ denotes the total number of documents co-citing d_1 and d_2 in the target document set. Note that this study denotes a weighted edge between d_1 and d_2 as Edge (d_1, d_2, w).

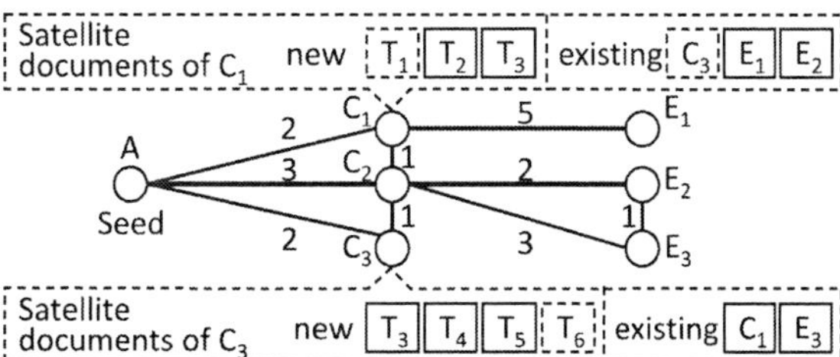

Fig. 1. Initial co-citation network and satellite documents.

The proposed technique specifies satellite documents by investigating documents one hop from the seed. This study defines host documents as source documents that are used to specify satellite documents. Using the title words of the host document as a query, the satellite documents are specified on the basis of a standard full-text search method; the seed document is excluded from the search target. For example, in Figure 1, Document C_1, a host document that is one hop from the seed, specifies six satellite documents. In the experiments in this study, the tf-idf retrieval function of the Indri search engine, which has been developed as part of the Lemur Project, was used. The top N documents ranked by this full-text search were adopted as satellite documents (e.g., $N = 10$).

In addition, as an optional process, the proposed technique attempts to check the appropriateness of each host document as a source because inappropriate host documents may yield noise. To check appropriateness, this technique uses the strength of co-citation context (see e.g., [6] and [7]) identified by parsing the full-text of documents that cite the seed and each host. More specifically, this technique examines reference positions within the text and if references to both the document and the seed appear within a paragraph in one or more citing documents, the document is selected as a host document because a seed and host co-cited in a strong context are expected to be closely related. For example, in Figure 1, if one or more documents cite Documents A and C_3 in the same paragraph, Document C_3 would be selected as a host document. Conversely, if no documents cite them in the same paragraph, Document C_3 would not be selected as a host document.

2.2 Incorporating satellite documents

If a satellite document is new, a new node is created with an undirected edge of weight 1 connecting the new node to its host. When two host documents share a new satellite document, one new node and two edges between the new node and each host node are created. In Figure 1, Document T_3 is specified by host Documents C_1 and C_3; therefore, a new node T_3, Edge (T_3, C_1, 1), and Edge (T_3, C_3, 1) are created. In addition, if a new document has co-citation linkages with documents already existing in the initial network or with other new documents, new edges are created and weights are assigned using Eq. (1).

When a satellite document already exists in a given network, the linkage between the satellite document and its host is used to create a new edge or recalculate the weight of a given edge. If the linkage is new for the network, an undirected edge of weight 1 is created between the satellite and its host. If the linkage already exists in the initial network, the weight of the existing edge is recalculated as

$$w\,(d_1, d_2) = \text{cociting}\,(d_1, d_2) + 1. \qquad (2)$$

Some new linkages may be duplicated in the specified results. In such cases, the proposed technique treats them as one combined link and creates one new edge. For example, in Figure 1, Document C_1 has satellite document C_3 and vice versa; therefore, only Edge (C_1, C_3, 1) is incorporated into the network.

2.3 Ranking the documents in the network

To calculate document scores, the RWR algorithm is applied to the enlarged network. This algorithm iteratively investigates the entire network, and the similarity between a seed node and each node in the network is calculated (see, e.g., [3] and [8]). Specifically, the walker starts at a seed node and then either proceeds to the connected nodes on the basis of a probability calculated by weights or returns back to the seed node; these steps are repeated iteratively until convergence. The long-term visit rate of each node is used as a document score; these rates are given by the steady state of

$$\vec{p} = (1 - r)\widetilde{w}\vec{p} + r\vec{s}. \tag{3}$$

Here, $\vec{p}$ is an n-dimensional vector (with n being the number of nodes in the network), $\vec{s}$ is an n-dimensional vector with 1 for the seed node and 0 for the others, and r is a return probability. This study uses the following 11 values of r in the experiments: 0.01, 0.1, 0.2, 0.3, 0.4, 0.5, 0.6, 0.7, 0.8, 0.9, and 0.99. Also, $\widetilde{w}$ is a transition probability matrix, and each transition probability between two nodes is the weight of an edge, which is normalized by the summation of the weights of the edges connected to the current node. In the case shown in Figure 1, the probability "A to C_1" is 0.286 given as 2/(2+3+2). Therefore, $\widetilde{w}$ is an asymmetric matrix, i.e., one direction can be different from another direction, e.g., the probability "C_1 to A" is not equal to 0.286.

3   EXPERIMENTAL SETUP

As described in Section 2.1, the proposed technique has an optional process. Therefore, this study evaluates the search performance of two retrieval methods. First, *Proposed (all)* omits the optional process and simply identifies all documents one hop from the seed as host documents. Second, *Proposed (context)* selects host documents using the strength of the co-citation context. For both retrieval methods, the parameter N (i.e., the number of retrieved documents per host document) was set to 10 and 100. In addition, the study evaluates the search performance of a baseline method that applies the RWR algorithm only to the initial co-citation network. In this experiment, the three retrieval methods take up to two hops from the seed to create each initial co-citation network; three or more hops are out of scope.

To create a special test collection, the Open Access Subset of PubMed Central was used. The test collection was constructed by selecting approximately 152,000 documents from the subset with the condition that the document had at least one citation linkage with a document in the subset. The test collection contained 100 seed documents that were randomly selected from all the documents under the condition that each seed document had co-citation linkages with 10 or more documents.

In addition, this experiment adopted nDCG@K as a metric to evaluate the search performance (with $K = 5$, 10, 50, and 100). A document was considered relevant depending on the degree to which it shared MeSH Descriptors with the target seed document. More specifically, the Jaccard coefficient (JC) was used, i.e., when nDCG was calculated, the experiment used a relevance score of 3 for documents whose JC was 0.3 or more, 2 for documents whose JC was 0.2–0.3, and 1 for documents whose JC was 0.1–0.2.

4   RESULTS

Search runs for 100 seed documents were executed using each method.

4.1   Evaluation of incorporated documents

First, the experiment examined whether the newly incorporated documents were relevant (see Figure 1). Table 1 shows the average number of relevant incorporated documents; a document is relevant if the JC is 0.1 or more. Further, Table 1 lists the average ratio of the relevant documents, which is the total number of relevant documents over 100 search runs divided by the total number of new documents over the 100 search runs.

As shown in the table, the numbers of relevant documents were relatively large. For example, *Proposed (all)* incorporated more than 50 new relevant documents per seed. Therefore, the proposed technique has the potential to improve the search performance.

Further, the ratio of relevant documents for *Proposed (context)* was higher than that of *Proposed (all)*. This result indicates that the checking process using the co-citation context tends to exclude inappropriate host documents.

Table 1. Statistics of the incorporated documents.

	Propsed (all)		Proposed (context)	
N	10	100	10	100
Number of relevant documetns	50.23	265.36	7.38	44.50
Number of incorporated documents	298.53	2390.03	29.18	261.34
Ratio	0.168	0.111	0.253	0.170

4.2   Evaluation of the ranked retrieval results

Table 2 shows the average scores of nDCG@K and the results of the paired t-test between the baseline method and each retrieval method using the proposed technique. Note that this table shows only the scores of the best results ranked by Eq. (3) using the aforementioned 11 different r-values.

Table 2. Average scores of nDCG@K.

		Proposed $N = 10$		Propsed $N = 100$	
K	Baseline (r)	all (r)	context (r)	all (r)	context (r)
5	0.226 (0.9)	0.226 (0.99)	0.232* (0.99)	0.224 (0.9)	**0.234**** (0.9)
10	0.223 (0.99)	0.221 (0.99)	0.227** (0.99)	0.226 (0.99)	**0.230**** (0.99)
50	0.188 (0.99)	0.191* (0.99)	0.189** (0.99)	**0.197**** (0.99)	0.191 (0.99)
100	0.174 (0.99)	0.181** (0.99)	0.177* (0.99)	**0.188**** (0.99)	0.180** (0.99)

* P < 0.05, ** P < 0.01

In Table 2, the maximum scores of the five retrieval results at each K are shown in bold. These are the results of *Proposed (context)* and *Proposed (all)* with N = 100, with the paired t-tests showing statistically significant differences. Therefore, the retrieval methods using the proposed technique tended to outperform the baseline method.

Furthermore, the scores of *Proposed (context)* were higher than those of the baseline method in all cases, with the paired t-tests indicating a statistically significant difference in most cases. Conversely, some scores of *Proposed (all)*, i.e., with N = 10 at K = 10 and with N = 100 at K = 5, were lower than those of the baseline method. This suggests that the checking process had a stable and positive impact on improving the search performance.

5   CONCLUSION

This study proposed a technique to enlarge co-citation networks by incorporating satellite documents in scientific paper searches. Retrieval methods using the proposed technique tended to outperform the baseline method, which was based on the initial co-citation network.

6   ACKNOWLEDGMENTS

This work was supported by JSPS KAKENHI Grant Number JP26730163.

7   REFERENCES

1. He, Q., Pei, J. Kifer, D., Mitra, P. and Giles. C. L. Context-aware citation recommendation. In Proceedings of the 19th International World Wide Web Conference (WWW2010), 421-430 (2010)
2. Sugiyama, K. and Kan, M. Exploiting Potential Citation Papers in Scholarly Paper Recommendation, In Proceedings of the 13th ACM/IEEE Joint Conference on Digital Libraries (JCDL 2013), 153-162 (2013)
3. Eto, M. Document retrieval method using random walk with restart on weighted co-citation network, In Proceedings of the 77th ASIS&T Annual Meeting (2014)
4. Eto, M. Spread co-citation relationship as a measure for document retrieval. Proceedings of the fifth ACM workshop on Research advances in large digital book repositories and complementary media, 7-8 (2012)
5. Tong, H., Faloutsos, C. and Pan, J. 2008. Random walk with restart: fast solutions and applications. Knowledge and Information Systems, 14, 3, 327-346 (2008)
6. Gipp, B. and Beel, J. Citation proximity analysis (CPA) - A new approach for identifying related work based on co-citation analysis. In Proceedings of the 12th ISSI Conference. 2, 571-575 (2009)
7. Eto, M. Evaluations of context-based co-citation searching, Scientometrics 94, 2, 651-673 (2013)
8. Gori, M. and Pucci, A. Research paper recommender systems: A random-walk based approach. In Proceedings of IEEE/WIC/ACM Web Intelligence, 778-781 (2006)

Making Sense of Massive Amounts of Scientific Publications: the Scientific Knowledge Miner Project

Francesco Ronzano, Ana Freire, Diego Saez-Trumper and Horacio Saggion

Department of Information and Communication Technologies
Universitat Pompeu Fabra
Carrer Tanger 122-140, Barcelona, Spain
`first.last@upf.edu`

Abstract. The World Wide Web has become the hugest repository ever for scientific publications and it continues to increase at an unprecedented rate. Nevertheless, this information overload makes the exploration of this content a very time-consuming task. In this landscape, the availability of text mining tools to characterize and explore distinctive features of the scientific literature is mandatory. We present the Scientific Knowledge Miner (SKM) Project, that aims to investigate new approaches and frameworks to facilitate the extraction of knowledge from scientific publications across different disciplines. More specifically, we will focus on citation characterization, recommendation and scientific document summarization.

Keywords: text mining, information extraction, recommender systems, indexing, crawling, online resources.

1 Introduction:

During the last decade the amount of scientific information available on-line increased at an unprecedented rate. Recent estimates reported that a new paper is published every 20 seconds [1]. PubMed[1], Elsevier' Scopus[2] and Thomson Reuther's ISI Web of Knowledge[3] respectively contain more than 24, 57 and 90 million papers. In this scenario, the exploration of scientific literature has turned into an extremely complex and time-consuming task. The availability of text mining tools able to extract, aggregate and turn scientific unstructured textual contents into well organized and interconnected knowledge is fundamental.

However, scientific publications are characterized by several structural (title, abstract, figures, citations...), linguistic and semantic peculiarities that make them difficult to analyze by relying on general purpose text mining tools. One of the special features of scientific papers is their network of citations, that are starting to be exploited in several context including opinion mining [2, 7] and scientific text summarization [3, 8]. Besides citations, the interpretation of the semantics of the actual textual contents of

---

[1] `http://www.ncbi.nlm.nih.gov/pubmed`

[2] `http://www.scopus.com`

[3] `http://www.webofknowledge.com`

scientific papers usually needs the availability of knowledge repositories with an adequate coverage of scientific concepts and relations that could not be found on global domain knowledge resources like WordNet, DBPedia, FreeBase or BabelNet.

Considering both the peculiar structural and semantic features of scientific publications and the huge amounts of papers that need to be taken into account when we mine scientific literature, customized information extraction, semantic indexing, search and content aggregation approaches are required in order to fully take advantage of the knowledge exposed by scientific articles.

In this context, we present the Scientific Knowledge Miner (SKM) Project. It aims at developing both knowledge resources and a complex scientific knowledge mining infrastructure that will be exploited to support fine-grained semantic analysis and large-scale studies of scientific document collections. In the context of the SKM Project, we are going to analyze publications by relying and extending the Dr. Inventor Scientific Text Mining Framework [9] (DRI Framework), a freely available Java-based library. The DRI Framework enables the automated analysis and characterization of several facets of publications including the identification of the scientific discourse category of sentences (Approach, Background, Future Work, etc.), the characterization of the purpose of citations and the annotation of Named Entities that occur inside the textual contents of a paper[4]. By performing fine-grained semantic analysis of articles and aggregating and merging this information across collections of papers, the scientific literature analysis supported by the SKM Project are characterized by a different, deeper level granularity when compared to platforms like CiteSeer and GoogleScholar: these platforms mainly aggregate scientific papers by extracting and normalizing a structured set of metadata, including titles, authors, citation counts, etc. In the SKM Project, the DRI Framework will be properly complemented by ad-hoc data normalization, indexing and content visualization infrastructures that will allow the integration of information across papers and the execution of large-scale experiments.

2   Overview of the SKM Project

The core objective of the SKM Project is the investigation of new approaches, the extension and development of software tools and the creation of new datasets that will facilitate the extraction of knowledge from scientific publications across different disciplines. In particular, we have identified three core research topics that we would like to explore thanks to the SKM Project:

1. The analysis, the characterization and the navigation of collections of research papers in order to test new, alternative metrics to evaluate their quality;
2. The investigation of new, state of the art multi-document summarization approaches, tailored to scientific publications;
3. The evaluation of new approaches to scientific content recommendation that relies on both the contents of a paper and its relations with other scientific results.

---

[4] We rely on Babelfy: http://babelfy.org/

To investigate these research topics, we will carry out the following activities:

- extension and improvement of the Dr. Inventor Text Mining Framework[5], a Java library that integrates several Document Engineering and Natural Language Processing tools customized to enable and ease the analysis of the textual contents of scientific publications, both in PDF and JATS XML format. To get more information on the framework, the interested reader can refer to [9]. In the SKM Project will extend the Framework by implementing semi-supervised or unsupervised methods for citation classification (polarity and purpose) and semantically aware relation extraction (e.g. causal inference), both features useful to support information extraction and automated semantic enrichment of scientific texts;
- enrichment with new features of the SUMMA document summarization Java library [10]. In particular, SUMMA will be able to support the summarization of scientific texts by relying on citation-based summarization approaches (both sentence and paper assessment based on peers opinion). We will also implement state of the art multi-document summarization customized to scientific papers, based on the extraction and aggregation of relevant sentences across publications in order to automatically create surveys;
- implementation of new methodologies for semantic enrichment, interlinking, indexing and navigation of corpora of scientific papers. We will develop Web crawling approaches specialized to repositories of scientific publications and model relevant structured Web contents (such as conference Websites) in order to complement, enrich or interlink the information mined from scientific publications. In the meanwhile, we will complement this activities by the definition of proper content indexing, normalization, search and aggregation methodologies and infrastructures to enable the aggregation and browsing of the information extracted from huge collections of scientific publications;
- creation and sharing of semantically enhanced scientific datasets to train and validate new information extraction approaches. To this purpose we will take advantage of Annote[6], the Web based collaborative annotation tool we developed in the context of Dr. Inventor to support annotators in carrying out complex annotation tasks such as rhetorical sentence classification or summarization.

3   SKM scientific publication mining infrastructure

In this section we introduce the high-level architecture of the infrastructure to crawl, process, index and visualize the contents of corpora of scientific publications in the context of the SKM Project (see Figure 1).

Our initial target collections of contents to analyze include open access Web sites of publishers, conferences as well as any kind of on-line repository of scientific publications. The crawler gathers papers and metadata (name of the conference, editors of a journal paper, etc.) from the input Web sites. The original paper (in PDF or XML) is stored in a repository together with its metadata. Then, the contents of each paper are

---

[5] `http://backingdata.org/dri/library/`

[6] `http://penggalian.org/annote/` - username: user, password: pswd

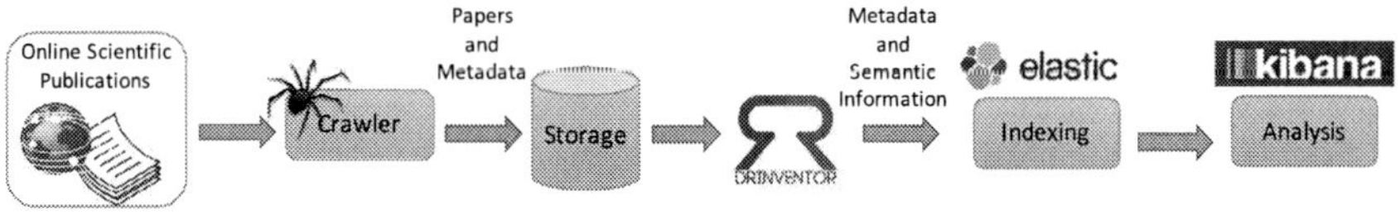

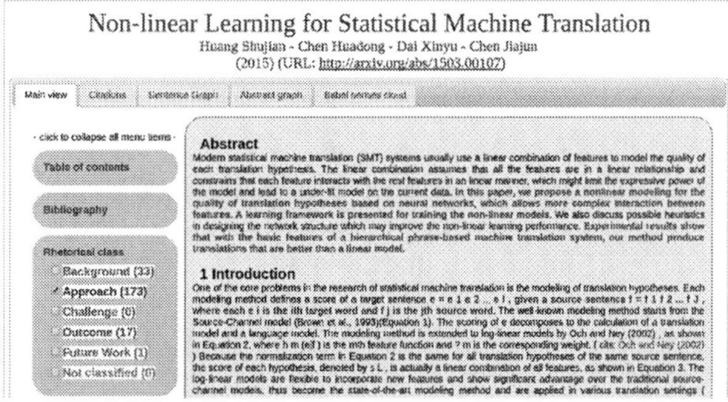

Fig. 1. Steps/components of our architecture

analyzed thanks to the DRI Framework. Both the metadata of a paper and the semantic information mined by the DRI Framework are properly indexed thanks to a mature open source engine: Elastic Search[7]. This platform is based on Lucene and has been designed to efficiently search across multiple documents, stored using the JSON format. Contents from different papers are linked by applying title and author normalization procedures. We will explore and analyze the collections of papers by directly querying Elastic Search by a graphical interface named Kibana. In Figure 2 we show some preliminary visualization of the information mined from a paper by the DRI Framework. These visualizations can be accesse on-line at: http://backingdata.org/dri/viz/.

Fig. 2. Web based visualization of the information extracted from a paper thanks to the DRI Framework. In particular, we can see highlighted in bold the sentences of the paper classified as approach.

4 Scientific information analysis use cases

In this section we briefly present the three core use cases we are going to investigate in the context of the SKM Project. Even if our initial investigations will be focused on the exploration of these three application scenarios, the scientific publication mining infrastructure that constitutes the core of the SKM Project (see Section 3) can be easily adapted and thus exploited in any other context related to the analysis of large corpora of papers.

---

[7] https://www.elastic.co/products

4.1 Characterization of citations' purpose and polarity

The network of citations across papers constitutes one of the most characteristic traits of scientific publications: when a paper cites the work presented in another one the author explicitly identifies a relevant connection among both works. The count of the citation that a paper receives constitute the basis of the most common metrics exploited to evaluate the scientific production of papers, journals and researchers (i.e. h-index). The effectiveness of citation-based research evaluation metrics would benefit from the possibility to take into account not only the number of citations a paper receives but also the purpose and the polarity of each one of them. Several classification schemata and approaches have been proposed to characterize aspects related to the purpose and polarity of citations [2,12]. By relying on and extending the set of annotated citation included in the Dr. Inventor Multi-Layered Annotated Corpus of Scientific Papers [5][8], we aim at exploring new approaches to citation purpose and polarity classification, by placing special attention on their robustness across domains and on the limited availability of manually annotated data.

4.2 Scientific document summarization

Nowadays, the possibility to automatically identify the most relevant contents across a set of scientific publications is essential to deal with and perform screenings of the huge amount of articles currently available on-line. Several approaches to scientific papers summarization have been proposed [3,8,11]. Most of them extend general purpose document summarization methodologies by considering information facets that are characteristic of scientific publications. In particular, the sentences of the papers in which the article to summarize is cited provide valuable material to improve the quality of scientific summarization. Also the possibility to consider the rhetorical structure (background, approach, future work, etc.) of the different excerpts of the contents of a paper to summarize provides valuable information to generate summaries that include contents better balanced across the sections of a paper. In the SKM Project, we aim at investigating different strategies to improve content and graph-based summarization approaches by considering typed citation networks and by relying on the automated characterization of the rhetorical structure of scientific publications implemented by the DRI Framework.

4.3 Recommender system for citations

Citation recommendation is a complex task because of the difficulty in matching excerpts of the source paper to the contents of huge amounts of other candidate articles to be cited. Among the many approaches proposed, many of them rely on text classification as well as on question answering and query ranking [4,6]. The goal of the SKM Project is to develop a recommender system for citations, that helps authors to find relevant articles by relying both on the semantic information extracted by the DRI Framework and on the data aggregated across corpora of papers crawled from the Web. In order to test our system, we will define a prediction task, where learning from the past, we will try to predict which citations a given article will contain.

---

[8] http://sempub.taln.upf.edu/dricorpus/

5 Conclusions

We introduced Scientific Knowledge Miner (SKM), a project that will facilitate the extraction of knowledge from scientific publications. We briefly described the SKM scientific publication mining infrastructure that will be exploited to analyze corpora of scientific papers, thus supporting large-scale investigations of scientific contents. We also presented our future venues of research by describing the three main application scenarios that we plan to investigate in the near future in the context of the SKM Project: characterization of the purpose and polarity of citation, summarization of scientific document and citation recommedation.

Acknowledgements. This work is supported by the Spanish Ministry of Economy and Competitiveness under the Maria de Maeztu Units of Excellence Programme (MDM-2015-0502), by the European Project Dr. Inventor (FP7-ICT-2013.8.1 - Grant: 611383), the Catalonia Trade and Investment Agency (*Agència per la competitivitat de l'empresa*, ACCIÓ) and the TUNER project (TIN2015-65308-C5-5-R, MINECO/FEDER, UE).

References

1. The rise of open access. Science 342(6154), 58–59 (2013)
2. Abu-Jbara, A., Ezra, J., Radev, D.R.: Purpose and polarity of citation: Towards nlp-based bibliometrics. In: HLT-NAACL. pp. 596–606 (2013)
3. Abu-Jbara, A., Radev, D.: Coherent citation-based summarization of scientific papers. In: Proc. of 49th Annual Meeting of the ACL: Human Language Techologies. pp. 500–509. ACL (June 2011)
4. Balog, K., Ramampiaro, H., Takhirov, N., Nørvåg, K.: Multi-step classification approaches to cumulative citation recommendation. In: Proc. of the 10th Conference on Open Research Areas in Information Retrieval. pp. 121–128. LE CENTRE DE HAUTES ETUDES INTERNATIONALES D'INFORMATIQUE DOCUMENTAIRE (2013)
5. Fisas, B., Ronzano, F., Saggion, H.: A multi-layered annotated corpus of scientific papers. In: LREC Conference (2016)
6. He, Q., Kifer, D., Pei, J., Mitra, P., Giles, C.L.: Citation recommendation without author supervision. In: Proc. of the fourth ACM international conference on Web search and data mining. pp. 755–764. ACM (2011)
7. Nakov, P.I., Schwartz, A.S., Hearst, M.A.: Citances: Citation sentences for semantic analysis of bioscience text. In: In Proc. of the SIGIR'04 workshop on Search and Discovery in Bioinformatics (2004)
8. Ronzano, F., Saggion, H.: Taking advantage of citances: citation scope identification and citation-based summarization. In: Text Analytics Conference (2014)
9. Ronzano, F., Saggion, H.: Knowledge extraction and modeling from scientific publications. In: Semantics, Analytics, Visualisation: Enhancing Scholarly Data Workshop co-located with the 25th International World Wide Web Conference April 11, 2016 - Montreal, Canada (2016)
10. Saggion, H.: Summa: A robust and adaptable summarization tool. In: Traitement Automatique des Langues. vol. 49.2 (2008)
11. Teufel, S., Moens, M.: Summarizing scientific articles: experiments with relevance and rhetorical status. Computational linguistics 28(4), 409–445 (2002)
12. Teufel, S., Siddharthan, A., Tidhar, D.: Automatic classification of citation function. In: Proc. 2006 conference on empirical methods in NLP. pp. 103–110. ACL (2006)

Exploring the leading authors and journals in major topics by citation sentences and topic modeling

Ha Jin Kim[1], Juyoung An[1], Yoo Kyung Jeong[1], Min Song[1]

[1]Department of Library and Information Science, Yonsei University, 50 Yonsei-ro, Seodaemun-gu, Seoul, South Korea
{hajin_228, anjy, yk.jeong, min.song}@yonsei.ac.kr

Abstract. Citation plays an important role in understanding the knowledge sharing among scholars. Citation sentences embed useful contents that signify the influence of cited authors on shared ideas, and express own opinion of citing authors to others' articles. The purpose of the study is to provide a new lens to analyze the topical relationship embedded in the citation sentences in an integrated manner. To this end, we extract citation sentences from full-text articles in the field of Oncology. In addition, we adopt Author-Journal-Topic (AJT) model to take both authors and journals into consideration of topic analysis. For the study, we collect the 6,360 full-text articles from PubMed Central and select the top 15 journals on Oncology. By applying AJT model, we identify what the major topics are shared among researchers in Oncology and which authors and journal lead the idea exchange in sub-disciplines of Oncology.

Keywords: text mining; citation analysis; topic modelling; bibliometrics

1   Introduction

As the size of data on the web continues to increase in an exponential manner, finding valuable meaning between data becomes of paramount importance in many research areas. In the information science field, citations are challenging, pivotal materials to discover the relationship between academic documents because citations present the description of authors' ideas and the hidden relationship between authors and documents. The earliest works focused mainly on classifying the citation behaviors and discovering the citation reasons with limited data such as the location of citation sentences and the number of references [1,2].

Since the mid-1990s, with the development of computer technology, citation content analysis was elaborated by applying data analysis techniques like text-mining or natural language processing. Zhang et al. [3] present citation analysis based on sematic and syntactic approaches. Semantic-based citation analysis is performed by qualitative analysis to discover the citation motivation and citation classification. On the other hand, syntactic-based citation analysis can be conducted by citation location and citation frequency, which reveals the hidden relation of authors by using meta-data of documents such as journal, venue of publication, affiliation of authors, etc. Following their study, Ding et al. [4] propose a theoretical methodology through content citation analysis. However, these analyses are somewhat limited to the explicit context that primarily represents their own ideas and arguments.

The main goal of the paper is to discover the implicit topical relationships buried in citation sentences by utilizing the citation information from the author's perspective of sharing other authors' point of view. Implicitness of the topical relationship is realized by using citation sentences as the input for the topic modeling technique. In this study, a citation sentence indicates the sentence including citation expression consisting of year and author of the cited work. In general, the citation sentence contains brief content of cited work and opinion that the author of citing work on the cited work. We claim that citation sentences reveal interesting characteristics of scholarly communication such as influence, idea exchange, justification for citer's arguments, etc. We assume that using citation sentences for topic analysis reveals aforementioned characteristics. To explore such intellectual space created by citation sentences, we take both authors and journals into consideration of topic analysis. To this end, we applied Author-Conference-Topic (ACT) model proposed by Tang et al. [5] for our topic analysis in relation with both authors and journals, which is called Author-Journal-Topic (AJT) topic model. ACT model is a probabilistic topic model for simultaneously extracting topics of papers, authors, and conferences. There are a few studies to analyze content of citation sentences. Most of previous studies focus on how the topic of document influences citation and vice versa [6,7,8] using Topic Modeling. Kataria, Mitra, and Bhatia [8] adapt citation to Author-Topic model [9] with the assumption that the context surrounding the citation anchor could be used to get topical information about the cited authors. These studies including Tang et al. [10]'s ACT model are the examples of combining topic modelling methods and citation content analysis. However, most previous studies used metadata of documents. In this work, we focus on identifying the landscape of the oncology field from a perspective of citation. By using citation sentences, our results can indicate which authors are actively cited and which journals lead a certain topic.

The rest of the paper is organized as follows: Section 2 describes the proposed approach. Section 3 analyzes the topic modeling results. Section 4 concludes the paper with the future work.

2 Methodology

2.1 Main idea

The basic assumption of the proposed approach is that citation sentences embed useful contents signifying the influence of cited authors on shared ideas of citing authors. Citation sentences are also considered as an invisible intellectual place for idea exchanging since citations are effective means of supporting and expressing their own arguments by using other works. In the similar vein, Di Marco and Mercer [11] claim that citation sentences play a major role in creating the relationship among relevant authors within the similar research fields. With these assumptions, we are to explore the implicitness of topic relationships resided in citation sentences from the integrated perspective by incorporating the citing authors and journal titles into interpreting the topical relationships.

As shown in Figure 1, we utilized various features including citing authors, citing sentences and journal titles for topic analysis. Authors in Figure 1 mean the citing authors who write a paper and who cite other's work. Citation sentences are the sentences written by the authors when they cite other's work in the paper, and journal titles are the journal names publishing the citing authors' paper. By employing AJT model with these three parameters , we can discover which topics are the most salient ones referred to frequently by researchers and who are the leading authors sharing other authors' ideas in the research field and which journal leads such endeavor.

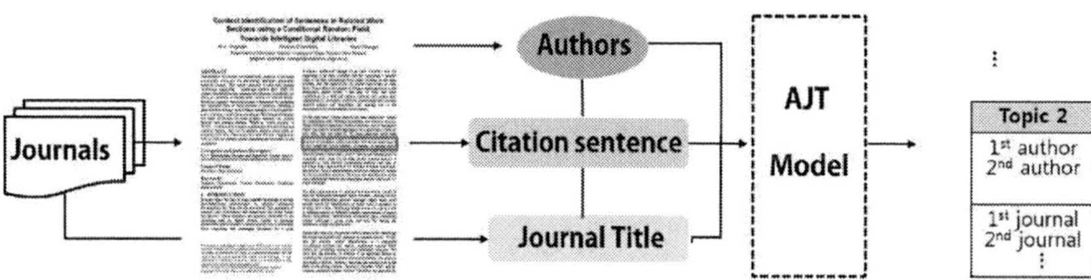

Fig. 1. Three parameters for AJT model

2.2   Data collection

For this study, we compile the dataset on the field of Oncology from PubMed Central that provides the full-text in the biomedical field. We select top 15 journals of Oncology by Thomson Reuter's JCR and journal's impact factor, and from these 15 journals, we are able to collect 6,360 full-text articles.

2.3   Method

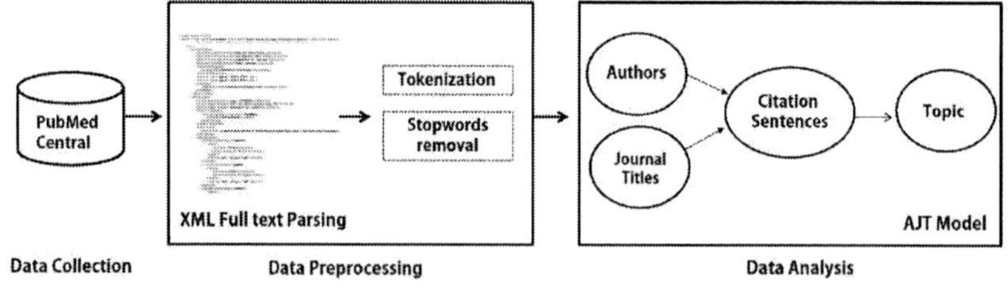

Fig. 2. Workflow

Figure 2 describes the workflow of our study. As mentioned earlier, with the full-text articles collected from PubMed Central, we extract the citation sentences. Most citation sentences are kept in the following format: (author, year), (reference number) [reference number]. An example of such format is "(<xref rid="bib00" ref-

type="bibr">Author name, 2000</xref>)". We use the regular expression technique to parse and extract the citation sentences, when the tag <xref rid=>, </xref> appears on the sentences after parsing XML records with the Java-based SAX parser.

We also parse other metadata for AJT model such as the name of authors and journal titles. The author tags, <surname> </surname> and <given-names></given-names> inside the <contrib-gourp></contrib-group>, denote the list of authors who wrote the paper. For journal, we extract the titles when the journal tags, <journal-title> and </journal-title>, are included in the tag of <journal-meta> and </journal-meta>. We also pre-process extracted sentences by removing both functional and general words and applying the Porter's stemming algorithm to improve the input for AJT Model.

2.4 AJT Model

For our study, we apply ACT [10] model with several metadata such as citation sentences, journal titles and citing authors to develop AJT model. Our AJT model utilizes journal titles and citation sentences instead of conference and abstract on documents. The change of model is needed to analyze most influential topics in Oncology and to find leading authors who frequently mention the active topics and to detect the journals involved in such topics.

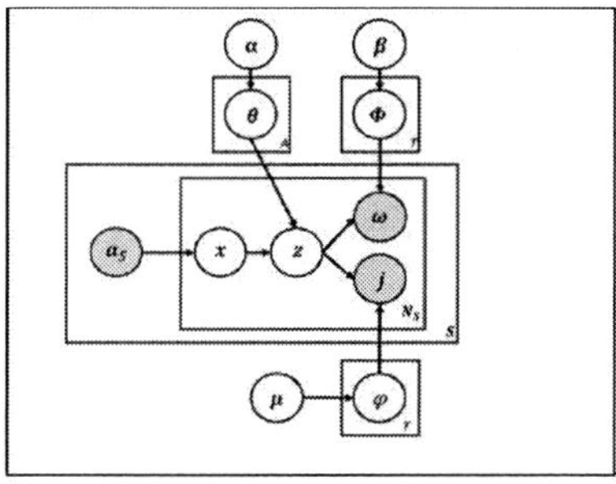

SYMBOL	Description	SYMBOL	Description
T	number of topics	ω_{Si}	the i_{th} word token in sentence S
S	number of citing sentences	z_{Si}	the topic assigned to word token ω_{Si}
V	number of words	x_{Si}	the chosen citing author associated with the word token ω_{Si}
A	number of citing authors	θ_x	multinomial distribution over topics specific to an citing author x
J	number of journal titles	Φ_z	multinomial distribution over words specific to topic z
N_S, A_S	number of word tokens and citing authors in S	φ_z	multinomial distribution over journal titles specific to topic z
ω_S, a_S, j_S	vector form of word tokens/authors/journals in S	α, β, μ	dirichlet priors to multinomial distribution θ, φ and Φ

Fig. 3. Graphical representation and Notions of AJT model, which applies ACT model (Applied Tang, J., Jin, R., & Zhang, J., 2008, p.1056, Figure 1, Table 1)

Like ACT model, AJT model assumes that each citing author is related to distribution over topics and each word in citation sentences is derived from a topic. In the AJT model, the journal titles are related to each word. To determine a word (ω_Si) in citation sentences (S), citing authors (x_Si) are consider for a word. Each citing author is associated with a distributed topic. A topic is generated from the citing author-topic distribution. The words and journal titles are generated from a specific topic. AJT model presents (1) the distribution θ of A citing authors-topics, the distribution of $\varnothing$ of T topic-words, and the distribution φ of T topic-journal titles; and (2) the following topic z_Si and citing author x_Si for each word ω_Si. The detailed descriptions of the algorithm are provided in the Tang et al.'s paper [5,10].

3   Results and Analyses

For AJT model, we set the number of topics to 15 and finally select 8 topics as major topics. Since we discovered that there are similar topics on our results, we calculated the similarity between 15 topics to select the most representative topics. The topical similarities are measured by each word on topics and we calculated the similarities of two topics where each topic are represented in an array of a term vector. Through this process, we chose 8 topics which have high topical similarities (over 0.5). Each topic presents top 5 words from topic-word distribution, and 5 most related authors and journal titles are displayed along with each topic. By performing several times on the pilot studies, we decided to choose top 5 words which are quite appropriate to describe each topics.

The results of AJT-based topic modeling is shown in Table 1. We label topic 1 "breast cancer" whose top words include breast, expression women, and growth. Since the dataset is compiled with citation sentences, it implies that the topic "breast cancer" is a popular topic where researchers share and exchange ideas and facts related to breast cancer. In relation to the topic "breast cancer", the active authors of breast cancer are Johnston Stephen RD, Colditz Graham A, and Sternlicht Mark D, and they share ideas with others on breast cancer from our results. In terms of journals that provide a common place for idea sharing and communication, the journal "Breast Cancer Research" is the top journal of topic 1, and its impact factor is 5.49. Authors such as Kurzrock Razelle, and Axelrod Haley in group 4 are the leading researchers sharing ideas on the topic "targeted therapy." The topic 4 is associated with the targeted therapy represented by words like mutations, treatments, therapy and disease. The two most influential journals in topic 4 are "Oncotarget" and "Journal of Thoracic Oncology" whose impact factors are 6.36 and 5.28 respectively, which indicates that these two journals are the major journals encouraging authors to share ideas and collaborate with each other on cancer targeted therapy subject area. Authors like Zitgel Laurence, Galluzzi Lorenzo, and Kroemer Guido in the author group 7 are the ones that actively share ideas about the topic "Cancer Immunology." Top concepts that are related to this topic are cell, immune, clinical and antitumor. The top journal of the topic "Cancer Immunology" is Oncoinmmunology whose impact factor is 6.266. Romagnani Paola and Salem Husein K in topic 8 "Stem Cell" are the authors that communicate and share ideas actively with each other in the given field, and the journal "Stem Cells" (impact factor: 6.523) is the leading journal.

Table 1. The Results of AJT-based Topic Modeling in Oncology

Topic1	Topic2	Topic3	Topic4
Breast cancer	Cancer epigenetics	Leukemia	Targeted therapy
breast	methylation	expression	mutations
expression	DNA	mutations	clinical
mammary	expression	AML	treatment
risk	gene	treatment	survival

women	histone	leukemia	resistance
Author group1	**Author group2**	**Author group3**	**Author group4**
Johnston Stephen RD	Gray Steven G.	Tefferi A	Muller Patricia AJ
Colditz Graham A	Mahlknecht Ulrich	Anderson K C	Vousden Karen H
Sternlicht Mark D	Tollefsbol Trygve O.	Ratajczak Janina	Zaravinos Apostolos
Reis-Filho Jorge S	Lichtenstein Anatoly V	Schöffski P	Dienstmann Rodrigo
Esteva Francisco J	Williams David E	Gjertsen B T	Shtivelman Emma
Journal group1	**Journal group2**	**Journal group3**	**Journal group4**
Breast Cancer Research	Clinical Epigenetics	Leukemia	Oncotarget
Annals of Oncology	Oncoimmunology	Pigment Cell & Melanoma Research	Journal of Thoracic Oncology
Cancer Cell	JNCI	Annals of Oncology	Annals of Oncology Cancer Cell
Clinical Epigenetics	Molecular Cancer	Cancer Cell	Clinical Epigenetics
JNCI	Annals of Oncology	Breast Cancer Research	Oncoimmunology

Topic5	**Topic6**	**Topic7**	**Topic8**
Molecular cancer	Oncogene pathway	Cancer Immunology	Stem cell
expression	cell	cell	stem
p53	activity	immune	expression
mutant	activation	expression	differentiation
gene	protein	clinical	MSCs
survival	apoptosis	responses	growth
Author group5	**Author group6**	**Author group7**	**Author group8**
Clarke Paul A	Melino Gerry	Zitvogel Laurence	Romagnani Paola
Workman Paul	Martelli Alberto M	Galluzzi Lorenzo	Salem Husein K
Hoelder Swen	McCubrey James A	Kroemer Guido	Thiemermann Chris
Akhavan David	Blagosklonny Mikhail V	Eggermont Alexander	Lako Majlinda
Cassidy Liam D	Steelman Linda S	Vacchelli Erika	Mellough Carla B
Journal group5	**Journal group6**	**Journal group7**	**Journal group8**
Cancer Cell	Oncotarget	Oncoimmunology	Stem Cells
Neuro-Oncology	Annals of Oncology	Annals of Oncology	Annals of Oncology
Oncotarget	Cancer Cell	Breast Cancer Research	Cancer Cell
Molecular Oncology	Clinical Epigenetics	Cancer Cell	Clinical Epigenetics
Molecular Cancer	Oncogene	Clinical Epigenetics	Molecular Cancer

We visualize topic keywords obtained from results of AJT-based topic model. We construct the co-occurrence network and analyze which topic words play an important role in this domain. Each node in the network represents a topic word, and an edge represents a co-occurrence frequency between keywords. The size of nodes represents degree centrality and the color means network clusters obtained by using modularity algorithm. This network consists of 100 nodes and 1,436 edges. As shown in Figure 4, each topic belongs to a specific community, but shares some important topic keywords. Especially, the topic words positioned at the center is represented core-keywords in Oncology. Figure 4 indicates that these words are the essential concepts of the Oncology domain. Along with the results of AJT-based topic models, we can infer the major journals and authors develop their own research area based on these core-concepts.

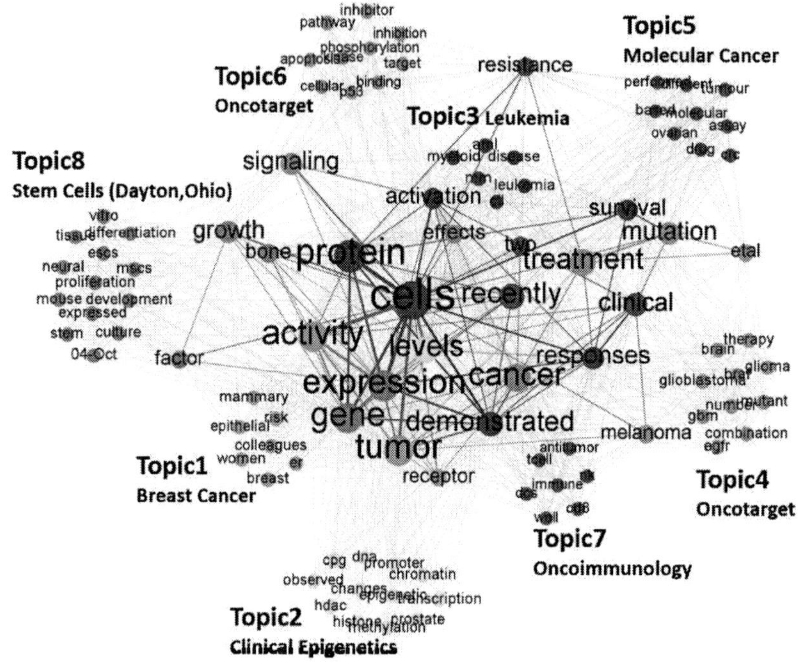

Fig. 4. Network of topic keywords

The above results imply that the proposed approach identifies which topics are frequently shared, who facilitates to exchange ideas, and which journals provide a placeholder for it. Identification of the triple relationship among authors, journals, and topics sheds new insight on understanding the well-discussed topics driven by the leading journals and authors that play a mediator role in the development of Oncology.

4   Conclusion

One of the major research problems in bibliometrics is how to map out the intellectual structure of a research field. The proposed approach tackles such research problem by utilizing citation sentences and AJT model. By using citation sentences as the input for AJT model to find latent meaning, AJT model suggests a new way to detect leading authors and journals in sub-disciplines represented by discovered topics in a certain field. Achieving this is not feasible by traditional frequency-based citation analysis.

One of the interesting observations is that the top-ranked journals in the discovered topics derived from AJT model are not ranked top in terms of JCR. For example, the "Oncotarget" journal is the top-ranked journal in three topics in our analysis, but the ranking of the journal is 20 according to JCR. Since we only report on preliminary results of our approach, we undertake in-depth analysis to investigate why this difference exists. We also conduct various statistical tests on the results. Based on the reported results in this paper, though, we claim that AJT can be used for discovering latent meaning associated citation sentences and the major players leading the field.

As a follow-up study, we will conduct a comparative study that compares the proposed approach with the general topic modeling technique such as LDA. We also plan to investigate whether there is a different impact of using citation sentences and general meta-data such as abstract and title for topic analysis on facilitating idea sharing and scholarly communication. In addition, we would like to consider the window size of citation sentences enriching citation context and to discover the authors' relationships among the neighboring citation sentences.

5   Reference

1. Garfield, E. (1955). Citation indexes for science: A new dimension in documentation through association of ideas. Science, 122(3159): 108–111. doi: 10.1126/ science.122.3159.108.
2. Moravcsik, M. J., & Murugesan, P. (1975). Some results on the function and quality of citations. Social studies of science, 5(1), 86-92.
3. Zhang, G., Ding, Y., and Milojević, S. (2013). Citation content analysis (cca): A framework for syntactic and semantic analysis of citation content. Journal of the American Society for Information Science and Technology, 64(7): 1490-1503.
4. Ding, Y., Zhang, G., Chambers, T., Song, M., Wang, X., and Zhai, C. (2014). Content-based citation analysis: The next generation of citation analysis. Journal of the Association for Information Science and Technology, 65(9): 1820-1833.
5. Tang, J., Zhang, J., Yao, L., Li, J., Zhang, L., & Su, Z. (2008). Arnetminer: extraction and mining of academic social networks. In Proceedings of the 14th ACM SIGKDD international conference on Knowledge discovery and data mining (pp. 990-998). ACM.
6. Dietz, L., Bickel, S., & Scheffer, T. (2007). Unsupervised prediction of citation influences. In Proceedings of the 24th international conference on Machine learning (pp. 233-240). ACM.
7. Nallapati, R. M., Ahmed, A., Xing, E. P., & Cohen, W. W. (2008). Joint latent topic models for text and citations. In Proceedings of the 14th ACM SIGKDD international conference on Knowledge discovery and data mining (pp. 542-550). ACM.
8. Kataria, S., Mitra, P., & Bhatia, S. (2010). Utilizing Context in Generative Bayesian Models for Linked Corpus. In AAAI (Vol. 10, p. 1)
9. Steyvers, M., Smyth, P., Rosen-Zvi, M., & Griffiths, T. (2004). Probabilistic author-topic models for information discovery. In Proceedings of the tenth ACM SIGKDD international conference on Knowledge discovery and data mining (pp. 306-315). ACM.

50

10. Tang, J., Jin, R., & Zhang, J. (2008). A topic modeling approach and its integration into the random walk framework for academic search. In Data Mining, 2008. ICDM'08. Eighth IEEE International Conference on (pp. 1055-1060). IEEE.

11. Di Marco, C., & Mercer, R. E. (2004). Hedging in scientific articles as a means of classifying citations. In Working Notes of the American Association for Artificial Intelligence (AAAI) Spring Symposium on Exploring Attitude and Affect in Text: Theories and Applications, 50-54.

What papers should I cite from my reading list? User evaluation of a manuscript preparatory assistive task

Aravind Sesagiri Raamkumar, Schubert Foo, Natalie Pang

Wee Kim Wee School of Communication and Information,
Nanyang Technological University, Singapore
{aravind002,sfoo,nlspang}@ntu.edu.sg

Abstract. Literature Review (LR) and Manuscript Preparatory (MP) tasks are two key activities for researchers. While process-based and technological-oriented interventions have been introduced to bridge the apparent gap between novices and experts for LR tasks, there are very few approaches for MP tasks. In this paper, we introduce a novel task of shortlisting important papers from the reading list of researchers, meant for citation in a manuscript. The technique helps in identifying the important and unique papers in the reading list. Based on a user evaluation study conducted with 116 participants, the effectiveness and usefulness of the task is shown using multiple evaluation metrics. Results show that research students prefer this task more than research and academic staff. Qualitative feedback of the participants including the preferred aspects along with critical comments is presented in this paper.

Keywords: manuscript preparation; shortlisting citations; scientific paper information retrieval; scientific paper recommender systems; digital libraries

1   Introduction

The Scientific Publication Lifecycle comprises of different activities carried out by researchers [5]. Of all these activities, the three main activities are literature review, actual research work and dissemination of results through conferences and journals. These three activities in themselves cover multiple sub-activities that require specific expertise and experience [16]. Prior studies have shown researchers with low experience, face difficulties in completing research related activities [9, 15]. These researchers rely on assistance from supervisors, experts and librarians for learning the required skills to pursue such activities. Scenarios where external assistance have been traditionally required are (i) selection of information sources (academic search engines, databases and citation indices), (ii) formulation of search queries, (iii) browsing of retrieved results and (iv) relevance judgement of retrieved articles [9]. Apart from human assistance, academic assistive systems have been built for alleviating the expertise gap between experts and novices in terms of research execution. Some of these interventions include search systems with faceted user interfaces for better display of search results [2], bibliometric tools for visualizing citation networks [7] and scientific paper recommender systems [3, 14], to name a few.

In the area of manuscript writing, techniques have been proposed to recommend articles for citation contexts in manuscripts [11]. In the context of manuscript publication, prior studies have tried to recommend prospective conference venues [25] most suited for the research in hand. One unexplored area is helping researchers in identifying the important and unique papers that can be potentially cited in the manuscript. This identification is affected by two factors. The first factor is the type of research where citation of a particular paper makes sense due to the particular citation context. The second factor is the type of article (for e.g., conference full paper, journal paper, demo paper) that the author is intending to write. For the first factor, there have been some previous studies [11, 14, 21]. The second factor represents a task that can be explored since the article-type places a constraint on the citations that can be made in a manuscript, in terms of dimensions such as recency, quantity, to name a few.

In our research, we address this new manuscript preparatory task with the objective of shortlisting papers from the reading list of researchers based on article-type preference. By the term 'shortlisting', we allude to the nature of the task in identifying important papers from the reading list This task is part of a functionality provided by an assistive system called Rec4LRW meant for helping researchers in literature review and manuscript preparation. The system uses a corpus of papers, built from an extract of ACM Digital Library (ACM DL). It is hypothesized that the Rec4LRW system will be highly beneficial to novice researchers such as Ph.D. and Masters students and also for researchers who are venturing into new research topics. A user evaluation study was conducted to evaluate all the tasks in the system, from a researcher's perspective.

In this paper, we report the findings from the study. The study was conducted with 116 participants comprising of research students, academic staff and research staff. Results from the six evaluation measures show that the participants prefer to have the shortlisting feature included in academic search systems and digital libraries. Subjective feedback from the participants in terms of the preferred features and the features that need to be improved, are also presented in the paper.

The reminder of this work is organized as follows. Section two surveys the related work. The Rec4LRW system is introduced along with dataset, technical details and unique UI features in section three. In section four, the shortlisting technique of the task is explained. Details about the user study and data collection are outlined in Section five. The evaluation results are presented in section six. The concluding remarks and future plans for research are provided in the final section.

2 Related Work

Conceptual models and systems have been proposed in the past for helping researchers during manuscript writing. Generating recommendations for citation contexts is an approach meant to help the researcher in finding candidate citations for particular placeholders (locations) in the manuscript. These studies make use of content oriented recommender techniques as there is no scope for using Collaborative Filtering (CF) based techniques due to lack of user ratings. Translation models have been specifically used in [13, 17] as they are able to handle the issue of vocabulary mismatch gap between the user query and document content. The efficiency of the approaches is dependent on the comprehensiveness of training set data as the locations and corresponding citations data are recorded. The study in [11] is the most sophisticated, as it does not expect the user to mark the citation contexts in the input paper unlike other studies where the contexts have to be set by the user. The proposed model in the study learns the placeholders in previous research articles where citations are widely made so that the citation recommendation can be made on occurrence of similar patterns. The methods in these studies are heavily reliant on the quality & quantity of training data; therefore they are not applicable to systems which lack access to full text of research papers.

Citation suggestions have also been provided as part of reference management and stand-alone recommendation tools. ActiveCite [21] is a recommendation tool that provides both high level and specific citation suggestions based on text mining techniques. Docear is one of the latest reference management software [3] with a mind map feature that helps users in better organizing their references. The in-built recommendation module in this tool is based on Content based (CB) recommendation technique with all the data stored in a central server. The Refseer system [14], similar to ActiveCite, provides both global and local (particular citation context) level recommendations. The system is based on the non-parametric probabilistic model proposed in [12]. These systems depend on the quality and quantity of full text data available in the central server as scarcity of papers could lead to redundant recommendations.

Even though article-type recommendations have not been practically implemented, the prospective idea has been discussed in few studies. The article-type dimension has been highlighted as part of the user's 'Purpose' in the multi-layer contextual model put forth in [8] and as one of the facets in document contextual information in [6]. The article type indirectly refers to the goal of the researcher. It is to be noted that goal or purpose related dimensions have been considered for research in other research areas of recommender systems namely course recommendations [23] and TV guide recommendations [20]. Our work, on the other hand, is the first to explore this task of providing article-type based recommendations with the aim of shortlisting important and unique papers from the cumulative reading list prepared by researchers during their literature review. Through this study, we hope to open new avenues of research which requires a different kind of mining of bibliographic data, for providing more relevant results.

3   Assistive System

3.1   Brief Overview

The Rec4LRW system has been built as a tool aimed to help researchers in two main tasks of literature review and one manuscript preparatory task. The three tasks are (i) Building an initial reading list of research papers, (ii) Finding similar papers based on a set of papers, and (iii) Shortlisting papers from the final reading list for inclusion in manuscript based on article-type choice. The usage context of the system is as follows. Typically, a researcher would run the first task for one or two times at the start of the literature review, followed by selection of few relevant seed papers which are then used for task 2. The second task takes these seed papers as an input to find topically similar papers. This task is run multiple times until the researcher is satisfied with the whole list of papers in the reading list. The third task (described in this paper), is meant to be run when the researcher is at the stage of writing manuscripts for publication. It is observed that the researcher would maintain numerous papers in his/her reading list while performing research (could be more than 100 papers for most research studies). The third task helps the researcher in identifying both important and unique papers from the reading list. The shortlisted papers count varies as per the article-type preference of the researcher. The recommendation mechanisms of the three tasks are based on seven features/criteria that represent the characteristics of the bibliography and its relationship with the parent research paper [19].

3.2 Dataset

A snapshot of the ACM Digital Library (ACM DL) is used as the dataset for the system. Papers from proceedings and journals for the period 1951 to 2011 form the dataset. The papers from the dataset have been shortlisted based on full text and metadata availability in the dataset, to form the sample set/corpus for the system. The sample set contains a total of 103,739 articles and corresponding 2,320,345 references.

3.3 User-Interface (UI) Features

In this sub-section, the unique UI features of the Rec4LRW system are presented. Apart from the regular fields such as author name(s), abstract, publication year and citation count, the system displays the fields:- author-specified keywords, references count and short summary of the paper (if the abstract of the paper is missing). Most importantly, we have included information cue labels beside the title for each article. There are four labels (1) Popular, (2) Recent, (3) High Reach and (4) Survey/Review. A screenshot from the system for the cue labels (adjacent to article title) is provided in Figure 1.

The display logic for the cue labels are described as follows. The recent label is displayed for papers published between the years 2009 and 2011 (the most recent papers in the ACM dataset is of 2011). The survey/review label is displayed for papers which are of the type - literature survey or review. For the popular label, the unique citation counts of all papers for the selected research topic are first retrieved from the database. The label is displayed for a paper if the citation count is in the top 5% percentile of the citation counts for that topic. Similar logic is used for the high reach label with references count data. The high reach label indicates that the paper has more number of references than most other articles for the research topic, thereby facilitating the scope for extended citation chaining. Specifically for task 3, the system provides an option for the user to view the papers in the parent cluster of the shortlisted papers. This feature helps the user in serendipitously finding more papers for reading. The screenshot for this feature is provided in Figure 1.

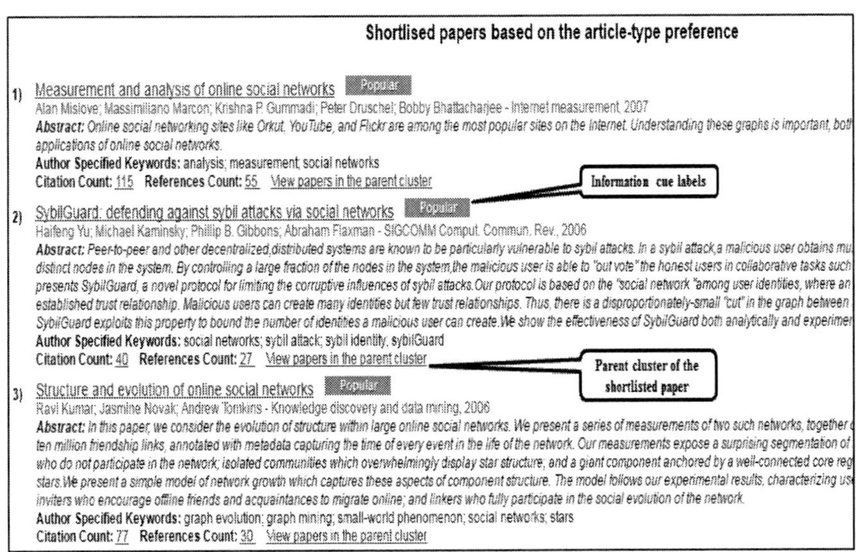

Fig. 1. Sample list of shortlisted papers for the task output

4 Technique For Shortlisting Papers From Reading List

The objective of this task is to help researchers in identifying important (based on citation counts) and unique papers from the final reading list. These papers are to be considered as potential candidates for citation in the manuscript. For this task, the Girvan–Newman algorithm [10] was used for identifying the clusters in the citations network. The specific goal of clustering is to identify the communities within the citation network. From the identified clusters, the top cited papers are shortlisted. The algorithm is implemented as the *EdgeBetweennessClusterer* in JUNG library. The algorithm was selected as it is the one of the most prominent community detection algorithms based on link removal. The other algorithms considered were voltage clustering algorithm [24] and bi-component DFS clustering algorithm [22]. Based on internal trail tests, the Girvan–Newman algorithm was able to consistently identify meaningful clusters using the graph constructed with the citations and references of the papers from the reading list.

As a part of this task, we have tried to explore the notion of varying the count of shortlisted papers by article-type choice. For this purpose, four article-types were considered: conference full paper (cfp), conference poster (cp), generic research paper (gp)[1] and case study (cs). The article-type classification is not part of the ACM metadata but it is partly inspired by the article classification used in Emerald publications. The number of papers to be shortlisted for these article-types was identified by using the historical data from ACM dataset. First, the papers in the dataset were filtered by using the title field and section field for the four article-types. Second, the average of the references count was calculated for the filtered papers for each article-type from previous step. The average references count for the article-types gp, cs, cfp and cp are 26, 17, 16 and 6 respectively. This new data field is used to set the number of papers to be retrieved from the paper clusters. The procedure for this technique is given in Procedure 1.

Procedure 1 shortlistpapers(P)

Input: P – set of papers in the final reading list
     AT – article-type choice of the user
1: $RC \leftarrow$ the average references count retrieved for AT
2: $R \leftarrow$ list of retrieved citations & references of papers from P
3: $G \leftarrow$ directed sparse graph created with papers from R
4: run *edge betweenness* algorithm on G to form cluster set C
5: $S \leftarrow$ final list of shortlisted papers
6: **if** $|C| > RC$ **then**
7:   **while** $|S| = RC$
8:      **for** each cluster in C **do**
9:        sort papers in the cluster on citation count
10:        $s \leftarrow$ top ranked paper from the cluster
11:        add s to S
12:      **end for**
13:   **end while**
14: **else**
15:      $N \leftarrow 0$
16.   **while** $|S| = RC$
17:        $N \leftarrow N+1$
18:      **for** each cluster in C **do**
19:        sort papers in the cluster on citation count
20:        $s \leftarrow N$ ranked paper from the cluster
21:        add s to S
22:      **end for**
23:     **end while**
24: **end if**
25: display papers from S to user

---

[1] A paper is qualified as a generic research paper when it doesn't fall quality under the requirements of all the other article-types

5   User Evaluation Study

In IR and RS studies, offline experiments are conducted for evaluating the proposed technique/algorithm with baseline approaches. Since the task addressed in the current study is a novel task, the best option was to perform a user evaluation study with researchers. Considering the suggestions from [4], the objective of the study was to ascertain the usefulness and effectiveness of the task to researchers. The specific evaluation goals were (i) ascertain the agreement percentages of the evaluation measures and (ii) identify the top preferred and critical aspects of the task through the subjective feedback of the participants. An online pre-screening survey was conducted to identify the potential participants. Participants needed to have experience in writing conference or journal paper(s) as a qualification for taking part in the study.

All the participants were required to evaluate the three tasks and the overall system. In task 1, the participants had to select a research topic from a list of 43 research topics. On selection of topic, the system provides the top 20 paper recommendations which are meant to be part of the initial LR reading list. In task 2, they had to select a minimum of five papers from task 1 in order for the system to retrieve 30 topically similar papers. For the third task, the participants were requested to add at least 30 papers in the reading list. The paper count was set to 30 as the threshold for highest number of shortlisted papers was 26 (for the article-type 'generic research paper'). The three other article-types provided for the experiment were conference full paper, conference poster and case study. The shortlisted papers count for these article-types was fixed by taking average of the references count of the related papers from the ACM DL extract. The participant had to then select the article-type and run the task so that the system could retrieve the shortlisted papers. The screenshot of the task 3 from the Rec4LRW system is provided in Figure 1.

In addition to the basic metadata, the system provides the feature "View papers in the parent cluster" for the participant to see the cluster from which the paper has been shortlisted. The evaluation screen was provided to the user at the bottom of the screen (not shown in Figure 1). The participants had to answer seven mandatory survey questions and one optional subjective feedback question as a part of the evaluation. The seven survey questions and the corresponding measures are provided in Table 1. A five-point Likert scale was provided for measuring participant agreement for each question. The measures were selected based on the key aspects of the task. The measures *Relevance, Usefulness, Importance, Certainty, Good_List* and *Improvement_Needed* were meant to ascertain the quality of the recommendations. The final measure *Shortlisting_Feature* was used to identify whether participants would be interested to use this task in current academic search systems and digital libraries.

Table 1. Evaluation measures and corresponding questions

Measure	Question
Relevance	The shortlisted papers are relevant to my article-type preference
Usefulness	The shortlisted papers are useful for inclusion in my manuscript

Importance	The shortlisted papers comprises of important papers from my reading list
Certainty	The shortlisted list comprises of papers which I would definitely cite in my manuscript
Good_List	This is a good recommendation list, at an overall level
Improvement_Needed	There is a need to further improve this shortlisted papers list
Shortlisting_Feature	I would like to see the feature of shortlisting papers from reading list based on article-type preference, in academic search systems and databases

The response values 'Agree' and 'Strongly Agree' were the two values considered for the calculation of agreement percentages for the evaluation measures. Descriptive statistics were used to measure central tendency. Independent samples t-test was used to check the presence of statistically significant difference in the mean values of the students and staff group, for the testing the hypothesis. Statistical significance was set at $p < .05$. Statistical analyses were done using SPSS 21.0 and R. Participants' subjective feedback responses were coded by a single coder using an inductive approach [1], with the aim of identifying the central themes (concepts) in the text.

The study was conducted between November 2015 and January 2016. Out of the eligible 230 participants, 116 participants signed the consent form and completed the whole study inclusive of the three tasks in the system. 57 participants were Ph.D./Masters students while 59 were research staff, academic staff and librarians. The average research experience for Ph.D. students was 2 years while for staff, it was 5.6 years. 51% of participants were from the computer science, electrical and electronics disciplines, 35% from information and communication studies discipline while 14% from other disciplines.

6 Results and Discussion

6.1 Agreement Percentages (AP)

The agreement percentages (AP) for the seven measures by the participant groups are shown in Figure 2. In the current study, an agreement percentage above 75% is considered as an indication of higher agreement from the participants. As expected, the AP of students was consistently higher than the staff with the biggest difference found for the measures *Usefulness* (82.00% for students, 64.15% for staff) and *Good_List* (76.00% for students, 62.26% for staff). It has been reported in earlier studies that graduate students generally look for assistance in most stages of research [9]. Consequently, students would prefer technological interventions such as the current system due to the simplicity in interaction. Hence, the evaluation of students was evidently better than staff. The quality measures *Importance* (85.96% for students, 77.97% for staff) and *Shortlisting_Feature* (84.21% for students, 74.58% for staff) had the highest APs. This observation validates the usefulness of the technique in identifying popular/seminal papers from the reading list. Due to favorable APs for the most measures, the lowest agreement values were observed for the measure *Improve-*

ment_Needed (57.89% for students, 57.63% for staff). The results for the measure *Certainty* (70% for students, 62.26% for staff) indicate some level of reluctance among the participants in being confident of citing the papers. Citation of a particular paper is subject to the particular citation context in the manuscript, therefore not all participants would be able to prejudge their citation behavior. In summary, participants seem to acknowledge the usefulness of the task in identifying important papers from the reading list. However, there is an understandable lack of inclination in citing these papers. This issue is to be addressed in future studies.

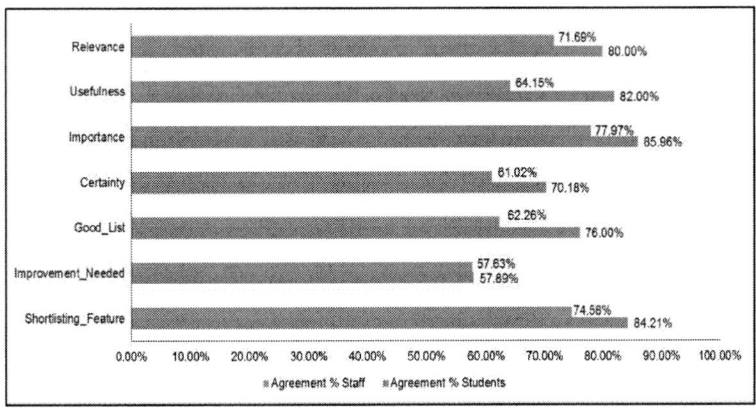

Fig. 2. Agreement percentage results by participant group

6.2   Qualitative Data Analysis

In Table 2, the top five categories of the preferred aspects and critical aspects are listed.

Preferred Aspects. Out of the total 116 participants, 68 participants chose to give feedback about the features that they found to be useful. 24% of the participants felt that the feature of the shortlisting papers based on article-type preference was quite preferable and would help them in completing their tasks in a faster and efficient manner. They also felt that the quality of the shortlisting papers was satisfactory. 15% of the participants felt that the information cue labels (popular, recent, high reach and literature survey) were helpful for them in relevance judgement of the shortlisted papers. This particular observation of the participants was echoed for the first two tasks of the Rec4LRW system, thereby validating the usefulness of information cue labels in academic search systems and digital libraries. Around 11% of the participants felt the option of viewing papers in the parent cluster of the particular shortlisted papers was useful in two ways. Firstly, it helped in understanding the different clusters formed with the references and citations of the papers in the reading list. Secondly, the clusters served as an avenue for finding some useful and relevant papers in serendipitous manner as some papers could have been missed by the researcher during the literature review process. The other features that the participants commended were the metadata provided along with the shortlisted papers (citations count, article summary) and the paper management collection features across the three tasks.

Table 2. Top five categories for preferred and critical aspects

Rank	Preferred aspects categories	Critical aspects categories
1	Shortlisting Feature & Rec. Quality (24%)	Rote Selection of Papers (16%)
2	Information Cue Labels (15%)	Limited Dataset Issue (5%)
3	View Papers in Clusters (11%)	Quality can be Improved (5%)
4	Rich Metadata (7%)	Not Sure of the Usefulness of the Task (4%)
5	Ranking of Papers (3%)	UI can be Improved (3%)

Critical Aspects. Out of the 116 participants, 41 participants gave critical comments about the task and features of the system catering to the task. Around 16% of the participants felt that the study procedure of adding 30 papers to the reading list as a precursor for running the task was uninteresting. The reasons cited were the irrelevance of some of the papers to the participants as these papers had to be added just for the sake of executing the task while some participants felt that the 30 papers count was too much while some could not comprehend why these many papers had to be added. Around 5% of the participants felt that the study experience was hindered by the dataset not catering to recent papers (circa 2012-2015) and the dataset being restricted to computer science related topics.

Another 5% of the participants felt that they shortlisting algorithm/technique could be improved to provide a better list of papers. A section of these participants needed more recent papers in the final list while others wanted papers specifically from high impact publications. Around 4% of the participants could not find the usefulness of the task in their work. They felt that the task was not beneficial. The other minor critical comments given by the participants were the ranking of the list could be improved, the task execution speed could be improved and more UI control features could be provided, such as sorting options and free-text search box.

7   Conclusion and Future Work

For literature review and manuscript preparatory related tasks, the gap between novices and experts in terms of task knowledge and execution skills is well-known [15]. A majority of the previous studies have brought forth assistive systems that focus heavily on LR tasks, while only a few studies have concentrated on approaches for helping researchers during manuscript preparation. With the Rec4LRW system, we have attempted to address the aforementioned gap with a novel task for shortlisting articles from researcher's reading list, for inclusion in manuscript. The shortlisting task makes use of a popular community detection algorithm [10] for identifying communities of papers generated from the citations network of the papers from the reading list. Additionally, we have also tried to vary shortlisted papers count by taking the article-type choice into consideration.

In order to evaluate the system, a user evaluation study was conducted with 116 participants who had the experience of writing research papers. The participants were instructed to run each task followed by evaluation questionnaire. Participants were requested to answer survey questions and provide subjective feedback on the features of the tasks. As hypothesized before the start of the study, students evaluated the task favorably for all measures. There was high level of agreement among all participants on the availability of important papers among the shortlisted papers. This finding validates the aim of the task in identifying the papers that manuscript reviewers would expected to be cited. In the qualitative feedback provided by the participants, majority of the participants preferred the idea of shortlisting papers and also thought the output of the task was of good quality. Secondly, they liked the information cue labels provided along with certain papers, for indicating the special nature of the paper. As a part of critical feedback, participants felt that the study procedure was a bit longwinded as they had to select 30 papers without reading them, just for running the task.

As a part of future work, the scope for this task will be expanded to bring in more variations for the different article-type choices. For instance, research would be conducted:- (i) to ascertain the quantity of recent papers to be shortlisted for different article-type choices, (ii) include new papers in the output so that the user is alerted about some key paper(s) which could have been missed during literature review, (iii) provide more user control in the system so that the user can select papers as mandatory to be shortlisted and (iv) Integrate this task with the citation context recommendation task [11, 14] so that the user can be fully aided during the whole process of manuscript writing.

Acknowledgements. This research is supported by the National Research Foundation, Prime Minister's Office, Singapore under its International Research Centres in Singapore Funding Initiative and administered by the Interactive Digital Media Programme Office.

References

[1]   A General Inductive Approach for Analyzing Qualitative Evaluation Data: *https://flexiblelearning.auckland.ac.nz/poplhlth701/8/files/general_inductive_approach.pdf.* Accessed: 2016-04-07.

[2]   Atanassova, I. and Bertin, M. 2014. Faceted Semantic Search for Scientific Papers. *PLoS Biology.* 2, (2014).

[3]   Beel, J. et al. 2013. Introducing Docear's Research Paper Recommender System. *Proceedings of the ACM/IEEE Joint Conference on Digital Libraries (JCDL)* (2013).

[4]   Beel, J. et al. 2013. Research Paper Recommender System Evaluation : A Quantitative Literature Survey. *Proceedings of the Workshop on Reproducibility and Replication in Recommender Systems Evaluation (RepSys) at the ACM Recommender System conference* (2013).

[5]   Björk, B.-C. and Hedlund, T. 2003. Scientific Publication Life-Cycle Model (SPLC). *ELPUB.* (2003).

[6]   Champiri, Z.D. et al. 2015. A systematic review of scholar context-aware recommender systems. *Expert Systems with Applications*. 42, 3 (2015), 1743–1758.

[7]   Chou, J.-K. and Yang, C.-K. 2011. PaperVis: Literature Review Made Easy. *Computer Graphics Forum*. 30, 3 (Jun. 2011), 721–730.

[8]   Dehghani, Z. et al. 2011. A multi-layer contextual model for recommender systems in digital libraries. *Aslib Proceedings*. 63, 6 (2011), 555–569.

[9]   Du, J.T. and Evans, N. 2011. Academic Users' Information Searching on Research Topics: Characteristics of Research Tasks and Search Strategies. *The Journal of Academic Librarianship*. 37, 4 (Jul. 2011), 299–306.

[10]   Girvan, M. and Newman, M.E.J. 2002. Community structure in social and biological networks. *Proceedings of the national academy of sciences*. National Acad Sciences.

[11]   He, Q. et al. 2011. Citation recommendation without author supervision. *Proceedings of the fourth ACM international conference on Web search and data mining - WSDM '11* (New York, New York, USA, 2011), 755.

[12]   He, Q. et al. 2010. Context-aware citation recommendation. *Proceedings of the 19th international conference on World wide web - WWW '10*. (2010), 421.

[13]   Huang, W. et al. 2012. Recommending Citations : Translating Papers into References. *Proceedings of the 21st ACM international conference on Information and knowledge management* (2012), 1910–1914.

[14]   Huang, W. et al. 2014. RefSeer : A Citation Recommendation System. *Digital Libraries (JCDL), 2014 IEEE/ACM Joint Conference on* (2014), 371–374.

[15]   Karlsson, L. et al. 2012. From Novice to Expert: Information Seeking Processes of University Students and Researchers. *Procedia - Social and Behavioral Sciences*. 45, (Jan. 2012), 577–587.

[16]   Levy, Y. and Ellis, T.J. 2006. A Systems Approach to Conduct an Effective Literature Review in Support of Information Systems Research. *Informing Science Journal*. 9, (2006).

[17]   Lu, Y. et al. 2011. Recommending citations with translation model. *Proceedings of the 20th ACM international conference on Information and knowledge management* (New York, New York, USA, 2011), 2017–2020.

[18]   Mcnee, S.M. 2006. *Meeting User Information Needs in Recommender Systems*. Proquest.

[19]   Sesagiri Raamkumar, A. et al. 2015. Rec4LRW – Scientific Paper Recommender System for Literature Review and Writing. *Proceedings of the 6th International Conference on Applications of Digital Information and Web Technologies* (2015), 106–120.

[20]   van Setten, M. et al. 2006. Goal-based structuring in recommender systems. *Interacting with Computers*. 18, 3 (May 2006), 432–456.

[21]   Shaoping, Z. 2010. *ActiveCite : An Interactive System for Automatic Citation Suggestion*.

[22]   Tarjan, R. 1972. Depth-first search and linear graph algorithms. *SIAM journal on computing*. 1, 2 (1972), 146–160.

[23]   Winoto, P. et al. 2012. Contexts in a Paper Recommendation System with Collaborative Filtering. *the International Review of Research in Open and Distance Learning*. 13, 5 (2012), 56–75.

[24]   Wu, F. and Huberman, B.A. 2004. Finding communities in linear time: a physics approach. *The European Physical Journal B-Condensed Matter and Complex Systems*. 38, 2 (2004), 331–338.

[25]   Xia, F. et al. 2013. Socially-aware venue recommendation for conference participants. *Ubiquitous Intelligence and Computing, 2013 IEEE 10th International Conference on and 10th International Conference on Autonomic and Trusted Computing (UIC/ATC)* (2013), 134–141.

Delineating Fields Using Mathematical Jargon

Jevin D. West[1] and Jason Portenoy[1]

Information School, University of Washington, `jevinw@uw.edu`

Abstract. Tracing ideas through the scientific literature is useful in understanding the origin of ideas and for generating new ones. Machines can be trained to do this at large scale, feeding search engines and recommendation algorithms. Citations and text are the features commonly used for these tasks. In this paper, we focus on a largely ignored facet of scholarly papers—the equations. Mathematical language varies from field to field but original formulae are maintained over generations (e.g., Shannon's Entropy equation). Here we extract a common set of mathematical symbols from more than 250,000 LaTeX source files in the arXiv repository. We compare the symbol distributions across different fields and calculate the jargon distance between fields. We find a greater difference between the experimental and theoretical disciplines than within these fields. This provides a first step at using equations as a bridge between disciplines that may not cite each other or may speak different natural languages but use a similar mathematical language.

Introduction

There has been considerable effort building and designing new recommendation algorithms to help scholars find relevant papers. Most of these methods depend on citations [14], full text [5] or usage data [3]. One feature that has been largely ignored are equations and the mathematical language surrounding these equations. These formal languages can tie together papers and ideas across fields and time periods. Shannon's famous entropy equation (also used in this paper) is an example of this kind of trace [7]. Unlike natural languages, formal languages such as mathematics are exempt from plagiarism rules. The norm is for an author to copy an equation from the original source. This provides a unique opportunity for tracing ideas back to their origins and for tracking them forward in time.

There have been attempts at utilizing the equations as a search facet. For example, Springer's LaTeX Search tool[1] allows authors to search formulae (in LaTeX format) from more than 8 million documents in Springer journals and articles. This is used both as a tool for searching similar formulae and for translating formulae to existing documents. But what if a researcher wants to find not just individual manuscripts with the same equations, but fields of study and groups of papers using similar language? What kind of formalism can be used to map jargon differences across the quantitative sciences?

---

[1] `http://latexsearch.com`

In this paper, we measure the communication efficiency or "jargon distance" between fields using mathematical symbols. The jargon metric is derived from a recent paper by Vilhena et al. [11] which measures the distance between disciplines using n-grams extracted from millions of papers in the JSTOR corpus. In our paper, we find that the metric separates fields that are different both in content and mathematical notation[2].

Our ultimate research goal is to find ways to utilize equations and formal notation in scholarly recommendation. The more proximate goal of this paper is to validate that equation jargon can delineate the relationship among fields at the scale of hundreds of thousands of papers in similar ways to citation and text-based clustering. We show in this paper that the jargon metric proposed in this paper does a reasonable job at identifying fields with similar attributes and language. The next steps will involve full-corpus scaling, extracting mathematical grammar, and incorporating the metric into citation-based recommendation algorithms [13,14].

Methods

Data

Research papers were downloaded from arXiv.org[3], an open-access e-print service in the fields of physics, mathematics, computer science, quantitative biology, quantitative finance, and statistics. For this study, we used a sample (N = 266,906) of papers published between 2000 and 2009. We downloaded papers using the arXiv's bulk data download, analyzing papers that had field designations in their filenames. We compiled a list of the LaTeX representations of 103 symbols commonly used in mathematical formulae[4]. These symbols included some commonly used Greek letters (e.g. "\alpha" [α], "\omega" [ω]), arrows (e.g. "\rightarrow" [$\rightarrow$]), binary operation/relation symbols (e.g. "=", ">", "\geq" [$\geq$], "\times" [$\times$]), and some other symbols (e.g. "\forall" [$\forall$]).[5] A shortcoming of this approach is that it does not take into account the ability of authors to redefine commands and refer to symbols with these new command names, but it gives a rough idea of the usage of these symbols over the corpus. Using the LaTeX source for the arXiv papers, we counted the occurrence of each of these symbols. We used field designations provided by the arXiv; however, the fields could be determined by other methods, including citation clustering [14], co-citations [8], and topic modeling [12]. We intend to combine the jargon metric with these different clustering methods in future studies.

---

[2] These content comparisons were based on inspection of sample papers in the respective fields. More rigorous inspection is needed.

[3] https://arxiv.org/help/bulk_data

[4] Modified from https://www.sharelatex.com/learn/List_of_Greek_letters_and_math_symbols

[5] Our list of symbols is not exhaustive; for example, it does not include certain structural elements of equations such as sums. We intend to expand the list in future analysis.

Jargon Distance

To measure the communication barrier between fields, we adapt a metric developed by Vilhena et al. [11]. In this study, the authors develop a model of communication to topographically map the JSTOR corpus. Instead of using n-grams from full text like the Vilhena study, we use the language of mathematics—such as symbolic notation and Greek letters—extracted from LaTeX source files.

The jargon distance (E_{ij}) between field i and j is determined by calculating the ratio between two things: (1) the entropy H of a random variable X_i with a probability distribution based on the frequency of mathematical symbols within field i and (2) the cross entropy[6] Q between the distributions in field i and j,

$$E_{ij} = \frac{H(X_i)}{Q(p_i||p_j)} = \frac{-\sum_{x \in \mathcal{X}} p_i(x) \log_2 p_i(x)}{-\sum_{x \in \mathcal{X}} p_i(x) \log_2 p_j(x)} \tag{1}$$

This calculation derives itself from a general communication heuristic whereby a mathematician communicates with another mathematician via a channel [7]. The mathematician writing the formulae in field i has a codebook P_i that maps mathematical concepts to codewords, which mathematician in field j with codebook P_j has to decode. Note that the metric is not symmetrical—field j may more efficiently decode concepts in field i than field j does for field i. The model assumes that the codebooks are optimized based on the frequency of different terms. This power-law assumption holds well for English words [15,16]. It also seems to hold for mathematical terms; we find a Zipfian distribution in our sample (see Figure 1).

This simple metric of communication efficiency has advantages. It is based on a model of communication, which has firm theoretical foundations and additional tools to build upon. Second, it is easy to calculate and can run an entire corpus over a relatively short amount of time[7].

Results

Table 1 shows the top 20 symbols in our sample. The full distribution of symbols follows a power-like law (see Figure 1). This is important given the assumption of the jargon distance metric. We find large numbers of equal signs and inequality symbols but far fewer of others.

After extracting the symbols and distributions of symbols across fields, we calculated jargon distances between fields. We wanted to know if similar fields had smaller jargon distances when compared to more dissimilar fields. To do

---

[6] The cross entropy is the the entropy of X_i plus the Kullback-Leibler divergence between p_i and p_j [4].

[7] We calculated distances for 200k papers in less than 5 minutes on a micro EC2 instance with Amazon's Web Services (AWS).

Table 1. Top 20 mathematical symbols and letters among the papers sampled.

Symbol	Count	Symbol	Count
$>$	131,163,440	β	2,970,664
$<$	124,248,288	γ	2,876,255
$=$	119,559,867	ρ	2,827,491
$\in$	9,586,274	ϕ	2,820,464
μ	5,655,959	δ	2,677,700
α	5,193,305	θ	2,483,652
π	4,021,629	τ	2,482,211
ν	3,382,075	ω	2,443,861
λ	3,360,273	$\times$	2,320,697
σ	3,207,950	Δ	2,273,644

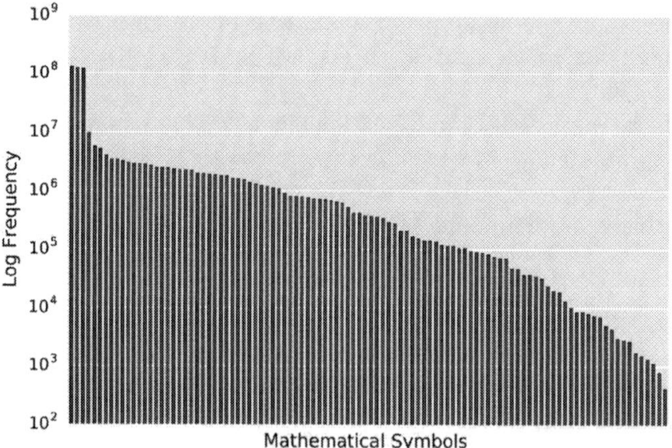

Fig. 1. Distribution of math symbols. The distribution of mathematical symbols in our sample. Most terms occur relatively infrequently compared to the equals ($=$) and inequality ($>$, $<$) symbols which occurred more than 10^8 times in equations and mathematical discussions.

this, we applied standard hierarchical clustering methods to the distance matrix in order to infer which fields were most like each other. We visualized the groupings using dendrograms. The dendrogram in Figure 2 was produced using a hierarchical clustering algorithm implemented in SciPy's linkage function[8]. We used UPGMA [9], which is an agglomerative method that uses average linkage as its criterion. The clustering is done on the adjacency matrix of fields where E_{ij} is the distance. Although the distance metric is not symmetric, for the clustering we symmetrize the matrix by taking the average of the the distances E_{ij} and E_{ji}.

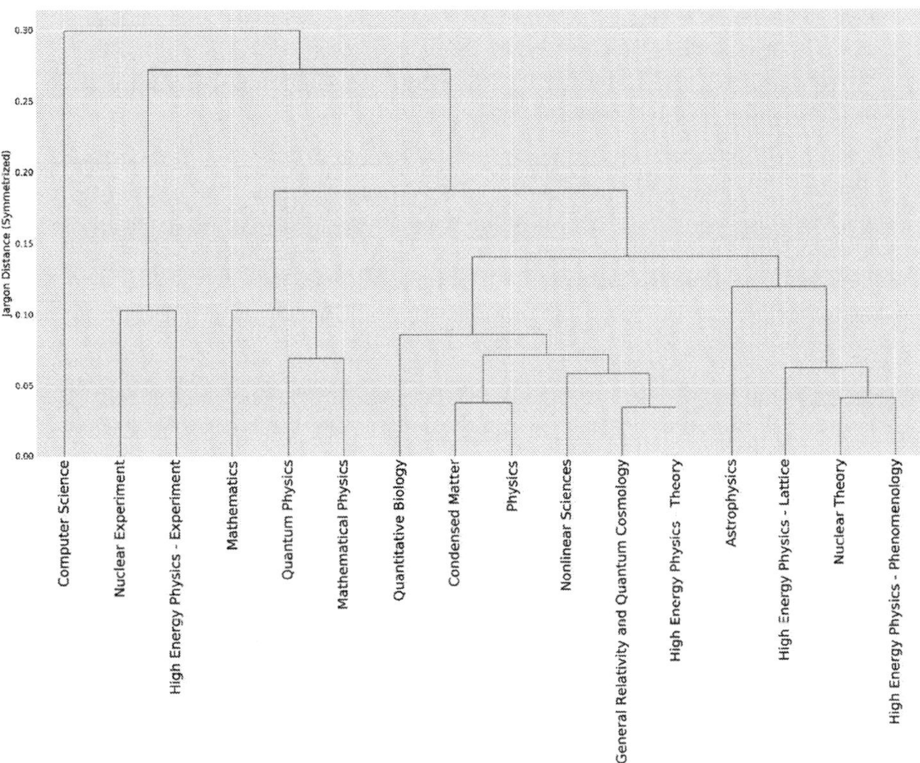

Fig. 2. Hierarchical Clustering. The dendrogram shows the relationships among the different fields represented in the arXiv. The jargon distance is used as the distance metric showing the relationship among disciplines within a sample of 266,906 papers in the arXiv. The distance between fields was determined using the mathematical jargon distance (E_{ij}) [11]. For this clustering, the distance between fields is the mean jargon distance of E_{ij} and E_{ji}.

---

[8] SciPy version 0.17.0 running on Python 2.7.6

We find a separation among theoretical and experimental sciences. Nuclear Experiment is most similar to High Energy Physics - Experiment (see Figure 2). We see Computer Science as an outlier to the rest of the fields. Mathematics shares a closer branch with Mathematical Physics than with any other discipline other than Quantum Physics. Quantitative Biology sits on its own but within the branch that includes Condensed Matter, Physics, Nonlinear Sciences, among others. We need to further investigate whether these similarities are real.

Figure 3 shows the distances between all fields using a heatmap. The darker colors represent larger jargon distances (lower communication efficiency between the writer and reader). The largest differences are between Computer Science and Experimental Physics, but Computer Science, in general, is quite different than almost all fields except Mathematics. Computer scientists and mathematicians seems to use similar symbols when conveying technical concepts. High Energy Physics (lattice) and High Energy Physics (phenomenology) are among the most similar, as one would expect.

Table 2 shows the top ten symbols for three fields: Computer Science, Nuclear Experiment, and High Energy Physics Experiment. The pairing from computer science to high energy physics experiment had a (mean) jargon distance of 0.171, whereas nuclear experiment to high energy physics experiment had a much smaller distance of 0.033. The top ten symbols help explain the differences (even though ten are not enough to see the full distribution differences).

Table 2. Comparing fields. This table compares two fields that have small jargon distances and two fields that have large jargon distances (see Figure 3). The (mean) jargon distance between the three pairings are the following (CS, Nuc Exp, **0.142**), (CS, HEP Exp, **0.171**), and (Nuc Exp, HEP Exp, **0.033**). The experimental sciences seem to use mathematical languages more similar to each other than to computer science. CS = Computer Science. Nuc Exp = Nuclear Experiment. HEP Exp = High Energy Physics Experiment.

CS		Nuc Exp		HEP Exp	
Symbol	Count	Symbol	Count	Symbol	Count
$=$	1,845,458	$>$	1,624,214	$>$	3,146,439
$>$	1,703,602	$<$	1,592,675	$<$	2,957,547
$<$	1,649,968	$=$	1,188,445	$=$	2,217,220
$\in$	253,658	$!=$	29,422	π	168,633
$\leq$	63,702	π	24,879	μ	100,176
α	63,302	$\in$	24,139	ν	85,847
μ	56,150	γ	18,637	$\in$	71,923
σ	45,041	$\cap$	17,218	γ	68,772
$\cap$	36,338	μ	14,692	η	65,464
λ	34,390	σ	13,867	$\rightarrow$	59,804

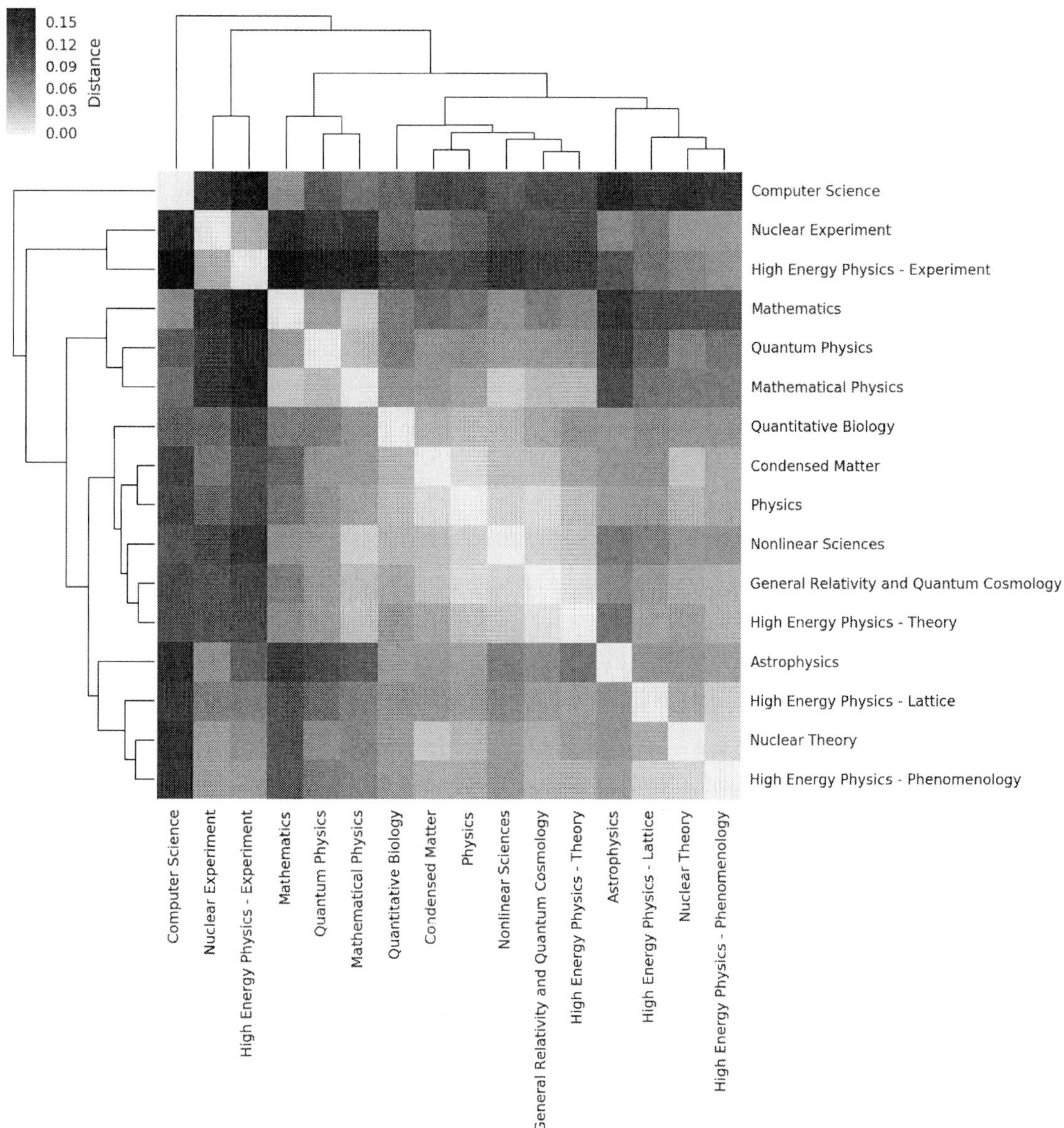

Fig. 3. Distance Matrix. The heatmap provides a visual representation of the distances between fields. We use the symmetrized version of the jargon distance matrix. The darker square represents a greater distance between two fields. For example, the frequency distribution of symbols in Computer Science is quite different than the mathematical notation found in Experimental High Energy Physics.

Discussion

Scientific papers contain many features that are used in search engines and recommendation algorithms: authors, titles, full text, citations, figures, etc. One feature largely ignored within the digital library community (at least relative to the other features) are equations. In this paper, we apply a model of communication efficiency between groups of papers first proposed by Vilhena et al. [11]. We find that field relationships (i.e., how fields are grouped hierarchcially) are recapitulated when using the jargon distance metric (Figure 2). The results are surprising given the simplicity of the data extraction and distance calculation. We only use isolated symbols and the frequency of these symbols to infer the groupings of fields. The resultant groups seem to assemble in logical ways (e.g., the experimental sciences group together, while the more theoretical fields assemble in another area of the tree). However, we see these results as preliminary evidence for using mathematical symbols as a way of clustering papers and topics.

We need to further investigate the true differences in fields. We plan to use citation based clustering as another means of field designation. We also plan to talk to scholars in the various fields to assess the validity of the clusters. In addition, we will extend our analysis to the full arXiv corpus. For corpora with no LaTeX available, we plan to use computer vision techniques from the viziometrics.org project for automatically extracting equations from PDFs [6]. We plan also to compare the jargon method to other well-known methods such as cosine similarity [10], LDA [1], and word2vec [2]. The primary difference we see from these methods is the communication theory underlying the jargon metric, but there needs to be analytic work for making this argument. In addition, we plan to expand beyond isolated symbols and analyze mathematical grammar.

Assuming the methods hold, our ultimate goal for this research project is to integrate our methods into existing recommendation engines at the scale of micro-fields. It is at these finer scales where the method could bridge seemingly disparate, emerging fields that are using similar mathematical language.

We also plan to extend this analysis to Science of Science questions, investigating the birth and death of ideas and the sociology surrounding these ideas. We see equations as an effective way of tracing ideas both forwards and backwards in time. The relative stability of equations and mathematical language provides a unique opportunity for tracking the movement of ideas across time and across disciplines.

Acknowledgements

We would like to thank three anonymous reviewers for their helpful feedback.

References

1. Blei, D.M., Ng, A.Y., Jordan, M.I.: Latent dirichlet allocation. the Journal of machine Learning research 3, 993–1022 (2003)

2. Goldberg, Y., Levy, O.: word2vec explained: Deriving mikolov et al.'s negative-sampling word-embedding method. arXiv preprint arXiv:1402.3722 (2014)
3. Kantor, P.B., Rokach, L., Ricci, F., Shapira, B.: Recommender systems handbook. Springer (2011)
4. Kullback, S., Leibler, R.A.: On information and sufficiency. The Annals of Mathematical Statistics 22(1), 79–86 (1951)
5. Lü, L., Medo, M., Yeung, C.H., Zhang, Y.C., Zhang, Z.K., Zhou, T.: Recommender Systems p. 97 (Feb 2012), http://arxiv.org/abs/1202.1112
6. P. Lee, West, J., B. Howe: Viziometrix: A platform for analyzing the visual information in big scholarly data. In: Proceedings of the 25th International Conference on World Wide Web. ACM (2016)
7. Shannon, C.E.: The mathematical theory of communication, vol. 27 (1948)
8. Small, H.: Co-Citation in Scientific Literature: A new measure of the relationship between two documents. Journal of the American Society for Information Science 24(4), 265–269 (1973)
9. Sokal, R.R.: A statistical method for evaluating systematic relationships. Univ Kans Sci Bull 38, 1409–1438 (1958)
10. Steinbach, M., Karypis, G., Kumar, V., et al.: A comparison of document clustering techniques. In: KDD workshop on text mining. vol. 400, pp. 525–526. Boston (2000)
11. Vilhena, D., Foster, J., Rosvall, M., West, J., Evans, J., Bergstrom, C.: Finding cultural holes: How structure and culture diverge in networks of scholarly communication. Sociological Science 1(June), 221–238 (2014), http://www.sociologicalscience.com/articles-vol1-15-221/
12. Wang, C., Blei, D.M.: Collaborative topic modeling for recommending scientific articles. In: Proceedings of the 17th ACM SIGKDD international conference on Knowledge discovery and data mining. pp. 448–456. ACM (2011)
13. Wesley-Smith, I., Dandrea, R., West, J.: An experimental platform for scholarly article recommendation. In: Proc. of the 2nd Workshop on Bibliometric-enhanced Information Retrieval (BIR2015). pp. 30–39 (2015)
14. West, J., Wesley-Smith, I., Bergstrom, C.: A recommendation system based on hierarchical clustering of an article-level citation network. IEEE Transactions on Big Data (in press) (2016)
15. Zipf, G.K.: The psycho-biology of language. Houghton, Mifflin (1935)
16. Zipf, G.K.: Human behavior and the principle of least effort. Addison-Wesley Press (1949)

A Study of Reuse and Plagiarism
in Speech and Natural Language Processing papers

Joseph Mariani [1], Gil Francopoulo [2], Patrick Paroubek [1]

1 LIMSI, CNRS, Université Paris-Saclay (France)
2 LIMSI, CNRS, Université Paris-Saclay + Tagmatica (France)

joseph.mariani@limsi.fr, gil.francopoulo@wanadoo.fr, pap@limsi.fr

Abstract

The aim of this experiment is to present an easy way to compare fragments of texts in order to detect (supposed) results of copy & paste operations between articles in the domain of Natural Language Processing, including Speech Processing (NLP). The search space of the comparisons is a corpus labelled as NLP4NLP, which includes 34 different sources and gathers a large part of the publications in the NLP field over the past 50 years. This study considers the similarity between the papers of each individual source and the complete set of papers in the whole corpus, according to four different types of relationship (self-reuse, self-plagiarism, reuse and plagiarism) and in both directions: a source paper borrowing a fragment of text from another paper of the collection, or in the reverse direction, fragments of text from the source paper being borrowed and inserted in another paper of the collection.

Keywords: Plagiarism Detection, Text reuse, Natural Language Processing, Speech Processing, Scientometrics, Informetrics

1. Introduction

Everything starts with a copy & paste and, of course the flood of documents that we see today could not exist without the practical ease of copy & paste. This is not new but what is new is that the availability of archives allows us to study a vast amount of papers in our domain (i.e. Natural Language Processing, NLP, both for written and spoken materials) and to figure out the level of reuse and plagiarism in this area.

2. Context

Our work comes after the various studies initiated in the Workshop entitled: "Rediscovering 50 Years of Discoveries in Natural Language Processing" on the occasion of ACL's 50th anniversary in 2012 [Radev et al 2013] where a group of researchers studied the content of the corpus recorded in the ACL Anthology [Bird et al 2008]. Among these studies, one was devoted to reuse and it is worth quoting Gupta and Rosso [Gupta et al 2012]: *"It becomes essential to check the authenticity and the novelty of the submitted text before the acceptance. It becomes nearly impossible for a human judge (reviewer) to discover the source of the submitted work, if any, unless the source is already known. Automatic plagiarism detection applications identify such potential sources for the submitted work and based on it a human judge can easily take the decision"*. Let's add that this subject is a specific and active domain ruled yearly by the PAN international plagiarism detection competition[1]. On our side, we also conducted a specific study of reuse and plagiarism in the papers published at the Language Resources and Evaluation conference (LREC), from 1998 to 2014 [Francopoulo et al 2016].

3. Objectives

Our aim is not to present the state-of-art or to compare the various metrics and algorithms for reuse and plagiarism detection, see [Hoad et al 2003] [HaCohen-Kerner et al 2010] for instance. We position our work as an extrinsic detection, the aim of which is to find near-matches between texts, as opposed to intrinsic detection whose aim is to show that different parts of a presumably single-author text could not have been written by the same author [Stamatatos et al 2011a], [Stein et al 2011], [Bensalem et al 2014].
In contrast, our main objective **is to deal with the entry level of the detection**. The main question is: Is there a *meaningful* difference in taking the verbatim raw strings compared with the result of a linguistic parsing? A secondary objective is to present and study a series of ascertainments about the practices of our specific field.

4. The corpus: NLP4NLP

The corpus is a large content of our own research field, i.e. NLP, covering both written and spoken language processing sub-domains and extended to a limited number of corpora, for which Information Retrieval and NLP activities intersect. This corpus was collected at IMMI-CNRS and LIMSI-CNRS (France) and is named NLP4NLP[2]. It currently contains 65,003 documents coming from various conferences and journals with either public or restricted access. This is a large part of the existing published articles in our field, apart from the workshop proceedings and the published books. The time period spans 50 years from 1965 to 2015. Broadly

---

[1] http://pan.webis.de
[2] www.nlp4nlp.org

speaking, and aside from the small corpora, one third comes from the ACL Anthology[3], one third from the ISCA Archive[4] and one third from IEEE[5].

The detail of NLP4NLP is presented in table 1, as follows:

short name	# docs	format	long name	language	access to content	period	# venues
acl	4264	conference	Association for Computational Linguistics Conference	English	open access *	1979-2015	37
acmtslp	82	journal	ACM Transaction on Speech and Language Processing	English	private access	2004-2013	10
alta	262	conference	Australasian Language Technology Association	English	open access *	2003-2014	12
anlp	278	conference	Applied Natural Language Processing	English	open access *	1983-2000	6
cath	932	journal	Computers and the Humanities	English	private access	1966-2004	39
cl	776	journal	American Journal of Computational Linguistics	English	open access *	1980-2014	35
coling	3813	conference	Conference on Computational Linguistics	English	open access *	1965-2014	21
conll	842	conference	Computational Natural Language Learning	English	open access *	1997-2015	18
csal	762	journal	Computer Speech and Language	English	private access	1986-2015	29
eacl	900	conference	European Chapter of the ACL	English	open access *	1983-2014	14
emnlp	2020	conference	Empirical methods in natural language processing	English	open access *	1996-2015	20
hlt	2219	conference	Human Language Technology	English	open access *	1986-2015	19
icassps	9819	conference	IEEE International Conference on Acoustics, Speech and Signal Processing - Speech Track	English	private access	1990-2015	26
ijcnlp	1188	conference	International Joint Conference on NLP	English	open access *	2005-2015	6
inlg	227	conference	International Conference on Natural Language Generation	English	open access *	1996-2014	7
isca	18369	conference	International Speech Communication Association	English	open access	1987-2015	28
jep	507	conference	Journées d'Etudes sur la Parole	French	open access *	2002-2014	5
lre	308	journal	Language Resources and Evaluation	English	private access	2005-2015	11
lrec	4552	conference	Language Resources and Evaluation Conference	English	open access *	1998-2014	9
ltc	656	conference	Language and Technology Conference	English	private access	1995-2015	7
modulad	232	journal	Le Monde des Utilisateurs de L'Analyse des Données	French	open access	1988-2010	23
mts	796	conference	Machine Translation Summit	English	open access	1987-2015	15
muc	149	conference	Message Understanding Conference	English	open access *	1991-1998	5
naacl	1186	conference	North American Chapter of the ACL	English	open access *	2000-2015	11
paclic	1040	conference	Pacific Asia Conference on Language, Information and Computation	English	open access *	1995-2014	19
ranlp	363	conference	Recent Advances in Natural Language Processing	English	open access *	2009-2013	3
sem	950	conference	Lexical and Computational Semantics / Semantic Evaluation	English	open access *	2001-2015	8
speechc	593	journal	Speech Communication	English	private access	1982-2015	34
tacl	92	journal	Transactions of the Association for Computational Linguistics	English	open access *	2013-2015	3
tal	177	journal	Revue Traitement Automatique du Langage	French	open access	2006-2015	10
taln	1019	conference	Traitement Automatique du Langage Naturel	French	open access *	1997-2015	19
taslp	6612	journal	IEEE/ACM Transactions on Audio, Speech and Language Processing	English	private access	1975-2015	41
tipster	105	conference	Tipster DARPA text program	English	open access *	1993-1998	3
trec	1847	conference	Text Retrieval Conference	English	open access	1992-2015	24
Total	67,937[6]					1965-2015	577
Total without duplicates	65,003					1965-2015	558

Table 1. Detail of NLP4NLP, with the convention that an asterisk indicates that the corpus is in the ACL Anthology.

A phase of preprocessing has been applied to represent the various sources in a common format. This format follows the organization of the ACL Anthology with two parts in parallel for each document: the metadata and the content. Each document is labeled with a unique identifier, for instance "lrec2000_1" is reified on the hard disk as two files: "lrec2000_1.bib" and "lrec2000_1.pdf".

For the metadata, we faced four different types of sources with different flavors and character encodings: BibTeX (e.g. ACL Anthology), custom XML (e.g. TALN), database downloads (e.g. IEEE) or HTML program of the conference (e.g. TREC). We wrote a series of small Java programs to transform these metadata into a common BibTeX format under UTF8. Each file comprises the author names and the title. The file is located in a directory which designates the year and the corpus.

Concerning the content, we faced different formats possibly for the same corpus, and the amount of documents being huge, we cannot designate the file type by hand individually. To deal with this, we wrote a program to self-detect the type and sub-type as follows:

- A small amount of texts are in raw text: we keep them in this format.
- The vast majority of the documents are in PDF format of different sub-types. First, we used PDFBox[7] to determine the sub-type of the PDF content: when the content is a textual content, we use PDFBox

---

[3] http://aclweb.org/anthology
[4] www.isca-speech.org/iscaweb/index.php/archive/online-archive
[5] https://www.ieee.org/index.html
[6] In the case of a joint conference, the papers are counted twice. This number reduces to 65,003, if we count only once duplicated papers. Similarly, the number of venues is 577 when all venues are counted, but this number reduces to 558 when the 19 joint conferences are counted only once.

again to extract the text, possibly with the use of the "Legion of the Bouncy Castle"[8] to extract the encrypted content. When the PDF is a text under the form of an image, we use PDFBox to extract the images and then Tesseract OCR[9] to transform the images into a textual content.

Then, and after some experiments, two filters are applied to avoid getting rubbish content:

- The content should be at least 900 characters.
- The content should be of good quality. In order to evaluate this quality, the content is analyzed by the morphological module of TagParser [Francopoulo 2007], a deep industrial parser based on a broad English lexicon and Global Atlas (a knowledge base containing more than one million words from 18 Wikipedias) [Francopoulo et al. 2013] to detect out-of-the-vocabulary (OOV) words. Based on the hypothesis that rubbish strings are OOV words, we retain a text when the ratio OOV / number of words is less than 9%.

We then apply a set of symbolic rules to split the abstract, body and reference section. The file is recorded in XML. It should be noted that we made some experiments with other strategies, given the fact that we are able to compare them with respect to a quantitative evaluation of the quality, as explained before. The first experiment was to use ParsCit[10] [Councill et al. 2008] but the evaluation of the quality was bad, specially when the content is not pure ASCII. The result on accentuated Latin strings, or Arabic and Russian contents was awful. We also tried Grobid[11] but we did not succeed to run it correctly on Windows.

A semi-automatic cleaning process was applied on the metadata in order to avoid false duplicates concerning middle names (for X Y Z, is Y a second given name or the first part of the family name?) and for this purpose, we use the specific BibTex format where the given name is separated from the family name with a comma. Then typographic variants (e.g. "Jean-Luc" versus "Jean Luc" or "Herve" versus "Hervé") were searched in a tedious process and false duplicates were normalized in order to be merged. The resulting number of different authors is 48,894.

Figures are not extracted because we are unable to compare images. See [Francopoulo et al 2015] for more details about the extraction process as well as the solutions for some tricky problems like joint conferences management or abstract / body / reference sections detection.

The majority (90%) of the documents come from conferences, the rest coming from journals. The overall number of words is roughly 270M. Initially, the texts are in four languages: English, French, German and Russian. The number of texts in German and Russian is less than 0.5%. They are detected automatically and are ignored. The texts in French are a little bit more numerous (3%), and are kept with the same status as the English ones. This is not a problem as our tool is able to process English and French.

The corpus is a collection of documents of a single technical domain, which is NLP in the broad sense, and of course, some conferences are specialized in certain topics like written language processing, spoken language processing, including signal processing, information retrieval or machine translation.

5. Definitions

As the terminology is fuzzy and contradictory among the scientific literature, we need first to define four important terms in order to avoid any misunderstanding.

The term "**self-reuse**" is used for a copy & paste when the source of the copy has an author who belongs to the group of authors of the text of the paste and when the source is cited.

The term "**self-plagiarism**" is used for a copy & paste when the source of the copy has similarly an author who belongs to the group of authors of the text of the paste, but when the source is not cited.

The term "**reuse**" is used for a copy & paste when the source of the copy has no author in the group of authors of the paste and when the source is cited.

The term "**plagiarism**" is used for a copy & paste when the source of the copy has no author in the group of the paste and when the source is not cited.

Said in other words, the terms "self-reuse" and "reuse" qualify a situation with a proper source citation, on the contrary of "self-plagiarism" and "plagiarism". Let's note that in spite of the fact that the term "self-plagiarism" seems to be contradictory as authors should be free to use their own wordings, we use this term because it is the usual habit within the community of plagiarism detection - some authors also use the term "recycling", for instance [HaCohen-Kerner et al 2010].

6. Directions

Another point to clarify concerns the expression "source papers". As a convention, we call "focus" the corpus corresponding to the source which is studied. The whole NL4NLP collection is the "search space". We examine

---

[7] https://pdfbox.apache.org

[8] http://www.bouncycastle.org/

[9] https://code.google.com/p/tesseract-ocr

[10] https://github.com/knmnyn/ParsCit

[11] https://github.com/kermitt2/grobid

the copy & paste operations in both directions: we study the configuration with a source paper borrowing fragments of text from other papers of the NLP4NLP collection, in other words, a backward study, and we also study in the reverse direction the fragments of the source paper being borrowed by papers of the NLP4NLP collection, in other words, a forward study.

7. Algorithm

Comparison of word sequences has proven to be an effective method for detection of copy & paste [Clough et al 2002a] and in several occasions, this method won the PAN contest [Barron-Cedeno et al 2010], so we will adopt this strategy. In our case, the corpus is first processed with the deep NLP parser TagParser [Francopoulo 2007] to produce a Passage format [Vilnat et al 2010] with lemma and part-of-speech (POS) indications.
The algorithm is as follows:
- For each document of the focus (the source corpus), all the sliding windows[12] of lemmas (typically 5 to 7, excluding punctuations) are built and recorded under the form of a character string key in an index locally to a document.
- An index gathering all these local indexes is built and is called the "focus index".
- For each document apart from the focus (i.e. outside the source corpus), all the sliding windows are built and **only the windows** contained in the focus index are recorded in an index locally to this document. This filtering operation is done to optimize the comparison phase, as there is no need to compare the windows out of the focus index.
- Then, the keys are compared to compute a similarity overlapping score [Lyon et al 2001] between documents D1 and D2, with the Jaccard distance: **score(D1,D2) = shared windows# / union# (D1 windows, D2 windows).** The pairs of documents D1 / D2 are then filtered according to a threshold in order to retain only significant similarity scoring situations.

8. Algorithm comments and evaluation

In a first implementation, we compared the raw character strings with a segmentation based on space and punctuation. But, due to the fact that the input is the result of PDF formatting, the texts may contain variable caesura for line endings or some little textual variations. Our objective is to compare at a higher level than hyphen variation (there are different sorts of hyphens), caesura (the sequence X/-/endOfLine/Y needs to match an entry XY in the lexicon to distinguish from an hyphen binding a composition), upper/lower case variation, plural, orthographic variation ("normalise" versus "normalize"), spellchecking (particularly useful when the PDF is an image and when the extraction is of low quality) and abbreviation ("NP" versus "Noun Phrase" or "HMM" versus "Hidden Markov Model"). Some rubbish sequence of characters (e.g. a series of hyphens) were also detected and cleaned.
Given that a parser takes all these variations and cleanings into account, we decided to apply a full linguistic parsing, as a second strategy. The syntactic structures and relations are ignored. Then a module for entity linking is called in order to bind different names referring to the same entity, a process often labeled as "entity linking" in the literature [Guo et al 2011][Moro et al 2014]. This process is based on the "Global Atlas" Knowledge Base [Francopoulo et al 2013] which comprises the LRE Map [Calzolari et al 2012]. Thus "British National Corpus" is considered as possibly abbreviated to "BNC", as well as less regular names like "ItalWordNet" possibly abbreviated to "IWN". Each entry of the Knowledge Base has a canonical form, possibly associated with different variants: the aim is to normalize into a canonical form to neutralize proper noun obfuscations based on variant substitutions. After this processing, only the sentences with at least a verb are considered.
We examined the differences between those two strategies concerning all types of copy & paste situations above the threshold, choosing the LREC source as the focus. The results are presented in Table 2, with the last column adding the two other columns without the duplicates produced by the couples of the same year.

Strategy	Backward study document pairs#	Forward study document pairs#	Backward + forward document pairs# after duplicate pruning
1. Raw text	438	373	578
2. Linguistic processing (LP)	559	454	736
Difference (LP-raw)	121	81	158

Table 2. Comparison of the two strategies on the LREC corpus

The strategy based on linguistic processing provides more pairs (+158) and we examined these differences. Among these pairs, the vast majority (80%) concerns caesura: this is normal because most conferences demand a double column format, so the authors frequently use caesura to save place[13]. The other differences (20%) are

---

[12] Also called "n-grams" in some NLP publications.
[13] Concerning this specific problem, for instance, PACLIC and COLING which are one column formatted give much better extraction quality than LREC and ACL which are two columns formatted.

mainly caused by lexical variations and spellchecking. Thus, the results show that using raw texts gives a more "silent" system. The drawback is that the computation is much longer[14], but we think that it is worth the value.

9. Tuning parameters

There are three parameters that had to be tuned: the window size, the distance function and the threshold. The main problem we had was that we did not have any gold standard to evaluate the quality specifically on our corpus and the burden to annotate a corpus was too heavy. We therefore decided to start from the parameters presented in the articles related to the PAN contest. We then computed the results, picked a random selection of pairs that we examined and tuned the parameters accordingly. All experiments were conducted with LREC as the focus and NLP4NLP as the search space.

In the PAN related articles, different window sizes are used. A window of five is the most frequent one [Kasprzak et al 2010], but our results show that a lot of common sequences like "the linguistic unit is the" overload the pairwise score. After some trials, we decided to select a size of seven tokens, in agreement with [Citron and Ginsparg 2014].

Concerning the distance function, the Jaccard distance is frequently used but let's note that other formulas are applicable and documented in the literature. For instance, some authors use an approximation with the following formula: score(D1,D2) = shared windows# / min(D1 windows#, D2 windows#) [Clough et al 2009], which is faster to compute, because there is no need to compute the union. Given that computation time is not a problem for us, we kept the most used function which is the Jaccard distance.

Concerning the threshold, we tried thresholds of 0.03 and 0.04 (3 to 4%) and we compared the results. The last value gave more significant results, as it reduced noise, while still allowing to detect meaningful pairs of similar papers.

After running the first trials, we discovered that using the Jaccard distance resulted in considering as similar a set of two papers, one of them being of small content. This may be the case for invited talks, for example, when the author only provide a short abstract. In this case, a simple acknowledgement to the same institution may produce a similarity score higher than the threshold. The same happens for some eldest papers when the OCR produced a truncated document. In order to solve this problem, we added a second threshold on the minimum number of shared windows that we set at 50 after considering the corresponding erroneous cases.

10. Special considerations concerning authorship and citations

As previously explained, our aim is to distinguish a copy & paste fragment associated with a citation compared to a fragment without any citation. To this end, we proceed with an approximation: we do not bind exactly the anchor in the text, but we parse the reference section and consider that, globally to the text, the document cites (or not) the other document. Due to the fact, that we have proper author identification for each document, the corpus forms a complex web of citations. We are thus able to distinguish self-reuse versus self-plagiarism and reuse versus plagiarism. We are in a situation slightly different from METER where the references are not linked. Let's recall that METER is the corpus usually involved in plagiarism detection competitions [Gaizauskas et al 2001][Clough et al 2002b].

11. Precision about the anteriority test

Given the fact that some papers and drafts of papers can circulate among researchers before the official published date, it is impossible to verify exactly when a document is issued; moreover we do not have any more detailed time indication than the year, as we don't know the precise date of submission. This is why we also consider the same year within the comparisons. In this case, it is difficult to determine which are the borrowing and borrowed papers, and in some cases they may even have been written simultaneously. However, if one paper cites a second one, while it is not cited by the second one, it may serve as a sign to consider it as being the borrowing paper.

12. Resulting files

The program computes a detailed result for each individual source as an HTML page where all similar pairs of documents are listed with their similarity score, with the common fragments displayed as red highlighted snippets and HTML links back to the original 67,937 documents[15]. For each of the 4 categories (Self-reuse, Self-Plagiarism, Reuse and Plagiarism), the program produces the list of couples of "similar" papers according to our criteria, with their similarity score, and the global results in the form of matrices displaying the number of papers

---

[14] It takes 25 hours instead of 3 hours on a mid-range mono-processor Xeon E3-1270 V2 with 32G of RAM.

[15] But the space limitations do not allow to present these results in lengthy details. Furthermore, we do not want to display personal results.

that are similar in each couple of the 34 sources, in the forward and backward directions (the using sources are on the X axis, while the used sources are on the Y axis). The total of used and using papers, and the difference between those totals, are presented, while the 7 (Table 3) or 5 (Table 4) top using or used sources are indicated in green.

We conducted a manual checking of the couples of papers showing a very high similarity: the 14 couples that showed a similarity of 1 were the duplication of a paper due to an error in editing the proceedings of a conference. We also found after those first trials erroneous results of the OCR for some eldest papers which resulted in files containing several papers, in full or in fragments, or where blanks were inserted after each individual character. We excluded those 86 documents from the corpus being considered.

Checking those results, we also mentioned several cases where the author was the same, but with a different spelling, or where references were properly quoted, but with a different wording, a different spelling (American English versus British English, for example) or an improper reference to the source. We had to manually correct those cases, and move the corresponding couples of papers in the correct category (from reuse or plagiarism to self-reuse or self-plagiarism in the case of authors names, from plagiarism to reuse, in the case of references).

13. Self-reuse and Self-Plagiarism

Table 3 provides the results of merging self-reuse (authors reusing their own text while quoting the source paper) and self-plagiarism (authors reusing their own text without quoting the source paper). As we see, it is a rather frequent phenomenon, with a total of 12,493 documents (i.e. 18% of the 67,937 documents!). In 61% of the cases (7,650 self-plagiarisms over 12,493), the authors do not quote the source paper. We found that 205 papers have exactly the same title, and that 130 papers have both the same title and the same list of authors! Also 3,560 papers have exactly the same list of authors. Given the large number of documents, it is impossible to conduct a manual checking of all the couples.

We see that the most used sources are the large conferences: ISCA, IEEE-ICASSP, ACL, COLING, HLT, EMNLP and LREC. The most using sources are not only those large conferences, but also the journals: IEEE-Transactions on Acoustics, Speech and Language Processing (and its various avatars) (TASLP), Computer Speech and Language (CSAL), Computational Linguistics (CL) and Speech Com. If we consider the balance between the using and the used sources, we clearly see that the flow of papers goes from conferences to journals. The largest flows of self-reuse and self-plagiarism concern ISCA and ICASSP, in both directions, but especially from ISCA to ICASSP, ICASSP and ISCA to TASLP (also in the reverse direction) and to CSAL, ISCA to Speech Com, ACL to Computational Linguistics, ISCA to LREC and EMNLP to ACL.

If we want to study the influence a given conference (or journal) has on another one, we must however recall that these figures are raw figures in terms of number of documents, and we must not forget that some conferences (or journals) are much bigger than others. For instance, LREC is a conference with more than 4,500 documents compared to LRE which is a journal with only 308 documents. If we relate the number of published papers that reuse another paper to the total number of published papers, we may see that 17% of the LRE papers (52 over 308) use content coming from the LREC conferences, without quoting them in 66% of the cases. Also the frequency of the conferences (annual or biennial) and the calendar (date of the conference and of the submission deadline) may influence the flow of papers between the sources.

The similarity scores range from 4% to 97% (Fig. 1). We see that about 4,500 couples of papers have a similarity score equal or superior to 10%; about 900 (1.3% of the total number of papers) have a score superior or equal to 30%. Looking at the ones with the largest similarity score, we found a few examples of important variants in the spelling of the same authors' names, and cases of republishing the corrigendum of a previously published paper or of republishing a paper with a small difference in the title and one missing author in the authors' list. In one case, the same research center is described by the same author in two different conferences with an overlapping of 90%. In another case, the difference of the two papers is primarily in the name of the systems being presented, funded by the same project agency in two different contracts, while the description has a 45% overlap!

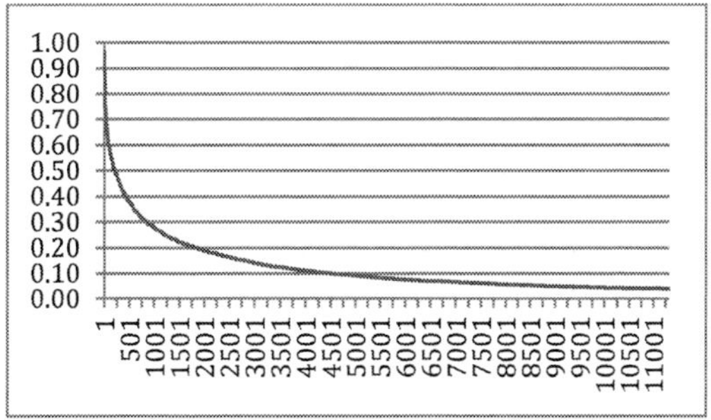

Fig. 1 Similarity scores of the couples detected as self-reuse / self-plagiarism

Used \ Using	acl	acmtslp	alta	anlp	cath	cl	coling	conll	csal	eacl	emnlp	hlt	icassps	ijcnlp	inlg	isca	jep	lre	lrec	ltc	modulad	mts	muc	naacl	paclic	ranlp	sem	speechc	tacl	tal	taln	taslp	tipster	trec	Total used	Total using	Difference
acl	22	8	1	4	8	136	78	25	31	22	83	85	29	31	7	48	0	20	71	4	0	19	1	51	8	5	26	1	2	0	0	24	4	9	863	625	238
acmtslp	1	0	0	0	0	0	0	0	2	0	0	2	3	2	0	6	0	1	1	0	0	0	0	2	0	0	1	0	1	0	0	2	0	0	24	93	-69
alta	3	0	2	0	0	1	5	0	1	2	5	0	0	1	0	4	0	0	4	0	0	0	0	0	0	1	0	0	0	0	0	0	0	4	33	14	19
anlp	7	0	0	1	3	5	8	1	1	2	1	4	0	0	0	1	0	0	5	0	0	1	0	2	1	0	0	0	0	0	0	0	2	5	50	50	0
cath	1	0	0	1	7	2	0	0	0	1	0	1	0	0	0	0	0	0	3	0	0	0	0	0	0	0	0	0	0	0	0	0	0	2	18	50	-32
cl	9	0	0	4	3	0	4	0	2	4	3	1	0	0	0	0	0	2	5	0	0	0	0	0	0	0	4	0	0	0	0	0	0	0	42	433	-391
coling	74	10	3	8	7	62	19	24	17	15	43	49	8	24	7	42	0	14	90	4	0	9	2	33	12	5	25	3	0	0	0	12	6	5	632	500	132
conll	26	1	1	1	1	20	18	8	5	6	16	11	2	14	2	2	0	2	10	1	0	3	0	7	0	5	13	0	1	0	0	3	0	0	179	151	28
csal	3	0	0	0	0	4	4	2	7	0	3	2	20	1	0	35	0	2	7	0	0	0	0	0	0	0	2	6	0	0	0	13	0	0	111	643	-532
eacl	16	2	0	2	5	31	12	6	3	1	8	13	3	1	2	9	0	0	21	1	0	1	0	13	1	1	4	0	0	0	0	5	0	1	162	130	32
emnlp	103	2	2	1	2	44	52	26	18	9	16	30	14	47	1	27	0	5	29	0	0	7	0	22	2	1	19	0	3	0	0	20	1	5	508	355	153
hlt	83	12	0	5	3	48	48	11	42	14	33	22	29	30	2	104	0	4	26	1	0	13	2	6	1	0	9	8	0	0	0	25	7	19	607	476	131
icassps	16	5	0	0	0	3	4	1	130	4	7	21	262	2	0	1005	0	0	19	0	0	2	0	14	2	0	0	65	0	0	0	746	0	3	2311	2160	151
ijcnlp	27	6	1	0	0	3	29	10	7	2	34	18	2	4	3	7	0	5	19	3	0	9	0	13	4	8	3	0	0	0	0	4	0	1	222	237	-15
inlg	7	0	0	1	1	6	5	2	0	3	1	3	0	1	2	4	0	1	6	0	0	1	0	4	0	0	0	0	0	0	0	1	0	0	49	35	14
isca	56	23	0	2	0	13	45	0	317	10	25	116	1531	10	4	879	0	10	133	19	0	12	0	38	6	0	1	233	0	0	0	669	0	5	4157	2460	1697
jep	0	0	0	0	0	0	0	0	0	0	0	0	0	0	0	0	10	0	0	0	0	0	0	0	0	0	0	0	0	6	0	0	0	0	16	18	-2
lre	2	1	0	0	0	2	3	0	0	0	0	1	0	0	0	2	0	2	6	0	0	0	0	1	1	0	0	0	0	0	0	1	0	0	22	146	-124
lrec	58	3	0	2	6	16	80	6	13	15	16	17	16	10	2	72	0	52	67	12	0	6	0	11	11	4	12	5	2	0	0	6	1	3	524	660	-136
ltc	4	0	0	0	0	0	0	0	0	0	0	0	0	2	0	15	0	1	35	10	0	2	0	0	6	6	1	4	0	0	0	0	0	0	86	71	15
modulad	0	0	0	0	0	0	0	0	0	0	0	0	0	0	0	0	0	0	0	0	0	0	0	0	0	0	0	0	0	0	0	0	0	0	0	0	0
mts	13	0	0	0	0	2	9	2	0	2	9	10	3	9	0	9	0	2	20	2	0	8	0	8	5	2	1	1	0	0	0	2	0	0	119	109	10
muc	2	0	0	2	0	2	3	0	0	1	0	7	0	0	0	0	0	0	0	0	0	0	10	1	0	0	0	0	0	0	0	0	18	1	47	28	19
naacl	46	10	0	2	1	24	30	7	12	11	22	5	15	22	3	30	0	3	16	1	0	9	0	3	0	0	9	1	0	0	0	8	0	3	293	251	42
paclic	4	0	0	0	1	0	12	1	1	1	1	0	2	8	0	3	0	5	18	7	0	3	0	0	21	7	1	0	0	0	0	1	0	0	97	85	12
ranlp	3	2	0	0	0	0	2	4	4	2	2	1	0	7	0	0	0	2	19	5	0	2	0	1	2	4	2	1	0	0	0	0	0	1	66	54	12
sem	25	2	0	0	0	7	16	14	4	1	12	12	0	8	0	0	0	13	12	1	0	1	0	8	1	4	53	0	0	0	0	0	0	1	195	188	7
speechc	0	0	0	0	0	1	1	0	11	0	0	4	17	0	0	48	0	0	2	0	0	0	0	0	0	0	0	1	0	0	0	17	0	0	102	344	-242
tacl	1	1	0	0	0	0	0	0	0	0	2	0	0	0	0	0	0	0	2	0	0	0	0	0	0	0	1	0	0	0	0	0	0	0	7	9	-2
tal	0	0	0	0	0	0	0	0	0	0	0	0	0	0	0	0	5	0	0	0	0	0	0	0	0	0	0	0	0	0	13	0	0	0	18	59	-41
taln	0	0	0	0	0	0	0	0	0	0	0	0	0	0	0	0	3	0	0	0	0	0	0	0	0	0	0	0	0	53	9	0	0	0	65	22	43
taslp	0	5	0	0	0	0	1	1	13	0	1	4	197	0	0	103	0	0	2	0	0	1	0	2	0	0	0	15	0	0	0	49	0	0	394	1610	-1216
tipster	3	0	0	3	0	0	6	0	0	0	1	5	0	0	0	0	0	0	2	0	0	0	13	1	0	0	0	0	0	0	0	0	2	7	43	65	-22
trec	10	0	4	11	2	1	6	0	2	2	11	32	7	3	0	5	0	0	10	0	0	0	0	10	0	1	1	0	0	0	0	2	24	287	431	362	69
Total using	625	93	14	50	50	433	500	151	643	130	355	476	2160	237	35	2460	18	146	660	71	0	109	28	251	85	54	188	344	9	59	22	1610	65	362	12493	12493	0

Table 3. Self-reuse and Self-Plagiarism Matrix, with indication of the 7 most using and used sources.

Used \ Using	acl	acmtslp	alta	anlp	cath	cl	coling	conll	csal	eacl	emnlp	hlt	icassps	ijcnlp	inlg	isca	jep	lre	lrec	ltc	modulad	mts	muc	naacl	paclic	ranlp	sem	speechc	tacl	tal	taln	taslp	tipster	trec	Total used	Total using	Difference
acl	1	0	0	0	1	1	2	2	0	0	4	3	0	3	0	2	0	0	1	1	0	0	1	1	1	1	3	0	0	0	0	0	0	0	28	7	21
acmtslp	0	0	0	0	0	0	0	0	0	0	0	0	0	0	0	0	0	0	0	0	0	0	0	0	0	0	0	0	0	0	0	0	0	0	0	0	0
alta	0	0	0	0	0	0	0	0	0	0	0	0	0	0	0	0	0	0	0	0	0	0	0	0	0	0	0	0	0	0	0	0	0	0	0	0	0
anlp	0	0	0	0	0	0	0	0	0	0	0	0	0	0	0	0	0	0	0	0	0	0	0	0	0	0	0	0	0	0	0	0	0	0	0	0	0
cath	0	0	0	0	0	0	0	0	0	0	0	0	0	0	0	0	0	0	0	0	0	0	0	0	0	0	0	0	0	0	0	0	0	0	0	2	-2
cl	0	0	0	0	0	0	1	0	0	0	1	1	0	1	0	0	0	0	4	0	0	1	0	1	2	0	0	0	0	0	0	0	0	0	12	5	7
coling	0	0	0	0	1	0	0	0	0	0	0	2	1	1	0	2	0	0	2	0	0	0	1	1	1	0	2	0	0	0	0	1	0	0	15	7	8
conll	0	0	0	0	0	0	0	0	0	0	2	0	0	0	0	0	0	0	0	0	0	0	0	0	0	0	1	0	0	0	0	0	0	0	3	5	-2
csal	0	0	0	0	0	0	0	0	0	0	0	1	1	0	0	3	0	0	0	0	0	0	0	1	1	0	0	0	0	0	0	0	0	0	7	6	1
eacl	0	0	0	0	0	0	0	0	0	0	0	2	0	0	0	0	0	0	0	0	0	0	0	0	0	0	0	0	0	0	0	0	0	0	2	2	0
emnlp	0	0	0	0	0	2	0	2	0	1	1	2	0	0	0	0	0	0	0	0	0	1	0	2	0	0	0	0	0	0	0	0	0	2	13	15	-2
hlt	2	0	0	0	0	1	0	1	1	0	2	1	1	1	0	2	0	0	0	1	0	1	0	0	1	0	0	0	0	0	0	0	0	2	17	17	0
icassps	0	0	0	0	0	0	0	0	1	0	1	2	3	0	0	32	0	0	0	0	0	0	0	2	0	0	0	2	0	0	0	5	0	0	48	37	11
ijcnlp	0	0	0	0	0	0	0	0	0	0	0	0	0	0	0	0	0	0	0	0	0	0	0	0	1	1	0	0	0	0	0	0	0	0	2	9	-7
inlg	0	0	0	0	0	0	0	0	0	0	0	0	0	0	0	0	0	0	0	0	0	0	0	0	0	0	0	0	0	0	0	0	0	0	0	0	0
isca	0	0	0	0	0	1	1	0	1	0	0	1	18	1	0	7	0	0	1	1	0	0	0	1	0	0	0	0	0	0	0	3	0	0	36	70	-34
jep	0	0	0	0	0	0	0	0	0	0	0	0	0	0	0	0	0	0	0	0	0	0	0	0	0	0	0	0	0	0	0	0	0	0	0	0	0
lre	0	0	0	0	0	0	0	0	0	0	0	0	0	0	0	0	0	0	0	0	0	0	0	0	0	0	0	0	0	0	0	0	0	0	0	1	-1
lrec	0	0	0	0	0	0	0	0	1	0	2	0	1	0	0	1	0	0	0	0	0	0	0	0	0	1	0	1	0	0	0	0	0	1	8	8	0
ltc	0	0	0	0	0	0	0	0	0	0	0	0	0	0	0	0	0	0	0	0	0	0	0	0	0	0	0	0	0	0	0	0	0	0	0	4	-4
modulad	0	0	0	0	0	0	0	0	0	0	0	0	0	0	0	0	0	0	0	0	0	0	0	0	0	0	0	0	0	0	0	0	0	0	0	0	0
mts	1	0	0	0	0	0	0	0	0	0	0	1	0	0	0	1	0	0	0	0	0	0	0	0	1	0	0	0	0	0	0	0	0	0	4	3	1
muc	1	0	0	0	0	0	1	0	0	0	0	0	0	0	0	0	0	0	0	0	0	0	1	0	0	0	0	0	0	0	0	0	0	0	3	3	0
naacl	1	0	0	0	0	0	0	0	1	0	1	1	1	0	0	1	0	0	0	1	0	0	0	1	2	0	0	0	0	0	0	0	0	0	9	10	-1
paclic	0	0	0	0	0	0	0	0	0	0	0	0	1	1	0	0	0	0	0	0	0	0	0	0	0	0	0	0	0	0	0	0	0	0	2	10	-8
ranlp	0	0	0	0	0	0	0	0	0	0	0	0	0	0	0	0	0	0	0	0	0	0	0	0	0	0	0	0	0	0	0	0	0	0	0	3	-3
sem	0	0	0	0	0	0	2	0	0	0	0	0	0	0	0	0	0	0	0	0	0	0	0	0	0	0	1	0	0	0	0	0	0	0	3	7	-4
speechc	0	0	0	0	0	0	0	0	0	0	0	0	0	1	0	2	0	0	0	0	0	0	0	0	0	0	0	0	0	0	0	1	0	0	4	5	-1
tacl	0	0	0	0	0	0	0	0	0	0	0	0	0	0	0	0	0	0	0	0	0	0	0	0	0	0	0	0	0	0	0	0	0	0	0	0	0
tal	0	0	0	0	0	0	0	0	0	0	0	0	0	0	0	0	0	0	0	0	0	0	0	0	0	0	0	0	0	0	0	0	0	0	0	0	0
taln	0	0	0	0	0	0	0	0	0	0	0	0	0	0	0	0	0	0	0	0	0	0	0	0	0	0	0	0	0	0	0	0	0	0	0	0	0
taslp	0	0	0	0	0	0	0	0	1	1	0	0	10	0	0	16	0	0	0	0	0	0	0	0	0	0	0	2	0	0	0	0	0	0	30	10	20
tipster	0	0	0	0	0	0	0	0	0	0	0	0	0	0	0	0	0	0	0	0	0	0	0	0	0	0	0	0	0	0	0	0	2	0	2	2	0
trec	1	0	0	0	0	0	0	0	0	0	1	0	1	0	0	1	0	1	0	0	0	0	0	0	0	0	0	0	0	0	0	0	0	8	13	13	0
Total using	7	0	0	0	2	5	7	5	6	2	15	17	37	9	0	70	0	1	8	4	0	3	3	10	10	3	7	5	0	0	0	10	2	13	261	261	0

Table 4. Reuse and Plagiarism Matrix, with indication of the 5 most using and used sources

14. Reuse and Plagiarism

Table 4 provides the results of merging reuse (authors reusing fragments of the texts of other authors while quoting the source paper) and plagiarism (authors reusing fragments of the texts of other authors without quoting the source paper). As we see, there are very few cases altogether. Only 261 papers (i.e. less than 0.4% of the 67,937 documents) reuse a fragment of papers written by other authors that they quote. In 60% of the cases (156 plagiarisms over 261), the authors do not quote the source paper, but these possible cases of plagiarism only represent 0.23% of the total number of papers. Given those small numbers, we were able to conduct a manual checking of those couples.

Among the couple papers placed in the "Reuse" category, it appeared that 12 have a least one author in common, but with a somehow different spelling and should therefore be placed in the "Self-reuse" category. Among the couples of papers placed in the "Plagiarism" category, 25 have a least one author in common, but with a somehow different spelling and should therefore be placed in the "Self-plagiarism" category and 14 correctly quote the source paper, but with variants in the spelling of the authors' names, of the paper's title or of the conference or journal source or forgetting to place the source paper in the references and should therefore be placed in the "Reuse" category. It therefore resulted in 107 cases of "reuse" and 117 possible cases of plagiarism (0.17% of the papers) that we studied more closely. We found the following explanations:

- The paper cites another reference from the same authors of the source paper (typically a previous reference, or a paper published in a Journal) (46 cases)
- Both papers use extracts of a third paper that they both cite (31 cases)
- The authors of the two papers are different, but from the same laboratory (typically in industrial laboratories or funding agencies) (11 cases)
- The authors previously co-authored papers (typically as supervisor and PhD student or postdoc) but are now in a different laboratory (11 cases)
- The authors of the papers are different, but collaborated in the same project which is presented in the two papers (2 cases)
- The two papers present the same short example, result or definition coming from another source (13 cases)

If we exclude those cases, only 3 cases of possible plagiarism remain that correspond to the same paper which appears as a patchwork of 3 other papers, while sharing several references with them.

The similarity scores range from 4% to 42% (Fig. 2). Only 34 couples of papers have a similarity score equal or higher than 10%. For example, the couple showing the highest similarity score comprises a paper published in 1998 and a paper published in 2000 which both describe *Chart parsing* using the words of the initial paper published 20 years earlier in 1980, that they both properly quote. Among the three remaining possible cases of plagiarism, the highest similarity score is 10%, with a shared window of 200 tokens.

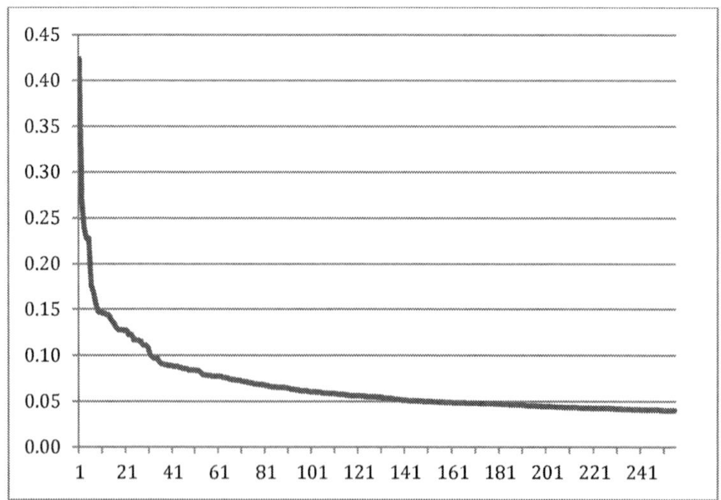

Fig. 2 Similarity scores of the couples detected as reuse / plagiarism

15. Time delay between publication and reuse

We now consider the duration between the publication of a paper and its reuse (in all 4 categories) in another publication. It appears that 38% of the similar papers were published on the same year, 71% within the next year,

83% over 2 years and 93% over 3 years (Figure 3 and 4). Only 7% reuse material from an earlier period. The average duration is 1.22 years. 30% of the similar papers published on the same year concern the couple of conferences ISCA-ICASSP.

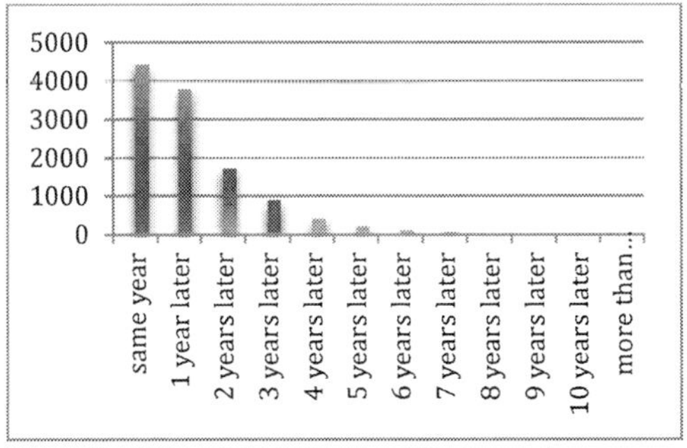

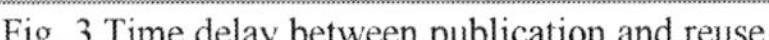

Fig. 3 Time delay between publication and reuse

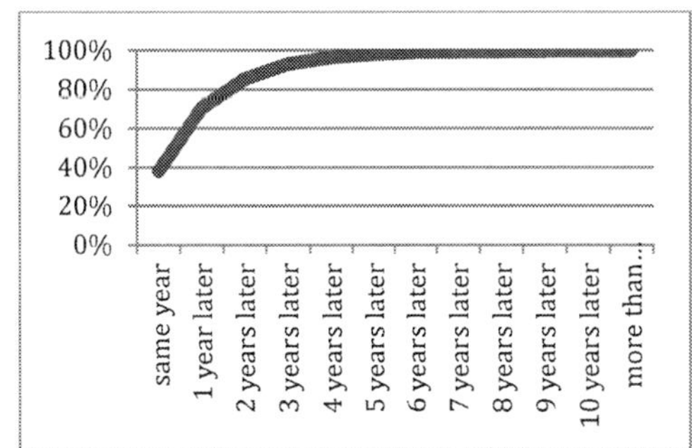

Fig. 4 Time delay between publication and reuse (in %)

We now consider the reuse of conference papers in journal papers (Figures 5 and 6). We observe here a similar time schedule, with a delay of one year: 12% of the reused papers were published on the same year, 41% within the next year, 68% over 2 years, 85% over 3 years and 93% over 4 years. Only 7% reuse material from an earlier period. The average duration is 2.07 years.

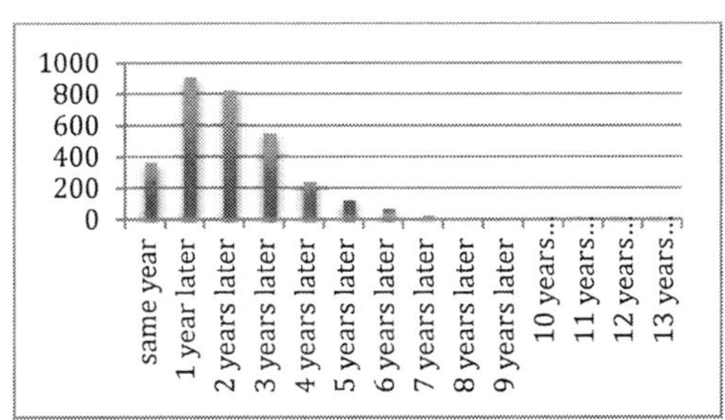

Fig. 5 Time delay between publication in conferences and reuse in journals

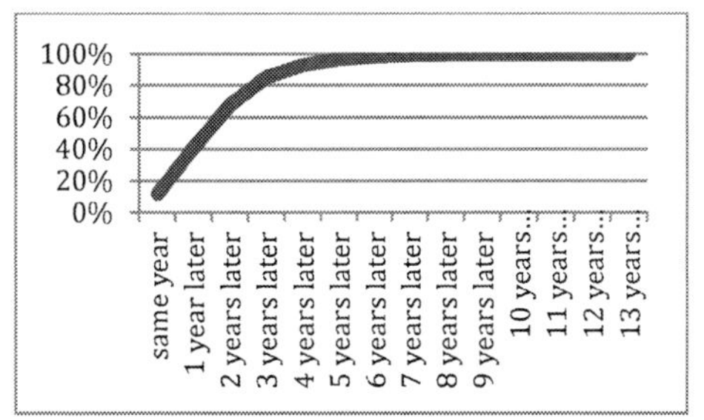

Fig. 6 Time delay between publication in conferences and reuse in journals (in %)

16. Discussion

The first obvious ascertainment is that self-reusing is much more important than reusing the content of others. With a comparable threshold of 0.04, when we consider the total of the two directions, there are 4843 self-reuse and 7650 self-plagiarism detected pairs, compared with 105 reuse and 156 plagiarism detected pairs. Globally, the source papers are quoted only in 39% of the cases on average, a percentage which falls down from 39% to 23% if the papers are published on the same year.

Plagiarism may raise legal issues if it violates copyright, but the *right to quote*[16] exists in certain conditions: "National legislations usually embody the Berne convention limits in one or more of the following requirements:

- the cited paragraphs are within a reasonable limit,
- clearly marked as quotations and fully referenced,
- the resulting new work is not just a collection of quotations, but constitutes a fully original work in itself",
- we could also add that the cited paragraph must have a function in the goal of the citing paper.

Obviously, most of the cases reported in this paper comply with the right to quote. The *limits of the cited paragraph* vary from country to country. In France and Canada, for example, a limit of 10% of both the copying and copied texts seems to be acceptable. As we've seen, we stay within those limits in all cases in NLP4NLP.

Self-reuse and self-plagiarism are of a different nature. Let's recall that they concern papers that have at least one author in common. Of course, a copy & paste operation is easy and frequent but there is another phenomena to take into account which is difficult to distinguish from copy & paste: this is the style of the author. Everybody has habits to formulate its ideas, and, even on a long period, most authors seem to keep the same chunks of prepared words. As we've seen, almost 40% of the cases concern papers that are published on the same year: authors submit two similar papers at two different conferences on the same year, and publish the two papers in

---

[16] https://en.wikipedia.org/wiki/Right_to_quote

both conferences if both are accepted. It is very difficult to prevent those cases as none of the papers are published when the other is submitted. Another frequent case is the publication of a paper in a journal after its publication in a conference. Here also, it is a natural and usual process, sometimes even encouraged by the journal editors after a pre-selection of the best papers in a conference.

As a tentative to moderate these figures and to justify self-reuse and self-plagiarism of previously published material, it is worth quoting Pamela Samuelson [Samuelson 1994]:

- The previous work must be restated to lay the groundwork for a new contribution in the second work,
- Portions of the previous work must be repeated to deal with new evidence or arguments,
- The audience for each work is so different that publishing the same work in different places is necessary to get the message out,
- The authors think they said it so well the first time that it makes no sense to say it differently a second time.

She considers that 30% is an upper limit in the reuse of parts of a previously published paper.

We believe that following these two sets of principles regarding (self) reuse and plagiarism will help maintaining an ethical behavior in our community.

17. Further developments

A limitation of our approach is that it fails to identify copy & paste when the original text has been strongly altered. Our study of graphical variations of a common meaning is presently limited to geographical variants, technical abbreviations (e.g. HMM versus Hidden Markov Model) and resource names aliases from the LRE Map. We plan to deal with "rogeting" which is the practice of replacing words with supposedly synonymous alternatives in order to disguise plagiarism[17] by obfuscation, see [Potthast et al 2010][Chong et al 2011][Ceska et al 2009] for another presentation. Detecting paraphrases and transpositions of passive / active sentences, seems in contrast rather difficult to implement [Barron-Cedeno et al 2013]. A more tractable development is to artificially modify the n-gram to match as presented in [Nawab et al 2012]. Another track of development could be to simplify the input to retain only the plain words, a process labeled as "stopwords n-gram" by [Stamatatos 2011b].

Another direction of improvement is to isolate and ignore tables in order to reduce noise, but this is a complex task as documented in [Frey et al 2015]. Let's note that this is not a big problem in our approach, as we ignore sentences without any verb and as verbs are not very frequent within a table.

More generally, we could also study the position and rhetorical structure of the copy & paste in order to identify and justify their function.

We may finally explore whether copy & paste is more common for non native English speakers, given that it is frequent that they publish first in their native language at a national conference and then in English in an international conference or an international journal, in order to broaden their audience.

18. Conclusions

To our knowledge, this paper is the first which reports results on the study of copy & paste operations on corpora of NLP archives of this size. Based on a simple method of n-gram comparison after text processing using NLP, this method is easy to implement. Of course, this process makes a large number of pairwise comparisons (65,000*65,000), which still represents a practical computing limitation.

As our measures show, self-reuse and self-plagiarism are common practices. This is not specific to our field and is certainly related to the current tendency which is called "salami-slicing" publication caused by the publish-and-perish demand[18]. But we gladly notice that plagiarism is very uncommon in our community.

19. Bibliographical references

1. Barron-Cedeno Alberto, Potthast Martin, Rosso Paolo, Stein Benno, Eiselt Andreas (2010). Corpus and Evaluation Measures for Automatic Plagiarism Detection, Proceedings of LREC, Valletta, Malta.
2. Barron-Cedeno Alberto, Vila Marta, Marti Maria Antonia, Rosso Paolo (2013). Plagiarism Meets Paraphrasing Insights for the Next Generation in Automatic Plagiarism Detection, Computational Linguistics.
3. Bensalem Imene, Rosso Paolo, Chikhi Salim (2014). Intrinsic Plagiarism Detection using N-gram Classes, Proceedings of the Conference on Empirical Methods in Natural Language Processing, Doha, Qatar.
4. Bird Steven, Dale Robert, Dorr Bonnie J, Gibson Bryan, Joseph Mark T, Kan Min-Yen, Lee Dongwon, Powley Brett, Radev Dragomir R, Tan Yee Fan (2008). The ACL Anthology Reference Corpus: A Reference Dataset for Bibliographic Research in Computational Linguistics, Proceedings of LREC, Marrakech, Morocco.
5. Calzolari Nicoletta, Del Gratta Riccardo, Francopoulo Gil, Mariani Joseph, Rubino Francesco, Russo Irene, Soria

---

[17] https://en.wikipedia.org/wiki/Rogeting
[18] To this regard, we must ourselves admit that the reader will find a certain degree of overlapping between this paper and the one we published at LREC 2016 also on reuse and plagiarism, but specifically related to the LREC papers, at least on the description of the NLP4NLP corpus.

Claudia (2012). The LRE Map. Harmonising Community Descriptions of Resources, Proceedings of LREC, Istanbul, Turkey.

6. Ceska Zdenek, Fox Chris (2009). The Influence of Text Pre-processing on Plagiarism Detection, Proceedings of the Recent Advances in Natural Language Processing, Borovets, Bulgaria.

7. Chong Miranda, Specia Lucia (2011). Lexical Generalisation for Word-level Matching in Plagiarism Detection, Proceedings of Recent Advances in Natural Language Processing, Hissar, Bulgaria.

8. Citron Daniel T., Ginsparg Paul (2014). Patterns of text reuse in a scientific corpus, PNAS 2015 112 (1) 25-30; published ahead of print December 8, 2014, doi:10.1073/pnas.1415135111

9. Clough Paul, Gaizauskas Robert, Piao Scott S L, Wilks Yorick (2002a). Measuring Text Reuse. Proceedings of ACL'02, Philadelphia, USA.

10. Clough Paul, Gaizauskas Robert, Piao Scott S L, (2002b). Building and annotating a corpus for the study of journalistic text reuse, Proceedings of LREC, Las Palmas, Spain.

11. Clough Paul, Stevenson Mark (2009). Developing a Corpus of Plagiarised Short Answers, Language Resources and Evaluation, Springer.

12. Councill, Isaac G., Giles, C. Lee and Kan, Min-Yen (2008), ParsCit: An open-source CRF reference string parsing package. In Proceedings of the Language Resources and Evaluation Conference (LREC 2008), Marrakesh, Morocco, May 2008

13. Francopoulo Gil (2007). TagParser: well on the way to ISO-TC37 conformance. Proceedings of ICGL (International Conference on Global Interoperability for Language Resources), Hong Kong.

14. Francopoulo Gil, Marcoul Frédéric, Causse David, Piparo Grégory (2013). Global Atlas: Proper Nouns, from Wikipedia to LMF, in LMF Lexical Markup Framework (Francopoulo, ed), ISTE Wiley.

15. Francopoulo Gil, Mariani Joseph, Paroubek Patrick (2015). NLP4NLP: the cobbler's children won't go unshod, in D-Lib Magazine: The magazine of Digital Library Research[19].

16. Francopoulo Gil, Mariani Joseph, Paroubek Patrick (2016). A Study of Reuse and Plagiarism in LREC papers. Proceedings of LREC 2016, Portorož, Slovenia.

17. Frey Matthias, Kern Roman (2015). Efficient Table Annotation for Digital Articles, in D-Lib Magazine: The magazine of Digital Library Research[20].

18. Gaizauskas Robert, Foster Jonathan, Wilks Yorick, Arundel John, Clough Paul, Piao Scott S L (2001). The METER Corpus: A Corpus for Analysing Journalistic Text Reuse. Proceedings of the Corpus Linguistics Conference, Lancaster, UK.

19. Guo Yuhang, Che Wanxiang, Liu Ting, Li Sheng (2011). A Graph-based Method for Entity Linking, International Joint Conference on NLP, Chiang Mai, Thailand.

20. Gupta Parth, Rosso Paolo (2012). Text Reuse with ACL: (Upward) Trends, Proceedings of the ACL-2012 Special Workshop on Rediscovering 50 Years of Discoveries, Jeju, Republic of Korea.

21. Hoad Timothy C, Zobel Justin (2003). Methods for identifying Versioned and Plagiarised Documents, Journal of the American Society for Information Science and Technology.

22. HaCohen-Kerner Yaakov, Tayeb Aharon, Ben-Dror Natan (2010). Detection of Simple Plagiarism in Computer Science Papers, in Proceedings of the 23rd International Conference on Computational Linguistics (COLING), Beijing, PRC.

23. Kasprzak Jan, Brandejs Michal (2010). Improving the Reliability of the Plagiarism Detection System Lab, in Proceedings of the Uncovering Plagiarism, Authorship and Social Software Misuse (PAN), Padua, Italy.

24. Lyon Caroline, Malcolm James, Dickerson Bob (2001). Detecting Short Passages of Similar Text in large document collections, Proc. of the Empirical Methods in Natural Language Processing Conference, Pittsburgh, PA USA.

25. Moro Andrea, Raganato Alessandro, Navigli Roberto (2014). Entity Linking meets Word Sense Disambiguation: a Unified Approach, Transactions of the Association for Computational Linguistics.

26. Nawab Rao Muhammad Adeel, Stevenson Mark, Clough Paul (2012). Detecting Text Reuse with Modified and Weighted N-grams, First Joint Conference on Lexical and Computational Semantics, Montréal, Canada.

27. Potthast Martin, Stein Benno, Barron-Cedeno Alberto, Rosso Paolo (2010). An Evaluation Framework for Plagiarism Detection, in Proceedings of the 23rd International Conference on Computational Linguistics (COLING), Beijing, PRC.

28. Radev Dragomir R, Muthukrishnan Pradeep, Qazvinian Vahed, Abu-Jbara, Amjad (203). The ACL Anthology Network Corpus, Language Resources and Evaluation 47: 919–944, Springer.

29. Samuelson Pamela (1994). Self-plagiarism or fair use? Communications of the ACM 37 (8):21-5.

30. Stamatatos Efstathios, Koppel Moshe (2011a). Plagiarism and authorship analysis: introduction to the special issue, Language Resources and Evaluation, Springer.

31. Stamatatos Efstathios (2011b). Plagiarism detection using stopword n-grams. Journal of the American Society for Information Science and Technology.

32. Stein Benno, Lipka Nedim, Prettenhofer Peter (2011). Intrinsic plagiarism analysis, Language Resources and Evaluation, Springer.

33. Vilnat Anne, Paroubek Patrick, Villemonte de la Clergerie Eric, Francopoulo Gil, Guénot Marie-Laure (2010). PASSAGE Syntactic Representation: a Minimal Common Ground for Evaluation. Proceedings of LREC 2010, Valletta, Malta.

---

[19] www.dlib.org/dlib/november15/francopoulo/11francopoulo.html

[20] www.dlib.org/dlib/november15/frey/11frey.html

How do practitioners, PhD students and postdocs in the social sciences assess topic-specific recommendations?

Philipp Mayr

GESIS - Leibniz Institute for the Social Sciences,
Unter Sachsenhausen 6-8
50667 Cologne, Germany
philipp.mayr@gesis.org

Abstract. In this paper we describe a case study where researchers in the social sciences (n=19) assess topical relevance for controlled search terms, journal names and author names which have been compiled by recommender services. We call these services Search Term Recommender (STR), Journal Name Recommender (JNR) and Author Name Recommender (ANR) in this paper. The researchers in our study (practitioners, PhD students and postdocs) were asked to assess the top n preprocessed recommendations from each recommender for specific research topics which have been named by them in an interview before the experiment. Our results show clearly that the presented search term, journal name and author name recommendations are highly relevant to the researchers topic and can easily be integrated for search in Digital Libraries. The average precision for top ranked recommendations is 0.749 for author names, 0.743 for search terms and 0.728 for journal names. The relevance distribution differs largely across topics and researcher types. Practitioners seem to favor author name recommendations while postdocs have rated author name recommendations the lowest. In the experiment the small postdoc group favors journal name recommendations.

Keywords: Recommendation services, bibliometric-enhanced IR, co-word analysis, author centrality, journal productivity, relevance assessment

1   Introduction

In metadata-driven Digital Libraries (DL) typically three major information retrieval (IR) related difficulties arise: (1) the vagueness between search and indexing terms, (2) the information overload by the amount of result records obtained by the information retrieval systems, and (3) the problem that pure term frequency based rankings, such as term frequency - inverse document frequency (tf-idf), provide results that often do not meet user needs [10]. Search term suggestion or other domain-specific recommendation modules can help users -

2   Philipp Mayr

e.g. in the social sciences [7] and humanities [4] - to formulate their queries by mapping the personal vocabularies of the users onto the often highly specialized vocabulary of a digital library. A recent overview of recommender systems in DL can be found in [2]. This strongly suggests the introduction of models in IR systems that rely more on the real research process and have therefore a greater potential for closing the gap between information needs of scholarly users and IR systems than conventional system-oriented approaches.

In this paper[1] we will present an approach to utilize specific information retrieval services [10] as enhanced search stratagems [1, 17, 5] and recommendation services within a scholarly IR environment. In a typical search scenario a user first formulates his query, which can then be enriched by a Search Term Recommender that adds controlled descriptors from the corresponding document language to the query. With this new query a search in a database can be triggered. The search returns a result set which can be re-ranked. Since search is an iterative procedure this workflow can be repeated many times till the expected result set is retrieved. These iterative search steps are typically stored in a search sessions log.

The idea of this paper is to assess if topic-specific recommendation services which provide search related thesaurus term, journal name and author name suggestions are accepted by researchers. In section 2 we will shortly introduce three different recommendation services: (1) co-word analysis and the derived concept of Search Term Recommendation (STR), (2) coreness of journals and the derived Journal Name Recommender (JNR) and (3) centrality of authors and the derived Author Name Recommender (ANR). The basic concepts and an evaluation of the top-ranked recommendations are presented in the following sections. We can show that the proposed recommendation services can easily be implemented within scholarly DLs. In the conclusion we assume that a users search should improve by using the proposed recommendation services when interacting with a scientific information system, but the relevance of these recommendations in a real interactive search task is still an open question (compare the experiences with the Okapi system [13]).

2   Models for information retrieval enhancement

The standard model of IR in current DLs is the tf-idf model which proposes a text-based relevance ranking. As tf-idf is text-based, it assigns a weight to term t in document d which is influenced by different occurrences of t and d. Variations of the basis term weighing process have been proposed, like normalization of document length or by scaling the tf values but the basic assumption stays the same. We hypothesize that recommendation services which are situated in the search process can improve the search experience of users in a DL.

The recommendation services are outlined very shortly in the following section. More details on these services can be found in [10].

---

[1] This paper is a slightly revised and updated version of a talk given at the EuroHCIR 2014 workshop in London.

2.1   Search Term Recommendation

Search Term Recommenders (STRs) are an approach to compensate the long known language problem in IR [3, 12, 7]: When searching an information system, a user has to come up with the "appropriate" query terms so that they best match the document language to get qualitative results. STRs in this paper are based on statistical co-word analysis and build associations between free terms (i.e. from title or abstract) and controlled terms (i.e. from a thesaurus) which are used during a professional indexation of the documents (see "Alternative Keywords" in Figure 1). The co-word analysis implies a semantic association between the free and the controlled terms. The more often terms co-occur in the text the more likely it is that they share a semantic relation. In our setup we use STR for search term recommendation where the original topical query of the researcher is expanded with semantically "near" terms[2] from the controlled vocabulary Thesaurus for the Social Sciences (TheSoz).

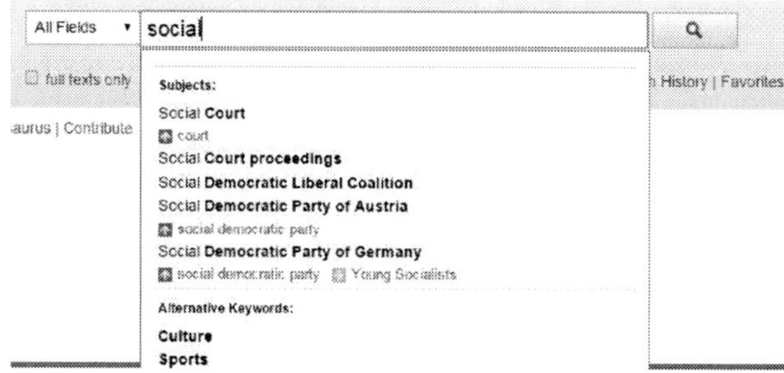

Fig. 1. Example search term "social" and search term recommendations

2.2   Recommending Journal Names

Journals play an important role in the scientific communication process. They appear periodically, they are topically focused, they have established standards of quality control and often they are involved in the academic gratification system. Metrics like the famous impact factor are aggregated on the journal level. In some disciplines journals are the main place for a scientific community to communicate and discuss new research results [11, 15]. In addition, journals or better journal names play an important role in the search process (see e.g. the famous search stratagem "journal run") [1, 8, 5]. The underlying mechanism for recommending journal names (JNR) in this paper is called Bradfordizing [16]. Bradfordizing is an alternative mechanism to re-rank journal articles according to core journals

---

[2] In the assessment we evaluated the "Alternative Keywords" generated from our STR implementation.

4   Philipp Mayr

to bypass the problem of very large and unstructured result sets. The approach of Bradfordizing is to use characteristic concentration effects (Bradfords law of scattering) that appear typically in journal literature. Bradfordizing defines different zones of documents which are based on the frequency counts in a given document set. Documents in core journals - journals which publish frequently on a topic - are ranked higher than documents which were published in journals from the following Bradford zones[3]. In IR a positive effect on the search result can be assumed in favor of documents from core journals [8, 9]. Bradfordizing is implemented as one re-ranking feature called "Journal productivity" in the digital library sowiport[4] [6]. In our setup of the assessment we evaluated the journal name recommendations, namely the top-ranked 5 core journals after Bradfordizing.

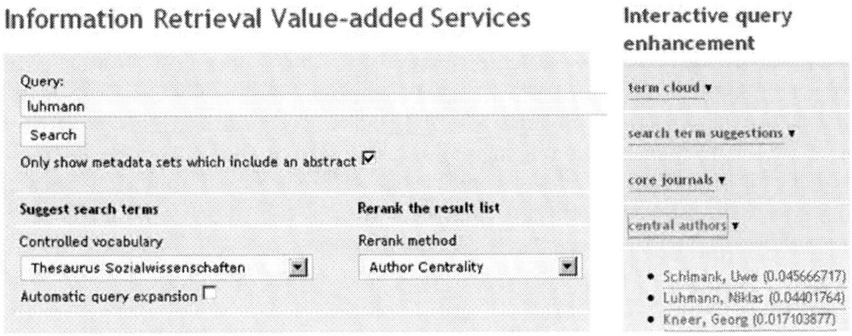

Fig. 2. Recommending author names in our retrieval prototype. Example search term "luhmann" and highly associated author names "central authors" in the right panel

2.3   Recommending Author Names

Collaboration in science is mainly represented by co-authorships between two or more authors who write a publication together. Transferred to a whole community, co-authorships form a co-authorship network reflecting the overall collaboration structure of a community. The underlying mechanism for recommending author names (ANR) in this paper is the author centrality measure betweenness. Author centrality is another way of re-ranking result sets (see Figure 2). Here the concept of centrality in a network of authors is an additional approach for the problem of large and unstructured result sets. The intention behind this ranking model is to make use of knowledge about the interaction and cooperation behavior in special fields of research. The (social) status and strategic position

---

[3] An explanation and visualization of Bradford Zones is given in [8].

[4] http://sowiport.gesis.org/

of a person in a scientific community is used too. The model is based on a network analytical view on a field of research and differs greatly from conventional text-oriented ranking methods like tf-idf. A concrete criterion of relevance in this model is the centrality of authors from retrieved publications in a co-authorship network. The model calculates a co-authorship network based on the result set to a specific query. Centrality of each single author in this network is calculated by applying the betweenness measure and the documents in the result set are ranked according to the betweenness of their authors so that publications with very central authors are ranked higher in the result list [10, 9]. From a recent study we know that many users are searching DL with author names [5]. In addition, author name recommendations basing on author centrality can be successfully be used as query expansion mechanism [14].

2.4 Implementation

All proposed services are implemented in a live information system using (1) the Solr search engine, (2) Grails Web framework to demonstrate the general feasibility of the approaches. Both Bradfordizing and author centrality as re-rank mechanism are implemented as plugins to the open source web framework Grails. Grails is the glue to combine the different modules and to offer an interactive web-based prototype. In general these retrieval services can be applied in different query phases.

In the following section we will describe a small case study with researchers using the recommendation services STR, JNR and ANR to find search terms, journal names and author names relevant to their research topics.

3   Assessment Study

The assessment study involved 19 researchers in the social sciences who agreed to name one or two of their research topics and take part in a short online assessment exercise. We have recruited the researchers (practitioners[5], PhD students and PostDocs) via email and telephone and they were asked to qualify their primary research topic in the form of 1-3 typical search terms they would enter in a search box. These search terms have been operationalized into a valid query for our prototype by us together with an individualized login for the single researcher. Individualized assessment accounts were sent to the researchers via email for each topic and contained a link to the online assessment tool and a short description how to evaluate the recommendations. All researchers were asked to assess the topical relevance of each recommendation in relationship to their research topic into relevant or not relevant (binary assessments). All researchers got three different assessment screens, always in the same order with a maximum of 5 recommendations for each recommender on one screen: first

---

[5] With practitioners we mean research staff/research associates who are working research related e.g. as information professionals, consultants or service staff, but are not working on a PhD thesis.

6   Philipp Mayr

all search term recommendations, second all author name recommendations and last all journal name recommendations. For each query, researchers got a set of max. 15 recommendations.

This is the list of all 23 evaluated researcher topics: [east Europe; urban sociology; equal treatment; data quality; interviewer error; higher education research; evaluation research; information science; political sociology; party democracy; data quality (2)[6], party system; factor structure; nonresponse; ecology; industrial sociology; sociology of culture; theory of action; atypical employment; lifestyle; Europeanization; survey design; societal change in the newly-formed German states].

4   Evaluation

In the following section we describe the evaluation of the recorded assessments. We calculated average precision AP for each recommender service. The precision P of each service was calculated by

$$P = \frac{r}{r + nr} \tag{1}$$

for each topic, where r is the number of all relevant assessed recommendations and $r+nr$ is the number of all assessed recommendations (relevant and not relevant).

We wanted to keep the assessment exercise for the researchers very short and hence we limited the list of recommendations of each service to a maximum of 5 controlled terms, journal names and author names. According to this restriction we decided to calculate $AP@1$, $AP@2$, $AP@4$ for each service. In very rare case one recommendation service generated just one or two recommendations.

5   Results

In sum 19 researchers assessed 23 topics in the online assessment study. This resulted in total 95 STR, 111 JNR and 107 ANR assessments (see Table 1). In average the researchers assessed 4.1 search term, 4.8 journal name and 4.6 author name recommendations per topic.

Table 1. Statistics of the assessment study

Researchers	Topics	STR Assessm.	JNR Assessm.	ANR Assessm.
19	23	95	111	107

Table 2 shows the evaluation results of all STR, JNR and ANR assessments. For this case study we did no statistically testing like t-test or Wilcoxon because

---

[6] Data quality is mentioned by two researchers and assessed two times.

of our very small sample. The following results should be read as plausibility tests without any statistical significance. We just want to demonstrate here the indicative relevance of this kind of recommender systems for scholarly search systems.

Table 2. Evaluation of the assessments. AP, AP@1, AP@2 and AP@4 for recommendation from STR, JNR and ANR

	STR	JNR	ANR
AP	0.743	0.728	0.749
AP@1	0.957	0.826	0.957
AP@2	0.826	0.848	0.864
AP@4	0.750	0.726	0.750

We can see that the average precision AP of ANR (0.749) and STR (0.743) is slightly better than JNR (0.728). Consulting the $AP@1$ measures ANR and STR are clearly better the JNR. That means that the first recommended author name or search term is rated more often relevant than the first journal name in a list of 4 or 5 recommendations. Surprisingly JNR (0.848) is slightly better than STR (0.826) in $AP@2$. If we look at the last row ($AP@4$) in Table 2 we can see that all three recommendation services move closer together when more recommendation are assessed.

Table 3 shows the average precision AP of STR, JNR and ANR for our three different researcher types (practitioners, PhD students and postdocs). From the 19 researchers in our user study we group 8 researchers into the practitioners group (mostly information professionals without PhD), 8 PhD students which had 1-4 years research experience and a small group of 3 postdocs with 4 and more years research experience. We can see clearly that the author name recommendations are rated highest by the practitioners (see AP of ANR = 0.836). Surprisingly the postdocs have evaluated ANR much lower than the other two groups (see AP of ANR = 0.467). In the experiment postdocs favor journal name recommendations. PhD students rate all three recommenders more or less the same.

Table 3. Evaluation of different researcher types. Average precision for recommendation from STR, JNR and ANR

	STR	JNR	ANR
AP Practitioners (N=8)	0.727	0.709	0.836
AP PhD students (N=8)	0.742	0.719	0.737
AP PostDocs (N=3)	0.750	0.800	0.467

8   Philipp Mayr

6   Conclusion

In this small case study typical researchers in the social sciences are confronted with specific recommendations which were calculated on the basis of researchers research topics. Looking at the precision values two important insights can be noted: (1) precision values of recommendations from STR, JNR and ANR are close together on a very high level - AP is close to 0.75 - and (2) each service retrieved a disjoint set of relevant recommendations. The different services each favor quite other - but still relevant - recommendations and relevance distribution differs largely across topics and researchers. A distinction between researcher types shows that practitioners are favoring author name recommendations (ANR) while postdocs are favoring journal name recommendations precompiled by our recommender services. This can be an artifact due to the small size of the postdoc group but this is also plausible. In terms of research topics author names typically are more distinctive than journal names. An experienced researcher (e.g. postdoc) who is familiar with an authors work can quickly rate an authors name relevance for a specific topic. In this context journal names are not that problematic because they published widely on different topics. This seems to be the case in our small sample (see third row in Table 3). PhD students who typically are unexperienced find all recommendations (terms, author names, journal names) helpful (see second row in Table 3).

The proposed models and derived recommendation services open up new viewpoints on the scientific knowledge space and also provide an alternative framework to structure and search domain-specific retrieval systems [10]. In sum, this case study presents limited results but show clearly that bibliometric-enhanced recommender services can support the retrieval process.

In a next step we plan to evaluate the proposed recommendation services in a larger document assessment task where the services are utilized as query expansion mechanisms [14] and interactive services [17]. However, a lot of research effort needs to be done to make more progress in coupling bibliometric-enhanced recommendation services with IR. The major challenge that we see here is to consider also the dynamic mechanisms which form the structures and activities in question and their relationships to dynamic features in scholarly information retrieval.

7   Acknowledgment

Our thanks go to all researchers in the study. The work presented here was funded by DFG, grant no. INST 658/6-1 and grant no. SU 647/5-2.

References

1. Bates, M.J.: Where should the person stop and the information search interface start? Information Processing & Management 26(5), 575–591 (jan 1990)
2. Beel, J., Gipp, B., Langer, S., Breitinger, C.: Research-paper recommender systems: a literature survey. International Journal on Digital Libraries (2015)
3. Blair, D.C.: Information retrieval and the philosophy of language. Annual review of information science and technology 37(1), 3–50 (2003)
4. Buchanan, G., Cunningham, S.J., Blandford, A., Rimmer, J., Warwick, C.: Information seeking by humanities scholars. In: Lecture Notes in Computer Science (including subseries Lecture Notes in Artificial Intelligence and Lecture Notes in Bioinformatics). vol. 3652 LNCS, pp. 218–229 (2005)
5. Carevic, Z., Mayr, P.: Survey on High-level Search Activities based on the Stratagem Level in Digital Libraries. In: 20th International Conference on Theory and Practice of Digital Libraries (TPDL 2016) (2016)
6. Hienert, D., Sawitzki, F., Mayr, P.: Digital Library Research in Action Supporting Information Retrieval in Sowiport. D-Lib Magazine 21(3/4) (2015), `http://www.dlib.org/dlib/march15/hienert/03hienert.html`
7. Hienert, D., Schaer, P., Schaible, J., Mayr, P.: A novel combined term suggestion service for domain-specific digital libraries. In: Lecture Notes in Computer Science (including subseries Lecture Notes in Artificial Intelligence and Lecture Notes in Bioinformatics). vol. 6966 LNCS, pp. 192–203 (2011)
8. Mayr, P.: Relevance distributions across Bradford Zones: Can Bradfordizing improve search? In: Gorraiz, J., Schiebel, E., Gumpenberger, C., Hörlesberger, M., Moed, H. (eds.) 14th International Society of Scientometrics and Informetrics Conference. pp. 1493–1505. Vienna, Austria (2013), `http://arxiv.org/abs/1305.0357`
9. Mutschke, P., Mayr, P.: Science Models for Search. A Study on Combining Scholarly Information Retrieval and Scientometrics. Scientometrics 102(3), 2323–2345 (2015)
10. Mutschke, P., Mayr, P., Schaer, P., Sure, Y.: Science models as value-added services for scholarly information systems. Scientometrics 89(1), 349–364 (jun 2011), `http://arxiv.org/abs/1105.2441`
11. Nicholas, D., Williams, P., Rowlands, I., Jamali, H.R.: Researchers' e-journal use and information seeking behaviour. Journal of Information Science 36(4), 494–516 (2010)
12. Petras, V.: Translating Dialects in Search: Mapping between Specialized Languages of Discourse and Documentary Languages. Ph.D. thesis, Berkeley, USA (2006)
13. Robertson, S.: Overview of the Okapi projects. Journal of Documentation 53(1), 3–7 (1997)
14. Schaer, P., Mayr, P., Lüke, T.: Extending Term Suggestion with Author Names. In: International Conference on Theory and Practice of Digital Libraries (TPDL 2012). pp. 317–322. Springer Berlin Heidelberg, Paphos, Cyprus (2012)
15. Talja, S., Maula, H.: Reasons for the use and non-use of electronic journals and databases: A domain analytic study in four scholarly disciplines. Journal of Documentation 59(6), 673–691 (2003)
16. White, H.D.: 'Bradfordizing' search output: how it would help online users. Online Review 5(1), 47–54 (1981)
17. Wilson, M.L., Kules, B., Schraefel, m.c., Ben Shneiderman: From Keyword Search to Exploration: Designing Future Search Interfaces for the Web. Foundations and Trends in Web Science 2(1), 1–97 (2010)

Overview of the CL-SciSumm 2016 Shared Task

Kokil Jaidka[1], Muthu Kumar Chandrasekaran[2], Sajal Rustagi[3], and
Min-Yen Kan[2,4]

[1] Big Data Experience Lab, Adobe Research India
[2] School of Computing, National University of Singapore, Singapore
[3] Dept. of Computer Science and Engineering, Indian Institute of Technology,
Roorkee, India
[4] Interactive and Digital Media Institute, National University of Singapore, Singapore
kokil@pmail.ntu.edu.sg

Abstract. The CL-SciSumm 2016 Shared Task is the first medium-scale
shared task on scientific document summarization in the computational
linguistics (CL) domain. The task built off of the experience and training
data set created in its namesake pilot task, which was conducted in 2014
by the same organizing committee. The track included three tasks involv-
ing: (1A) identifying relationships between citing documents and the referred document, (1B) classifying the discourse facets, and (2) generating
the abstractive summary. The dataset comprised 30 annotated sets of citing and reference papers from the open access research papers in the CL
domain. This overview paper describes the participation and the official
results of the second CL-SciSumm Shared Task, organized as a part of
the Joint Workshop onBibliometric-enhanced Information Retrieval and
Natural Language Processing for Digital Libraries (BIRNDL 2016), held
in New Jersey,USA in June, 2016. The annotated dataset used for this
shared task and the scripts used for evaluation can be accessed and used
by the community at: https://github.com/WING-NUS/scisumm-corpus.

1   Introduction

The CL-SciSumm task provides resources to encourage research in a promising
direction of scientific paper summarization, which considers the set of citation
sentences (i.e., "citances") that reference a specific paper as a (community created) summary of a topic or paper [21]. Citances for a reference paper are considered a synopses of its key points and also its key contributions and importance
within an academic community [19]. The advantage of using citances is that
they are embedded with meta-commentary and offer a contextual, interpreta-
tive layer to the cited text. The drawback, however, is that though a collection
of citances offers a view of the cited paper, it does not consider the context of
the target user [9] [24], verify the claim of the citation or provide context from
the reference paper, in terms the type of information cited or where it is in the
referenced paper [8].

CL-SciSumm explores summarization of scientific research, for the computational linguistics research domain. It encourages the incorporation of new kinds

of information in automatic scientific paper summarization, such as the facets of research information being summarized the research paper. Our previous task suggested that scholars in CL typically cite methods information from other papers. CL-SciSumm also encourages the use of citing mini-summaries written in other papers, by other scholars, when they refer to the paper. It is anticipated that these selected facts would closely reflect the most important contributions and applications of the paper. These insights have been explored in a smaller scope by previous work. We propose that further explorations can help to advance the state of the art. Furthermore, we expect that the CL-SciSumm Task could spur the creation of new resources and tools, to automate the synthesis and updating of automatic summaries of CL research papers.

Previous work in scientific summarization has attempted to automatically generate multi-document summaries by instantiating a hierarchical topic tree[6], generating model citation sentences[17] or implementing a literature review framework[8]. However, the limited availability of evaluation resources and human-created summaries constrains research in this area. In 2014, the CL-SciSumm Pilot task was conducted as a part of the larger BioMedSumm Task at TAC [5]. In 2016, our proposal was not successful with ACL; fortunately it was accepted as a part of the BIRNDL workshop [15] at JCDL-2016[6].

The development and dissemination of the CL-SciSumm dataset and the related Shared Task has been generously supported by the Microsoft Research Asia (MSRA) Research Grant 2016.

2   Task

Given: A topic consisting of a Reference Paper (RP) and up to ten Citing Papers (CPs) that all contain citations to the RP. In each CP, the text spans (i.e., citances) have been identified that pertain to a particular citation to the RP.

Task 1A: For each citance, identify the spans of text (cited text spans) in the RP that most accurately reflect the citance. These are of the granularity of a sentence fragment, a full sentence, or several consecutive sentences (no more than 5).

Task 1B: For each cited text span, identify what facet of the paper it belongs to, from a predefined set of facets.

Task 2: Finally, generate a structured summary of the RP from the cited text spans of the RP. The length of the summary should not exceed 250 words. This was an optional bonus task.

Evaluation: Participants were required to submit their system outputs from the test set to the task organizers. An automatic evaluation script was used to measure system performance for Task 1a, in terms of the sentence id overlaps between the sentences identified in system output, versus the gold standard created by human annotators. Task 1b was evaluated as a proportion of the

---

[5] http://www.nist.gov/tac/2014

[6] http://www.jcdl.org

correctly classified discourse facets by the system, contingent on the expected response of Task 1a. Task 2 was optional, and evaluated using the ROUGE-N [12] scores between the system output and three types of gold standard summaries of the research paper.

Data: The dataset comprises ten pairs of training sets, development and test sets. Each pair comprises the annotated citing sentences for a research paper and the discourse facets being referenced, and summaries of the research paper.

3   CL-SciSumm Pilot 2014

The CL Summarization Pilot Task [7] was conducted as a part of the Biomed-Summ Track at the Text Analysis Conference 2014 (TAC 2014) [7]. Ten pairs of annotated citing sentences and summaries were made available to the participants, who reported their performance on the same Tasks described above, as a cross-validation over the same dataset. System outputs for Task 1a were scored using word overlaps with the gold standard measured by the ROUGE–L score. Task 1b was scored using precision, recall and F_1. Task 2 was an optional task where system summaries were evaluated against the abstract using ROUGE–L. No centralized evaluation was performed. All scores were self-reported.

Three teams submitted their system outputs. clair_umich was a supervised system using lexical, syntactic and WordNet based features; MQ system used information retrieval inspired ranking methods; TALN.UPF used various TF-IDF scores.

During this task, the participants reported several errors in the dataset including text encoding and inconsistencies in the text offsets. The annotators also reported flaws in the xml encoding, and problems in the OCR export to XML. These issues hindered system building and evaluation. Accordingly, changes were made to the annotation file format and the XML transformation process in the current task.

4   Development

The CL-SciSumm 2016 task included the original training dataset of the Pilot Task, to encourage teams from the previous edition to participate. It also incorporated a new development corpus of ten sets for system training, and a separate test corpus of ten sets for evaluation. Additionally, it provided three types of summaries for each set in each corpus -

- the abstract, written by the authors of the research paper
- the community summary, collated from the reference spans of its citances
- human-written summary written by the annotators of the CL-SciSumm annotation effort

---

[7] http://www.nist.gov/tac/2014

For the general procedure followed to construct the CL-SciSumm corpus, please see [7]. There are two differences in the selection of citing papers (CP) for the training corpus, as compared to the development and test corpora. Firstly, the minimum numbers of CP provided in the former, which was 3, was increased to 8 in the construction of the latter. Secondly, the maximum number of CPs provided in the former was 10, but this limit was removed in the construction of the latter, so that up to 60 CPs have been provided for a single RP. This was done to have more citances of which potentially more would mention the RP in greater detail. This would also produce a wider perspective in the community summary.

4.1 Annotation

The annotators of the development and test corpora were five postgraduate students in Applied Linguistics, from University of Hyderabad, India. They were selected out of a larger pool of over twenty-five participants, who were all trained to annotate an RP and its CPs on their personal laptops, using the Knowtator[8] annotation package of the Protege editing environment[9].

The annotation scheme was unchanged from what was followed by [7]: Given each RP and its associated CPs, the annotation group was instructed to find citations to the RP in each CP. Specifically, the citation text, citation marker, reference text, and discourse facet were identified for each citation of the RP found in the CP. Inadvertently, we included the gold standard annotations for Task 1a and 1b when we released the test corpus. We alerted the participating teams to this mistake and requested them not to use that information for training their systems.

5 Overview of Approaches

The following paragraphs discuss the approaches followed by the participating systems, in no particular order. Except for the top performing systems in each of the sub-tasks, we do not provide detailed relative performance information for each system, in this paper. The evaluation scripts have been provided at the CL- SciSumm Github respository [10] where the participants may run their own evaluation and report the results.

The approach by [14] used the Transdisciplinary Scientific Lexicon (TSL) developed by [5] to build a profile for each discourse facet in citances and reference spans. Then a similarity function developed by [16] was used to select the best-matching reference span with the same facet as the citance. For Task 2, the authors used Maximal Marginal Relevance [3] to choose sentences so that they brought new information to the summary.

---

[8] http://knowtator.sourceforge.net/

[9] http://protege.stanford.edu/about.php

[10] github.com/WING-NUS/scisumm-corpus

Nomoto [20] proposed a hybrid model for Task 2, comprising TFIDF and a tripartite neural network. Stochastic gradient descent was performed on a training data comprising of triples of citance, the true reference and the set of false references for the citance. Sentence selection was based on a dissimilarity score similar to MMR.

Mao *et al.* [11] used an SVM classifier with a topical lexicon to identify the best matching reference spans for a citance, using ifd similarity, Jaccard similarity and context similarity. They finally submitted six system runs, each following a variant of similarities and approaches - the fusion method, the Jaccard Cascade method, the Jaccard Focused method, the SVM method and two voting methods.

Klampfl *et al.* [10] developed three different approaches based on summarization and classification techniques. They applied a modified version of an unsupervised summarization technique, termed it TextSentenceRank, to the reference document. Their second method incorporates similarities of sentences to the citation on a textual level, and employed classification to select from candidates previously extracted through the original TextSentenceRank algorithm. Their third method used unsupervised summarization of the relevant sub-part of the document that was previously selected in a supervised manner.

Saggion *et al.* [23] reported their results for the linear regression implementation of WEKA used together with the GATE system. They trained their model to learn the weights of different features with respect to the relevance of cited text spans and the relevance to a community-based summary. Two runs were submitted, using SUMMA [22] to score and extract all matched sentences and only the top sentences respectively.

Lu *et al.* [13] regarded Task 1a as a ranking problem, applying Learning to Rank strategies. In contrast, the group cast Task 1b as a standard text classification problem, where novel feature engineering was the team's focus. Along this vein, the group considered features of both citation contexts and cited spans.

Aggarwal and Sharma [1] propose several heuristics derived from bigram overlap counts between citances and reference text to identify the reference text span for each citance. This score is used to rank and select sentences from the reference text as output.

Baki *et al.* [18] used SVM with subset tree kernel, a type of convolution kernel. Computed similarities between three tree representations of the citance and reference text formed the convolution kernel. Their set-up scored better than their TF-IDF baseline method. They submitted three system runs with this approach.

The PolyU system [2], for Task 1a, use SVM-rank with lexical and document structural features to rank reference text sentences for every citance. Task 1b is solved using a decision tree classifier. Finally, they model summarization as a query–focussed summarization with citances as queries. They generate summaries (Task 2) by improvising on a Manifold Ranking method (see [2] for details).

Finally, the system submitted by Conroy and Davis [4] attempted to solve Task 2 with an adaptation of a system developed for the TAC 2014 BioMedSumm Task [11]. They provided the results from a simple vector space model, wherein they used a TF representation of the text and non- negative matrix factorization (NNMF) to estimate the latent weights of the terms for scientific document summarization. They also provide the results from two language models based on the distribution of words in human-written summaries.

6   System Runs

Performance of systems for Task 1a was measured by the number of sentences output by the system that overlap with the sentences in the human annotated reference text span (see section 4.1). These numbers were then used to calculate the precision, recall and F_1 score for each system. As Task 1b is a multi-label classification, this task was also scored by metrics - precision, recall and F_1 score.

Nine systems submitted outputs for Task 1. The following plots rank the systems for Task 1 by their F_1 scores. In the figures, all the systems have been identified by their participant number. Only the top performing systems for Tasks 1a, 1b and 2 have been identified by name in sections 6 and 7.

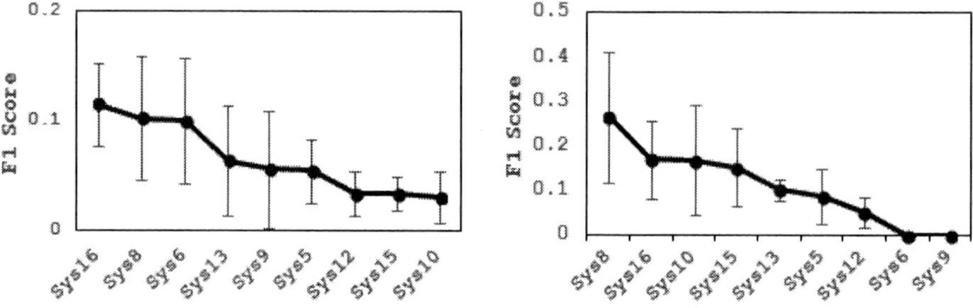

Fig. 1. System performances on Task 1a(left) and Task 1b(right).

Task 2, to create a summary of the reference paper from citances and the reference paper text, was evaluated against 3 types of gold standard summaries: the reference paper's abstract, a community summary and a human summary. A Java Implementation of ROUGE[12] was used to compare the gold summaries against summaries generated by systems. We calculated ROUGE–2 and ROUGE–4 F_1 scores for the system summaries against each of the 3 summary types. ROUGE–1 and ROUGE–3, which showed similar results have been omitted from this paper.

---

[11] http://www.nist.gov/tac/2014/BiomedSumm
[12] http://kavita-ganesan.com/content/rouge-2.0

Four of the nine system that did Task 1 also did the bonus Task 2. Following are the plots with their performance measured by ROUGE–2 and ROUGE–4 against the 3 gold standard summary types.

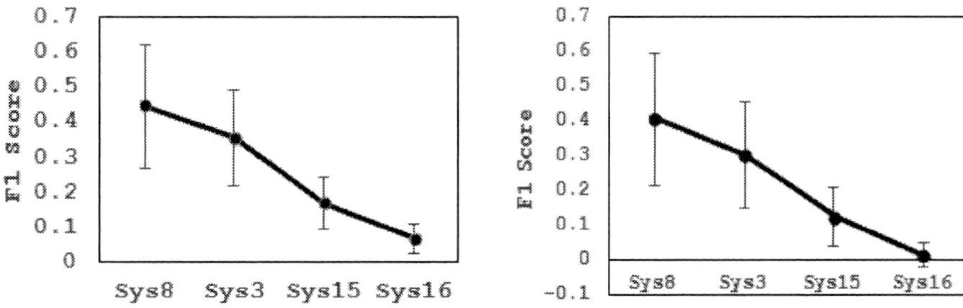

Fig. 2. Task 2 system performances on abstract summaries measured by ROUGE–2 (left) and ROUGE–4 (right)

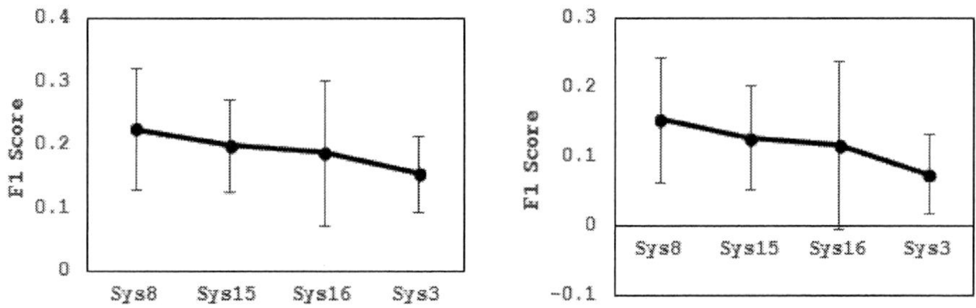

Fig. 3. Task 2 system performances on community summaries measured by ROUGE–2 (left) and ROUGE–4 (right)

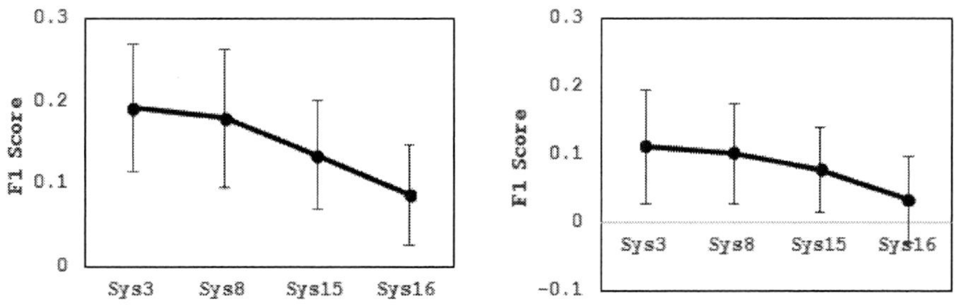

Fig. 4. Task 2 system performances on human summaries measured by ROUGE 2 (left) and 4 (right)

For Task 1a, the best performance was shown by *sys16*, developed by [2]. The next best performance was shown by *sys8* [11] and *sys6* [20].

For Task 1b, the best performance was shown by *sys8* [11], followed by the systems *sys16*[2] and *sys10*[23].

For Task 2, the system by [11], *sys8*, performed the best against abstract and community summaries, while *sys16* [2] performed well on community summaries. The system by *sys15* [1], was also a strong performer on these tasks. On human summaries, the best performance was seen from *sys3* [4].

The F_1 scores of all systems on Tasks 1a and 1b were generally low. However, the systems ranked in the first 3 places, did significantly better than systems ranked in the last 3 places.

On Task 2, all systems except *sys16* performed better when evaluated against abstracts, than against other summary types. Furthermore, system performances did not differ significantly from one another when evaluated against human and community summaries. However, when evaluated against abstracts, the best performing system significantly outperforms systems ranked in the lower half.

7 Conclusion

Ten systems participated in the CL-SciSumm Task 2016. A variety of heuristical, lexical and supervised approaches were used. Two of the best performing systems in Task 1a and 1b were also participants in the CL-SciSumm Pilot Task. The results from Task 2 suggest that automatic summarization systems may be adaptable to different domains, as we observed that the system by [4], which had originally been developed for biomedical human summaries, outperformed the others. We also note that systems performing well on Tasks 1a and 1b also do well in generating community summaries - this supports our expectations about the Shared Task, and validates the need to push the state-of-the-art in scientific summarization. In future work, other methods of evaluation can be used for comparing the performance of the different approaches, and a deeper analysis can lead to new insights about which approaches work well with certain kinds of data. However, such an inquiry was beyond the scope of this overview paper. We deem our Task a success, as it has spurred the interest of the community and the development of tools and approaches for scientific summarization. We are investigating other potential subtasks which could be added into our purview. We are also scouting for other related research problems, of relevance to the scientific summarization community.

Acknowledgement. The organizers of the CL-SciSumm16 shared task would like to thank Microsoft Research Asia, for their generous funding. We would also like to thank Vasudeva Varma and colleagues at IIIT-Hyderabad, India and University of Hyderabad, India for their efforts in convening and organizing our annotation workshops. We acknowledge the continued advice of Hoa Dang, Lucy Vanderwende and Anita de Waard from the pilot stage of this task and thank them for the same. We thank Rahul Jha and Dragomir Radev for sharing their software to prepare the XML versions of papers. We are grateful to Kevin B. Cohen and colleagues for their support, and for sharing their annotation schema, export scripts and the Knowtator package implementation on the Protege software - all of which have been indispensable for this Shared Task.

References

1. Aggarwal, P., Sharma, R.: Lexical and Syntactic cues to identify Reference Scope of Citance. In: Proc. of the Joint Workshop on Bibliometric-enhanced Information Retrieval and Natural Language Processing for Digital Libraries (BIRNDL2016). pp. 103–112. Newark, NJ, USA (June 2016)
2. Cao, Z., Li, W., Wu, D.: PolyU at CL-SciSumm 2016. In: Proc. of the Joint Workshop on Bibliometric-enhanced Information Retrieval and Natural Language Processing for Digital Libraries (BIRNDL2016). pp. 132–138. Newark, NJ, USA (June 2016)
3. Carbonell, J., Goldstein, J.: The use of MMR, diversity-based reranking for re-ordering documents and producing summaries. In: 21st annual international ACM SIGIR conference on Research and development in information retrieval. pp. 335–336. Association of Computational Linguistics (1998)
4. Conroy, J., Davis, S.: Vector space and language models for scientific document summarization. In: NAACL-HLT. pp. 186–191. Association of Computational Linguistics, Newark, NJ, USA (2015)
5. Drouin, P.: Extracting a bilingual transdisciplinary scientific lexicon. In: eLexicography in the 21st century: new challenges, new applications. pp. 43–53. Louvain-la-Neuve: Presses Universitaires de Louvain (2010)
6. Hoang, C., Kan, M.: Towards automated related work summarization. In: Proc. of COLING: Posters. pp. 427–435. ACL (2010)
7. Jaidka, K., Chandrasekaran, M.K., Elizalde, B.F., Jha, R., Jones, C., Kan, M.Y., Khanna, A., Molla-Aliod, D., Radev, D.R., Ronzano, F., et al.: The Computational Linguistics Summarization Pilot Task. In: Proceedings of Text Analysis Conference. Gaithersburg, USA (2014)
8. Jaidka, K., Khoo, C.S., Na, J.C.: Deconstructing human literature reviews–a framework for multi-document summarization. In: Proc. of ENLG. pp. 125–135 (2013)
9. Jones, K.S.: Automatic summarising: The state of the art. Information Processing and Management 43(6), 1449–1481 (2007)
10. Klampfl, S., Rexha, A., Kern, R.: Identifying Referenced Text in Scientific Publications by Summarisation and Classification Techniques. In: Proc. of the Joint Workshop on Bibliometric-enhanced Information Retrieval and Natural Language Processing for Digital Libraries (BIRNDL2016). pp. 122–131. Newark, NJ, USA (June 2016)

11. Li, L., Mao, L., Zhang, Y., Chi, J., Huang, T., Cong, X., Peng, H.: CIST System for CL-SciSumm 2016 Shared Task. In: Proc. of the Joint Workshop on Bibliometric-enhanced Information Retrieval and Natural Language Processing for Digital Libraries (BIRNDL2016). pp. 156–167. Newark, NJ, USA (June 2016)

12. Lin, C.Y.: Rouge: A package for automatic evaluation of summaries. Text summarization branches out: Proceedings of the ACL-04 workshop 8 (2004)

13. Lu, K., Mao, J., Li, G., Xu, J.: Recognizing reference spans and classifying their discourse facets. In: Proc. of the Joint Workshop on Bibliometric-enhanced Information Retrieval and Natural Language Processing for Digital Libraries (BIRNDL2016). pp. 139–145. Newark, NJ, USA (June 2016)

14. Malenfant, B., Lapalme, G.: RALI System Description for CL-SciSumm 2016 Shared Task. In: Proc. of the Joint Workshop on Bibliometric-enhanced Information Retrieval and Natural Language Processing for Digital Libraries (BIRNDL2016). pp. 146–155. Newark, NJ, USA (June 2016)

15. Mayr, P., Frommholz, I., Cabanac, G., Wolfram, D.: Editorial for the Joint Workshop on Bibliometric-enhanced Information Retrieval and Natural Language Processing for Digital Libraries (BIRNDL) at JCDL 2016. In: Proc. of the Joint Workshop on Bibliometric-enhanced Information Retrieval and Natural Language Processing for Digital Libraries (BIRNDL2016). pp. 1–5. Newark, NJ, USA (June 2016)

16. Mihalcea, R., Corley, C., Strapparava, C.: Corpus-based and knowledge-based measures of text semantic similarity. In: 21st national conference on Artificial Intelligence. pp. 775–780. AAAI (2006)

17. Mohammad, S., Dorr, B., Egan, M., Hassan, A., Muthukrishan, P., Qazvinian, V., Radev, D.R., Zajic, D.: Using citations to generate surveys of scientific paradigms. In: Proc. of NAACL. pp. 584–592. ACL (2009)

18. Moraes, L., Baki, S., Verma, R., Lee, D.: University of Houston at CL-SciSumm 2016: SVMs with tree kernels and Sentence Similarity. In: Proc. of the Joint Workshop on Bibliometric-enhanced Information Retrieval and Natural Language Processing for Digital Libraries (BIRNDL2016). pp. 113–121. Newark, NJ, USA (June 2016)

19. Nakov, P.I., Schwartz, A.S., Hearst, M.: Citances: Citation sentences for semantic analysis of bioscience text. In: Proceedings of the SIGIR'04 workshop on Search and Discovery in Bioinformatics. pp. 81–88 (2004)

20. Nomoto, T.: NEAL: A neurally enhanced approach to linking citation and reference. In: Proc. of the Joint Workshop on Bibliometric-enhanced Information Retrieval and Natural Language Processing for Digital Libraries (BIRNDL2016). pp. 168–174. Newark, NJ, USA (June 2016)

21. Qazvinian, V., Radev, D.: Scientific paper summarization using citation summary networks. In: Proceedings of the 22nd International Conference on Computational Linguistics-Volume 1. pp. 689–696. ACL (2008)

22. Saggion, H.: SUMMA: A Robust and Adaptable Summarization Tool. Traitement Automatique des Langues 49(2), 103–125 (2002)

23. Saggion, H., AbuRa'Ed, A., Ronzano, F.: Trainable Citation-enhanced Summarization of Scientific Articles. In: Proc. of the Joint Workshop on Bibliometric-enhanced Information Retrieval and Natural Language Processing for Digital Libraries (BIRNDL2016). pp. 175–186. Newark, NJ, USA (June 2016)

24. Teufel, S., Moens, M.: Summarizing scientific articles: experiments with relevance and rhetorical status. Computational Linguistics 28(4), 4099–445 (2002)

Lexical and Syntactic cues to identify Reference Scope of Citance

Peeyush Aggarwal[1], Richa Sharma[2]

[1]Bharti Vidyapeeth College of Engineering, Delhi, India
peeyushaggarwal94@gmail.com
[2]BML Munjal University, Gurgaon, India
richa.sharma@bml.edu.in

Abstract.

In this paper, we present our system addressing Task 1 of CL-SciSumm Shared Task at BIRNDL 2016. Our system makes use of lexical and syntactic dependency cues, and applies rule-based approach to extract text spans in the Reference Paper that accurately reflect the citances. Further, we make use of lexical cues to identify discourse facets of the paper to which cited text belongs. The lexical and syntactic cues are obtained on pre-processed text of the citances, and the reference paper. We report our results obtained for development set using our system for identifying reference scope of citances in this paper.

Keywords: Natural Language Processing, Syntactic Analysis, Scientific Document Summarisation, Bag of Words

1   Introduction

The scientific research community needs different viewpoints of research contributions in summarized form. Abstract of the research contribution presents summary from the author(s) perspective. Citations of a reference paper reflect the viewpoint of the citing authors for that reference paper, and possibly in a certain context only. Summary drawn for a reference paper from its citations can put forward a different and interesting context of that reference paper. There have been several efforts towards extracting reference scope of citances, and such citations-based summary in recent years like [1], [2] etc. Kokil et al. [3] have shown through their Computational Linguistics Summarization (CL-Summ) Pilot task that citation based summary of scientific documentation is important to create for understanding different perspectives of a reference paper. Further to that pilot task, Computational Linguistics Scientific Document Summarization (CL-SciSumm-2016[1]) shared task has been designed with the goal of exploring automated summarization of scientific contributions for the computational linguistics research domain.

---

[1] http://wing.comp.nus.edu.sg/cl-scisumm2016/

The organizers of CL-SciSumm shared task have divided the task into two parts: (1) For each citance, identify the spans of text (cited text spans) in the Reference Paper (RP) that most accurately reflect the citance, and identify the facet of the paper it belongs to; (2) Generate a structured summary of the RP from the cited text spans of the RP. Task-2 is optional. However, task-1 is required to create citations-based summary of the RP. This makes task-1 crucial and important step in creating citations-based summary of any scientific document [4]. The corpus of CL-SciSumm shared task has been created by sampling documents from ACL Anthology corpus and selecting their citing papers [9].

We have worked on task-1 ('a' and 'b') to develop our system for identifying the reference scope of the citance in the RP. We present the details of our system in Section – 2 below. This is followed by evaluation of our system, as presented in section 3, and observations in section 4. We finally present concluding remarks in Section 5.

2   Our System

In order to develop our system for the CL-SciSumm shared task, we first reviewed one sample topic (one RP and its citing papers) from the training set, and one from the development set. Manual review of these two samples revealed that though the shared task requires analysing the statements in the corpus semantically, but semantic analysis is challenging owing to the nature of the corpus. The corpus is a collection of scientific, technical articles making use of appropriate technical language, and therefore usage of varying, similar-meaning words is quite less. This makes the scope of using text semantic similarity measures quite minimal. Secondly, the citance from the citing paper refers to the text spans of RP in different contexts. These citing texts often do not refer to any meaningful content or information from RP except for a word or two. For example, the citing statement below does not convey much information about the RP except for two hinting words – *RFTagger* and *German*:

*For German, we show results for **RFTagger (Schmid and Laws, 2008)**.*

Having found most of such examples in manual review, we were discouraged to make use of sub-sequences (of words) overlap between the statement in Citing Paper (CP) and its corresponding, reflective statements in RP. The overlapping words between the statements in CP and in RP usually do not form a subsequence. Therefore, we resolved to work with lexical (n-grams in bag-of-words approach instead of sub-sequence of words), and syntactic cues to develop our system. Following sub-sections summarize our approach and the heuristics used in our system. We have implemented our solution approach using Python. During the course of development of our system, we observed various advantages that Python offered us. We shall discuss those in observations section 3. Figure 1 below summarizes an overview of our approach implemented to develop Python-based system for carrying out task-1 of CL-SciSumm:

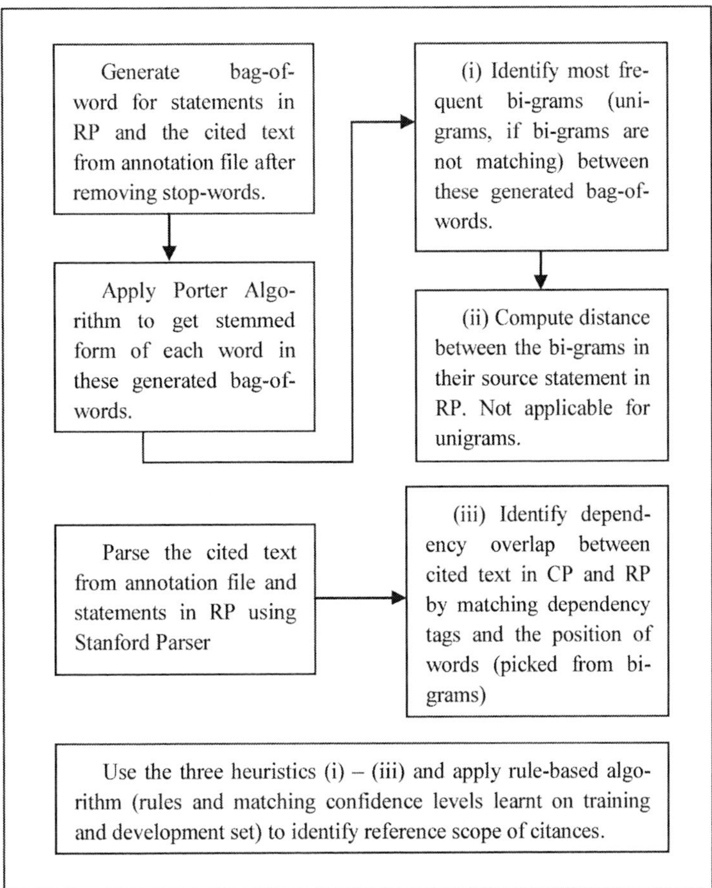

Fig. 1. System Overview

2.1 Generating Bag-of-words

Lexical cues, in our system, are gathered in terms of bi-grams (two lexical tokens from the bag-of-words) and unigrams (where bi-grams are not available). We are extending the notion of bi-grams, in our context of study, to group of two matching words between the cited text in CP and its reference scope in the RP. As discussed above, most of the citances refer to two (or more) lexical units in the reference scope of the RP. Therefore, we have limited the scope of our solution to bi-grams. We first parse the XML version of the reference paper to get individual statements in the RP for further processing. Then, we generate bag-of-words after removing stop-words from the citing text, and the statements of the RP. We have used most commonly used

Glasgow list of stop-words[2] for the purpose. We identify the (matching) bi-grams after converting the lexical units in bag-of-words to their stemmed form using Porter's Stemmer[3]. Porter's stemmer is often criticized for not returning the correct root form of a word. However, this limitation of Porter's stemmer does not affect the results in our case since we are applying it to both the bag-of-words to be used for matching (words/lexical units) purpose. Therefore, carrying out a regular expression comparison on both the bag-of-words did not add any discrepancy inadvertently.

2.2 Syntactic Dependency Analysis

Syntactic Dependency analysis has been extensively used for analysing statement at granular level for recognizing textual entailments [5] and question-answering systems [6]. Similarities in syntactic roles, and dependency overlaps between statements under analysis for semantic similarity have proved to be effective heuristics. Finding reference scope for citations could also benefit from dependency overlap, though similarity in syntactic roles is difficult to find between citations and their corresponding reference scope in RP. We have used Stanford dependency parser [7] to find dependency overlaps for the identified bi-grams between citing statement in CP and its reflective statement in RP. After obtaining parsed output, the words in the dependency relation are again converted to their stemmed form (using Porter's stemmer) to facilitate matching between different forms of same word like *use*, *using* etc.

2.3 Heuristics to identify Reference Scope of Citance

We have worked with following heuristics for task 1a of the CL-SciSumm task:

1. **Most frequent bi-grams.** We search for matching words (stemmed form) between the citing statement and the statements in RP. Having obtained a list of matching statements, we search for most frequent words in thus obtained list of statements from the RP. The count of matching words in the statements of the RP varies from zero to five-six. We observe that considering bi-grams for ranking statements in RP is if help. If none of the statements in the RP has been found to have matching words with bag-of-words of the citing statement, then we output such a citance relationship with '*NaN*'. There are instances where citing statements got stopped inadvertently due to incorrect marking of end of statement while preparing the corpus. In case only uni-gram is found to be matching between citing statement and the source statement in RP, then its weight in the matching statement is computed as the ratio of its occurrence count against the size of bag-of-words for that matching statement. The statement with highest weight is assigned rank $-$ 1. If more than two statements have exactly same weight with same words, then all

---

these statements are assigned rank – 1. In case, the word are different in such similar weighing statements, then the statement having most frequent word across various statements is assigned highest rank.

In case, two or more than two words are matching, then we rank the statements considering bi-grams for weight-assignment. We identify the most frequent bi-gram across various statements that have matching words with the citing statement. For the most frequent bi-gram, we assign weight to the statement as the ratio of count of occurrence of the words in bi-gram against the size of bag-of-words in each of the source statements from RP. The matching statement having highest weight is ranked highest, and is reported as the reflective statement for the cited statement under consideration. In case, more than one statement has similar weights then ranking algorithm considers rest of the two heuristics as discussed below.

2. **Distance between tokens in frequent bi-grams.** This heuristic considers the distance between the words or tokens in the most frequent bi-gram. This heuristic helps in resolving ranks of the matching statements from the RP when the heuristic in point 1 happens to assign similar weights to more than one statement. However, this heuristic is not applicable where unigrams have been found to be matching.

3. **Dependency Overlap Count.** We determine dependency overlap for the frequent bi-grams between the cited text in CP and its corresponding reflective statement in the RP. We extract those dependencies that have either of the words or tokens in the bi-gram. A match is said to be found if the dependency tag matches, the stemmed form of tokens also match, and the token is in the identical position (either governing position or dependent position). Following example illustrates how dependency overlap is found:

Considering the following citing statement from development set for topic, C02-1025:

S1: In such cases, neither global features (Chieu and Ng, 2002) nor aggregated contexts (Chieu and Ng, 2003) can help.

and one of the statements from RP:

S2: Such a classification can be seen as a not-always-correct summary of global features.
The parsed output for S1 and S2 is respectively:

Parsed Output for S1 in CP:

amod(cases-3, such-2)	prep_in(help-12, cases-3)
preconj(features-7, neither-5)	amod(features-7, global-6)
nsubj(help-12, features-7)	amod(contexts-10, aggregated-9)
conj_nor(features-7, contexts-10)	nsubj(help-12, contexts-10)
aux(help-12, can-11)	root(ROOT-0, help-12)

Parsed Output for S2 in RP:

predet(classification-3, Such-1)	det(classification-3, a-2)
nsubjpass(seen-6, classification-3)	aux(seen-6, can-4)
auxpass(seen-6, be-5)	root(ROOT-0, seen-6)
amod(summay-10, not-always-correct-9)	
det(summay-10, a-8)	prep_as(seen-6, summay-10)
amod(features-13, global-12)	prep_of(summay-10, features-13)

The most frequent bi-gram for this topic is: *global, features*. Searching for these words in the parsed output of S1 and S2, we get:

S1:

preconj(features-7, neither-5)
amod(features-7, global-6)
nsubj(help-12, features-7)
conj_nor(features-7, contexts-10)

S2:

amod(features-13, global-12)
prep_of(summay-10, features-13)

Matching the dependency tags and governing/dependent positions in the above-extracted dependencies of S1 and S2, we get dependency overlap count as *one* (matching dependency presented in italics above).

2.4 Rule-based System to identify Reference Scope in RP

We have developed rule-based system based on these three heuristics to report reference scope in RP for the cited text in CP. We have learnt threshold values for ranking and further processing the statements after several rounds of experimentation with these datasets. The statements having weight more than or equal to 0.2 are considered for further ranking and processing. We report the reflective source statement in RP for a citing statement in CP after considering highest weights, maximum dependency overlap count, and lowest distance between bi-grams. In case of more than one statement encountered having similar values for any of these three heuristics, we assign weights the highest priority, followed by dependency overlap count, and then distance. After these checks, if there is still more than one statement with same values of heuristics, then our system reports all of these statements as reference scope for the CP statement.

2.5 Heuristics to identify Facets

The next sub-task of task-1 is to identify discourse facet for the cited text span with reference to the RP. The discourse facet is helpful in identifying different contexts of citing a reference paper. The organizers of the CL-SciSumm have predefined five facets: aim_citation, hypothesis_citation, method_citation, implication_citation, and results_citation. Identifying correct discourse facet again calls for understanding semantics of the cited text span, though there are challenges involved with the same as discussed above. Our approach to identify discourse facet, therefore, is based on section headers in the paper. However, our approach has the drawback of not being able to identify hypothesis_citation and implication_citation. For rest of the three facets, following rules are observed:

1. If the cited text span lies in the introduction section, beginning of abstract, then it is indicative of aim_citation.
2. Discourse facet is marked as results_citation if the cited text span belongs to the sections having title as – Results, Observations, Discussion, Conclusion, or if the cited text span is one of the last 2 statements of the abstract.
3. If cited text span does not belong to the sections as mentioned in above two points, then the discourse facet is marked as method_citation.

3   Evaluation

We have computed ROUGE-N [8] metric with 'N' as 2 for bi-grams to evaluate our system. Table 1 below presents the average results for identifying reference scope (task – 1a) for each topic in the development set, and an average overall performance of the system for the development set for task -1a:

Table 1. Task 1a performance in terms of ROUGE-N for development set

Paper Id	Precision	Recall	F-measure
C02-1025	0.12	0.08	0.09
C08-1098	0.07	0.03	0.04
C10-1045	0.17	0.14	0.15
D10-1083	0.08	0.08	0.08
E09-2008	0.27	0.21	0.23
N04-1038	0.25	0.21	0.22
P06-2124	0.16	0.05	0.06
W04-0213	0.12	0.04	0.06
W08-2222	0.14	0.05	0.07
W95-0104	0.16	0.13	0.13
Average	0.16	0.10	0.11

For task 1b, we have computed accuracy of reporting discourse facet of the paper as the ratio of correctly identified facets in an annotation file for a topic and the total number of citances for that topic. Table 2 presents the discourse-facet accuracy corresponding to the development set:

Table 2. Discourse Facet Accuracy for development set

Paper Id	Accuracy
C02-1025	0.74
C08-1098	0.69
C10-1045	0.42
D10-1083	0.55
E09-2008	0.63
N04-1038	0.75
P06-2124	0.44
W04-0213	0.83
W08-2222	0.78
W95-0104	0.49
Average	0.63

4   Observations

The experiments with different datasets – training, development, and test set indicate that lexical and syntactic cues are indeed of help. But, lexical and syntactic analysis has its own limitations in terms of only regular expression match, and no semantic or contextual matching. We observe that the same approach does not perform uniformly with all the datasets, and performance does differ even within one dataset. For example – our system worked better with topics E09-2008 and N04-1038 as compared to other topics in development set, as evident from Table – 1. The evaluation results presented in Table – 1 correspond to ROUGE-N metric (N as 2). We have used this metric because our system is bi-gram in nature. Nevertheless, we are implementing ROUGE-S metric as well in order to cross-validate our evaluation and system performance.

It can be inferred from the discussion above that semantic-level analysis is inevitable to yield good results. The task of identifying reference scope for citances appears similar to the task of recognizing textual entailment (RTE), but is actually quite different. This is primarily because of different nature of corpus. Nevertheless, CL-SciSumm task can benefit from the RTE challenges and solution approaches to recognizing textual entailment. While working with CL-SciSumm corpus, we encountered several problems in the corpus in terms of its formatting, characters coding as well as annotations. However, these problems are not major, and could be fixed. Resolution of these concerns may provide useful pointers to semantic-level analysis needed for tasks like CL-SciSumm.

We have worked with three heuristics of lexical and syntactic nature to identify the reference scope of the cited text in the RP. The computation of values of these heuristics has been described in detail in section – 2. We observed after experiments with our system that computation methodology of our heuristics may further be refined. As of now, our system considers unigrams and bi-grams only. We have mitigated the challenges with lexical analysis by considering stemmed form of words to work with. We are further experimenting with different priorities for our heuristics, and tweaking our algorithms currently.

We have developed our system for CL-SciSumm task in Python language. We have observed that Python turned out to be a useful choice. Python is an interpreted language supporting both object-oriented and functional programming flavour. Python allowed us to develop codes in fewer lines with dividing the problems into sub-problems. We were thus able to code and test small snippets separately and merge those later to develop complete system.

5   Conclusion

In this paper, we have presented our system for CL-SciSumm task 1 to identify reflective statements from RP for a given citance in CP. The task is challenging as semantic-level analysis has limited applicability in this case. We have addressed the task using lexical and syntactic cues to extract text-spans from RP that correspond to the cited text in CP. We believe that further refinements to the corpus and to our system can yield better results. We do intend to further refine our heuristics and check the applicability of machine learning too.

6   References

1. Nakov, P.I., Schwartz, A.S. and Hearst. M.A.: Citances: Citation sentences for semantic analysis of bioscience text. In: SIGIR (2004).
2. Qazvinian, V. and Radev, D.R.: Identifying Non-explicit Citing Sentences for Citation-based Summarization. In Proceedings of Association for Computational Linguistics, (2010).
3. Jaidka, K., Chandrasekaran, M.K., Elizalde, B.F., Jha, R., Jones, C., Kan, M., Khanna, A., Molla-Aliod, D., Radev, D.R., Ronzano, F., et al.: The computational linguistics summarization pilot task. In: Proceedings of Text Ananlysis Conference, Gaithersburg, USA, (2014).
4. Abu-Jbara, A. and Radev, D.: Reference Scope Identification in Citing Sentences. In: Proceedings of Conference of the North American Chapter of the Association for Computational Linguistics: Human Language Technologies, pp 80–90, (2012).
5. Sharma, N., Sharma, R. and Biswas K.K..: Recognizing Textual Entailment using Dependence Analysis and Machine Learning. In: Proceedings of Conference of the North American Chapter of the Association for Computational Linguistics: Human Language Technologies - Student Research Workshop (SRW), Colorado, USA (2015).
6. Molla, D.: Towards semantic-overlap based measures for question answering. In: Proceedings of the Australasian Language Technology Workshop, Australia (2003).

7. Marneffe, M.C. de, Silveira, N., Dozat, T., Haverinen, K., Ginter, F., Nivre, J. and Manning, C.D.: Universal Stanford Dependencies: A cross-linguistic typology. In: LREC (2014).
8. Lin, C. and Hovy, E.H.: Automatic Evaluation of Summaries using N-gram co-occurence Statistics. In: Proceedings of Language Technology Conference (HLT-NAACL), Canada (2003).
9. Jaidka, K., Chandrasekran, M.K., Rustagi, S. and Kan, M.: Overview of the 2nd Computational Linguistics Scientific Document Summarization Shared Task (CL-SciSumm-2016), To appear in the Proceedings of the Joint Workshop on Bibliometric-enhanced Information Retrieval and Natural Language Processing for Digital Libraries (BIRNDL), Newark, New Jersey, USA (2016).

University of Houston at CL-SciSumm 2016:
SVMs with tree kernels and Sentence Similarity*

Luis Moraes, Shahryar Baki, Rakesh Verma and Daniel Lee

Computer Science Department
University of Houston, TX 77204

Abstract. This paper describes the University of Houston team's efforts toward the problem of identifying reference spans in a reference document given sentences from other documents that cite the reference document. We investigated the following approaches: cosine similarity with multiple incremental modifications and SVMs with a tree kernel. Although the best performing approach in our experiments is quite simple, it is not the best under every metric used for comparison. We also present a brief analysis of the dataset which includes information on its sparsity and frequency of section titles.

1 Introduction

The CL-SciSumm 2016 shared task poses the problem of automatic summarization in the Computational Linguistics (CL) domain. Single text summarization is hardly new, however, in addition to the reference text to be summarized we are also given citances i.e. sentences that cite our reference text.

The shared task is broken into multiple tasks with the unifying theme of leveraging citances. Task 1a is, given a citance, to identify the span of reference text that best reflects what has been cited. Task 1b asks us to classify the cited aspect according to a predefined set of facets: hypothesis, aim, method, results, and implication. Finally, Task 2 is generating a structured summary.

We experimented with the following approaches: SVMs with a tree kernel and cosine similarity based on TF/IDF weights for sentences. The best results when measuring by sentence inclusion are obtained by cosine similarity. However, ROUGE-L scores are better for the tree kernel approach.

We also study two characteristics of the dataset: sparsity and section importance. We define section importance as the normalized frequency of the section, i.e., the number of correct reference sentences that belong to this section across all the citances. We found that the introduction is the most cited section in this year's dataset. We also find that citances are less sparse than the average sentence within the corpus.

* Research supported in part by NSF grants CNS 1319212, DGE 1433817 and DUE 1241772

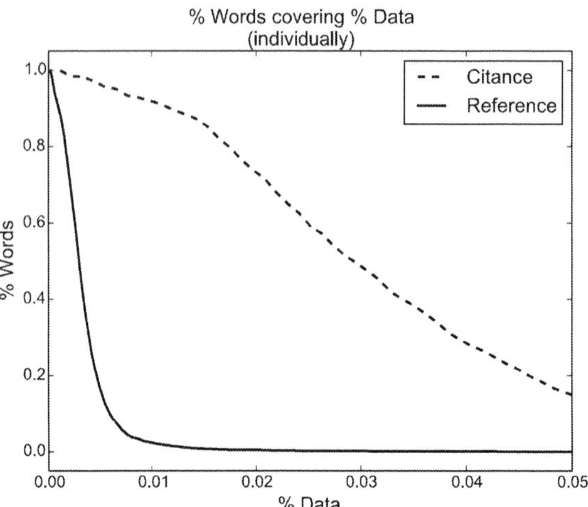

Fig. 1. The percentage of unique words in a set of sentences that appears in a percentage of all sentences. An indirect measure of sparsity.

2 Dataset

The dataset [3] consists of 30 total documents separated into three sets of 10 documents each: training, development, and test sets. For the following analysis no preprocessing has been done (for instance, stemming). There are 23784 unique words among the reference documents in the dataset. The citances contain 6415 unique words. The most frequent word among reference documents appears in 4125 sentences. The most frequent word among citances appears in 598 sentences. There are 6706 reference sentences and 913 citance sentences (a few annotations have more than one). The average reference sentence has approximately 22 words in this dataset whereas citances have an average of approximately 30 words.

In Figure 1 we can see how sparse the dataset is; the quicker the decay, the greater the sparsity. Noise in the dataset is one of the factors for the sparsity. We can see that citances, seen as a corpus, are in general less sparse than the reference texts. This can be an indication that citances have some common structure or semantics.

2.1 Citances

It should be noted that citances have a few peculiarities, such as an abundance of citation markers and proper names. Citation markers will sometimes include the names of authors, thus causing our sentences to have a greater frequency of proper names. Identifying and ignoring citation markers should reduce noise. This could justify the lesser sparsity (reoccuring authors), but could also justify greater sparsity (unique authors).

2.2 Frequency of Section Titles

For each cited reference sentence, we looked at the title of the section in which it appears. The titles that appeared with greatest frequency can be seen in Table 1. To extract these section titles we looked at the parent nodes of sentences within the XML document. The "title" and "abstract" sections are special since they refer to parent nodes of type other than SECTION. These results clearly show sentences that are cited are not uniformly distributed within a document.

Title	Frequency Relevant
introduction	25.55%
abstract	6.98%
title	5.58%
conclusion.	4.46%
the approach.	4.05%
potential for improvement.	3.35%
evaluation.	3.21%

Table 1. The frequency refers to how many times the section contained a relevant sentence. This was calculated from all the documents in the dataset.

3 Task 1a

In this task we are asked to identify the reference sentences referred to by a given citance. We approach the problem from two different perspectives. One of our systems follows the intuitive idea that the citance and the sentences to which it refers must share some similarity. Thus, we modify this system with the intent to capture more forms of similarity. Our second system abstracts further, instead of looking at the similarity between citance and reference sentences we look at the similarity between citance and reference sentence pairs, (c, r). We attempt to learn how to distinguish relevant and irrelevant pairs. We modify this system with the intent to improve the learned classifier.

3.1 TF/IDF Approach

This approach compares the TF/IDF vectors of the citance and the sentences in the reference document. Each reference sentence is assigned a score according to the cosine similarity between itself and the citance. Stopwords were removed for all configurations. A few of the modifications to this general approach follow:

Stemming. (ST) To remove the effect of using words in their different forms we used stemming to reduce words to their root form. For this purpose, we use the Snowball Stemmer, provided by the NLTK package [1].

Context Expansion. (CE) Citances by themselves only have a limited amount of semantic information. We expand the semantic content of a citance by including the sentences that occur directly before and after the citance when constructing its word vector.

WordNet Expansion. (WN) Another method for semantic expansion is to include the lemmas obtained from the synsets of each word in a sentence. This applies to both citances and sentences in the reference document. We use the Lesk algorithm, provided through the NLTK package [1], to perform wordsense disambiguation. This is a necessary step before obtaining the synset of a word from WordNet [7]. The lemmas for each synset are added to the word vector of the sentence; this augmented vector is used when calculating the cosine similarity instead.

Sentence Limiting. (SL) In order to reduce noise (due to OCR), we eliminate from consideration all sentences outside a certain range of number of words. For the TF/IDF approach we only consider reference sentences with more than 10 and less than 70 words. This process eliminates 1494 sentences out of 6706 total, roughly 22%. The test set has a total of 390 sentences that should be retrieved. Only 340 can still be retrieved once we restrict the number of words.

3.2 Tree Kernel Approach

We classify the (c, r) pairs of citance and reference sentence as relevant or irrelevant. We then rank the sentences according to how confident we are it is relevant.

SVM. The Support Vector Machine (SVM) is a classifier that learns a hyperplane to separate two classes [2]. The hyperplane with the largest margin is considered the best choice. Thus, learning becomes an optimization problem.

After training, an SVM will have a set of support vectors that define its hyperplane. The hyperplane can be thought of as a description of the boundary between classes. The output is the signed distance from the instance to this hyperplane: a positive distance implies the item belongs to the positive class; a negative distance implies the item is in the negative class.

Learning can be carried out with just the Gram Matrix, a matrix of the "distances" between pairs of data items. This is known as the kernel trick. By choosing a different kernel we implicitly transform the space where items reside. This broadens the utility of SVMs since the new space may allow for simpler separation between classes.

Subset Tree Kernel. Our kernel of choice is a convolutional kernel on trees. Although there are a few different formulations, we use the subset tree kernel which compares the number of common subset trees (subtrees that can have nonterminals as leaves) [9].

Parse trees may be ideally suited for the kernel, but we can easily produce "flat trees" for vector-like data. Flat trees can be understood as trees where all leaves are directly connected to the root. Therefore, in addition to the parse tree, we use a flat tree for the bag-of-words representation and the POS tags. For each sentence we have 3 different trees (similar to [9]), so for each (c, r) pair we have 6 trees total. The similarity between items is calculated by first finding the similarity between respective trees (using the subset tree kernel), then adding up each tree's contribution.

Class Imbalance. The way we modeled the problem makes it heavily imbalanced. The number of (c, r) pairs that are irrelevant is much larger than the number that are relevant. Due to this imbalance the classifier was trained with subsets of all possible pairs to reduce the influence of the majority class. We train SVMs with a random selection of negative items. We experimented with three different positive-to-negative ratios: $1:1$, $1:4$, $1:8$. We performed 5 runs for each configuration since the selection of negative items could help or hurt our performance.

Context Expansion. (CE) For the Tree kernel approach, context expansion consists in adding the sentence above and below a citance as part of the citance. This is only used in training; preliminary results showed little difference in performance when classifying more (c, r) pairs (those of the extra sentences).

Sentence Limiting. (SL) Similar to how we eliminated sentences from consideration in the TF/IDF approach, we do the same here. Since we randomly select negative items, it becomes of greater concern that we perform multiple runs. To get a sufficient number of runs we use a narrower range to reduce classification time; sentences must have more than 15 and less than 35 words. This process eliminates 3462 sentences out of 6706 total, roughly 51%. Out of the 390 relevant sentences in the test set, only 215 meet the criteria.

Implementation. We utilize SVM-LIGHT-TK [8, 4] for our experiments. We use the Stanford CoreNLP [6] for obtaining POS tags and parse trees from our data. First we train our SVM on all the relevant (c, r) pairs with a few select irrelevant pairs. Then, we classify all possible pairs in the reference text. The top 3 are selected as the output of our system.

4 Task 2

Task 2 consists in generating a summary for the reference text. For Task 2 we average the sentence scores given by each citance and extract sentences until we reach the 250 word limit. This was only performed for the Tree kernel approach and only against human summaries. Furthermore, we only evaluated the best performing run of each configuration (according to its performance in Task 1a).

5 Evaluation

The evaluation of our systems is done by comparison of several metrics which are detailed below. For the Tree kernel method, these values are averaged over 5 runs.

ROUGE-L. The ROUGE metrics are useful for evaluating summaries. In particular we look at the ROUGE-L metric [5], which has the fewest parameters. The ROUGE-L metric is based on the Longest Common Subsequence (LCS). Consequently, it is more lenient since sentences that share words will be considered as somewhat correct.

Top-3 Metrics. Our systems output the top 3 sentences, thus we compute recall, precision, and F_1 score for these sentences. If a relevant sentence appears in the top-3, then it factors into recall, precision, and F_1 score. Note that due to sentence limiting (SL) we impose a limit on the F_1 score attainable. Since we always return the top 3 sentences, for the 279 citances of the test set we return 837 total sentences. We can calculate the maximum attainable F_1 score. For the Tree kernel approach it is 35.04%. For the TF/IDF aproach it varies between 44.98% and 58.02%.

Mean Average Rank. We compute the average rank by obtaining the rank of all the relevant reference sentences of each citance. These are normalized according to the total number of sentences being considered. The normalized rank is a value within the interval $[0, 1]$. We average these ranks among the citances for a document. Finally we find the mean of these averages for all documents. For example, for a single reference text with two citances, each referring to a single sentence, we would average the normalized rank of these two sentences according to their appropriate citance. We then find the mean among the documents processed. Lower is better.

Method	ROUGE-L
TKern(1:1)+SL	58.78%
TKern(1:4)+SL	57.90%
TKern(1:8)+SL	57.76%
TKern(1:1)+SL+CE	**58.84%**
TKern(1:4)+SL+CE	58.12%
TKern(1:8)+SL+CE	57.87%

Table 2. F_1-score of ROUGE-L metric for Tree kernel approach.

Method	ROUGE-L	Method	ROUGE-L
TFIDF	**50.63%**	TFIDF+CE	48.05%
TFIDF+ST	50.35%	TFIDF+ST+CE	48.37%
TFIDF+SL	49.45%	TFIDF+SL+CE	47.48%
TFIDF+WN	46.61%	TFIDF+WN+CE	45.87%
TFIDF+ST+SL	49.10%	TFIDF+ST+SL+CE	47.47%
TFIDF+ST+WN	37.93%	TFIDF+ST+WN+CE	36.75%
TFIDF+SL+WN	45.85%	TFIDF+SL+WN+CE	45.40%
TFIDF+ST+SL+WN	38.29%	TFIDF+ST+SL+WN+CE	37.25%

Table 3. F_1-score of ROUGE-L metric for TF/IDF approach.

Method	P@3	R@3	F_1	Mean Avg.Rank
TKern(1:1)+SL	5.63%	12.10%	7.69%	0.262 (215/390)
TKern(1:4)+SL	4.85%	10.41%	6.61%	0.263 (215/390)
TKern(1:8)+SL	5.13%	11.02%	7.00%	0.245 (215/390)
TKern(1:1)+SL+CE	5.71%	12.25%	7.79%	0.261 (215/390)
TKern(1:4)+SL+CE	4.70%	10.10%	6.42%	0.262 (215/390)
TKern(1:8)+SL+CE	5.11%	10.97%	6.97%	0.252 (215/390)
TFIDF	7.88%	16.92%	10.75%	0.106 (298/390)
TFIDF+ST	8.60%	18.46%	11.73%	0.124 (329/390)
TFIDF+SL	8.72%	18.71%	11.89%	0.093 (276/390)
TFIDF+WN	4.77%	10.25%	6.51%	0.154 (331/390)
TFIDF+ST+SL	**8.96%**	**19.23%**	**12.22%**	0.112 (309/390)
TFIDF+ST+WN	5.61%	12.05%	7.66%	0.164 (336/390)
TFIDF+SL+WN	6.09%	13.07%	8.31%	0.137 (307/390)
TFIDF+ST+SL+WN	5.61%	12.05%	7.66%	0.144 (286/390)
TFIDF+CE	7.04%	15.12%	9.61%	0.159 (330/390)
TFIDF+ST+CE	7.04%	15.12%	9.61%	0.167 (349/390)
TFIDF+SL+CE	7.88%	16.92%	10.75%	0.137 (303/390)
TFIDF+WN+CE	4.65%	10.00%	6.35%	0.216 (354/390)
TFIDF+ST+SL+CE	7.76%	16.66%	10.59%	0.149 (325/390)
TFIDF+ST+WN+CE	4.89%	10.51%	6.68%	0.220 (**356**/390)
TFIDF+SL+WN+CE	5.25%	11.28%	7.17%	0.183 (326/390)
TFIDF+ST+SL+WN+CE	4.77%	10.25%	6.51%	0.189 (304/390)

Table 4. Recall, precision, and F_1 score at Top-3. Average rank of relevant sentences. In parentheses we have the number of relevant sentences with non-zero similarity.

Method	ROUGE-L
TKern(1:1)+SL	27.56%
TKern(1:4)+SL	26.05%
TKern(1:8)+SL	**27.68%**
TKern(1:1)+SL+CE	27.09%
TKern(1:4)+SL+CE	26.52%
TKern(1:8)+SL+CE	25.64%

Table 5. F_1-score of ROUGE-L metric for Task 2.

6 Discussion

6.1 TF/IDF Results

The TF/IDF approach is unexpectedly our best performing approach. Although some modifications hurt performance, upon closer inspection we see how they might improve our results in other ways. It is, however, surprising that the minimally modified TFIDF+SL+ST approach has the highest F_1 score. Furthermore, among the TF/IDF configurations, the unmodified TF/IDF approach has the highest ROUGE-L F_1 score. One of the considerations when using cosine similarity is whether or not we get any value at all due to sparsity. As we can see from Table 4, a portion of relevant sentences are indistinguishable since they have zero similarity. WordNet expansion, stemming, and context expansion provide a significant increase in non-zero similarities among relevant sentences. However, recall and precision decrease in turn. Sentence limits have the opposite effect: they increase recall and precision but also decrease the number of relevant sentences we can distinguish.

6.2 Tree Kernel Results

For the Tree kernel approach, we expected the inclusion of more negative items to increase our recall and precision. However, the configuration with $1\!:\!1$ ratio had the best performance. It is significant that this dominance occurs not only with regards to the ROUGE-L scores in Table 2 but also in terms of top-3 metrics in Table 4.

Average rank did improve with a greater number of negative items. We conjecture these negative items in training had the effect of lowering the rank of negative items in testing, thus improving the rank of positive items. This overall improvement came at the expense of recall and precision.

The performance variation between runs was calculated for each system as the maximum F_1 at top-3 score attained minus the minimum F_1 at top-3 score attained in these 5 runs. The system with the largest variation was Tkern(1:1)+SL, with 2.7% difference, whereas the system with the least variation was TKern(1:1)+SL+CE, with 0.9% difference.

The output had a curious behavior. For each reference text, the sentences chosen by the system were the same regardless of citance. Even after context expansion, the behavior persisted. Unfortunately, this did not translate into high ROUGE-L scores for Task 2. It is possible that tuning the method so this behavior does not occur would increase its performance.

Finally, it is interesting to note that the ROUGE-L scores for the Tree kernel approach were consistently higher than the scores for the TF/IDF approach.

7 Future Work

We investigated the effects of various modifications on the performance of a simple TF/IDF approach. In addition, an SVM with a tree kernel was also employed with mixed results. Although the traditional F_1

score points to one of the simplest approaches as the most effective, it is important to remember the two approaches tackled the same problem from different perspectives. Whether these two perspectives – similarity between citance and reference sentence and the similarity between (c, r) pairs – complement each other is worth exploring.

The characterization of citances also warrants further research. The peculiarities apparent (and those less apparent) could lead to improvements in these tasks.

References

1. Steven Bird, Edward Loper, and Ewan Klein. *Natural Language Processing with Python*. O'Reilly Media, Inc., 2009.
2. Corinna Cortes and Vladimir Vapnik. Support-vector networks. *Machine Learning*, 20(3):273–297, 1995.
3. Kokil Jaidka, Muthu Kumar Chandrasekaran, Sajal Rustagi, and Min-Yen Kan (2016). Overview of the 2nd Computational Linguistics Scientific Document Summarization Shared Task (CL-SciSumm 2016). In *Proceedings of the Joint Workshop on Bibliometric-enhanced Information Retrieval and Natural Language Processing for Digital Libraries (BIRNDL 2016)*, Newark, New Jersey, USA.
4. Thorsten Joachims. *Advances in Kernel Methods*, chapter Making Large-scale Support Vector Machine Learning Practical, pages 169–184. MIT Press, Cambridge, MA, USA, 1999.
5. Chin-Yew Lin and Franz Josef Och. Automatic evaluation of machine translation quality using longest common subsequence and skip-bigram statistics. In *Proceedings of the 42nd Annual Meeting on Association for Computational Linguistics*, page 605. Association for Computational Linguistics, 2004.
6. Christopher D. Manning, Mihai Surdeanu, John Bauer, Jenny Finkel, Steven J. Bethard, and David McClosky. The Stanford CoreNLP natural language processing toolkit. In *Association for Computational Linguistics (ACL) System Demonstrations*, pages 55–60, 2014.
7. George A. Miller. Wordnet: A lexical database for english. *Commun. ACM*, 38(11):39–41, 1995.
8. Alessandro Moschitti. Making tree kernels practical for natural language learning. In *EACL 2006, 11st Conference of the European Chapter of the Association for Computational Linguistics, Proceedings of the Conference, April 3-7, 2006, Trento, Italy*, pages 113–120. The Association for Computer Linguistics, 2006.
9. Alessandro Moschitti, Silvia Quarteroni, Roberto Basili, and Suresh Manandhar. Exploiting syntactic and shallow semantic kernels for question answer classification. In *ACL 2007, Proceedings of the 45th Annual Meeting of the Association for Computational Linguistics, June 23-30, 2007, Prague, Czech Republic*. The Association for Computational Linguistics, 2007.

Identifying Referenced Text in Scientific Publications by Summarisation and Classification Techniques

Stefan Klampfl, Andi Rexha, and Roman Kern

Know-Center GmbH
Inffeldgasse 13, 8010 Graz, Austria
{sklampfl,arexha,rkern}@know-center.at

Abstract. This report describes our contribution to the 2nd Computational Linguistics Scientific Document Summarization Shared Task (CL-SciSumm 2016), which asked to identify the relevant text span in a reference paper that corresponds to a citation in another document that cites this paper. We developed three different approaches based on summarisation and classification techniques. First, we applied a modified version of an unsupervised summarisation technique, TextSentenceRank, to the reference document, which incorporates the similarity of sentences to the citation on a textual level. Second, we employed classification to select from candidates previously extracted through the original TextSentenceRank algorithm. Third, we used unsupervised summarisation of the relevant sub-part of the document that was previously selected in a supervised manner.

Keywords: text summarisation, key sentence extraction, citation analysis

1   Introduction

Extractive summarisation of a textual document is the process of finding a representative subset of the document text that captures as much information about the original document as possible. A promising idea in the realm of scientific publications is to consider the set of sentences that cite a paper as a summary created by the research community. Here we describe our contribution to the 2nd Computational Linguistics Scientific Document Summarization Shared Task (CL-SciSumm 2016)[1] [6], which aims at exploring and encouraging novel techniques for scientific paper summarisation along this direction. This task takes place at the Joint Workshop on Bibliometric-enhanced Information Retrieval and Natural Language Processing for Digital Libraries (BIRNDL 2016)[2] [2] at the Joint Conference on Digital Libraries (JCDL '16) and is a follow-up on the

---

[1] http://wing.comp.nus.edu.sg/cl-scisumm2016/

[2] http://wing.comp.nus.edu.sg/birndl-jcdl2016/

2   Stefan Klampfl, Andi Rexha, and Roman Kern

CL Pilot Task that has been conducted as a part of the BiomedSumm Track at the Text Analysis Conference 2014 (TAC 2014)[3] [5].

The dataset provided for this year's task consists of a set of reference papers (RP), each of which is accompanied by a set of citing papers (CP). The goal is to identify the text span in the RP which corresponds to the citations in CP (Task 1A) as well as the discourse facet of the RP this text span belongs to (Task 1B). Human annotators have created the ground truth in the form of pairs of citation text and cited text on the granularity level of sentences.

For Task 1A, we implemented a number of approaches that employ both unsupervised and supervised techniques that differ in the way how information from the citing sentence in the CP is incorporated into the process. In total, we submitted three runs, corresponding to our three approaches for Task 1A: (i) *modified-tsr*, (ii) *tsr-sent-class*, and (iii) *sect-class-tsr*.

First, in a completely unsupervised setting, we applied a modified variant of our TextSentenceRank algorithm to the RP (*modified-tsr*). TextSentenceRank [9] is a graph based ranking algorithm, a refinement of the well-known TextRank algorithm, which is applied to text in order to extract key words and/or key sentences. For the task at hand, we investigated a specific weighting that takes into account the information provided by the CP.

As a second approach for Task 1A, we employed a supervised classification setting following an unsupervised preprocessing (*tsr-sent-class*). Through the original version of TextSentenceRank we pre-selected candidate sentences from the RP, independently from the CP, that are potential text spans for being cited. For a given citation in the CP, we then selected the corresponding candidate through supervised classification.

In our third option, we took a dual approach (*sect-class-tsr*). We first used supervised learning to identify the relevant sub-part (section) of the RP that corresponds to the citing sentence in the CP. Once the relevant section has been found, we used the original version of TextSentenceRank on this sub-part, independent from the CP, to identify referenced text spans.

For Task 1B, we used a similar classifier as for identification of the section. We used features derived from the citing sentence as well es from the extracted text span in the reference document to determine the discourse facet. This is applied in all three approaches to Task 1A.

In principle, TextSentenceRank is able to extract multiple candidate text spans scattered across the document, but since the task description required the extraction of consecutive referenced text, we decided to output a single sentence as the extracted reference span in all of our approaches.

This report is structured as follows. In sections 2 and 3 we explain our approaches for both Task 1A and Task 1B in detail. In section 4 we individually evaluate the classifiers that we used in our approaches and present our results for the overall task. In the end, in section 5 we conclude, discuss our findings, and give an outlook to potential future work.

---

[3] http://www.nist.gov/tac/2014/BiomedSumm/

2 Task 1A: Identification of the Referenced Text Spans

In this subsection we detail our three approaches for Task 1A, the identification of referenced text spans. We also introduce TextSentenceRank as a base method which is used in all three runs.

2.1 TextSentenceRank as a Method for Extracting Candidate Text Spans

This approach is inspired by graph based ranking algorithms, such as Google's PageRank [1], where vertices in a graph are ranked based on their importance given by the connectedness within the graph: the more likely a vertex is visited by random walk, the higher is its score in the ranking. The *TextSentenceRank* algorithm [9] is an application of such a graph based ranking method to natural language text, returning a list of relevant key terms and/or key sentences ordered by descending scores. It builds a graph where vertices correspond to sentences or tokens and connects them with edges weighted according to their similarity (textual similarity between sentences or textual distance between words). Furthermore, each sentence vertex is connected to the vertices corresponding to the tokens it contains[4].

The score $s(v_i)$ of a vertex v_i is given by

$$s(v_i) = (1 - d) + d \sum_{j \in I(v_i)} \frac{w_{ij}}{\sum_{v_k \in O(v_j)} w_{jk}} s(v_j), \tag{1}$$

where d is a parameter accounting for latent transitions between non-adjacent vertices (set to 0.85 as in [1, 7]), w_{ij} is the edge weight between v_i and v_j, and $I(v)$ and $O(v)$ are the predecessors and successors of v, respectively. The scores can be obtained algorithmically by an iterative procedure, or alternatively by solving an eigenvalue problem on the weighted adjacency matrix.

The TextSentenceRank algorithm is an extension to the original TextRank algorithm [7], which could either compute key terms or key sentences. It has been shown in [9] that by computing both key terms and key sentences at the same time, the performance of key term extraction can be improved.

When used for key sentence extraction, TextSentenceRank extracts the "most relevant" sentences in terms of how they are connected to other sentences in the document via co-occurring words. Here we pursue our intuition that such relevant sentences are also more likely to be cited and use TextSentenceRank as a base algorithm for extracting candidates for referenced text.

2.2 Run 1: A Modified Version of TextSentenceRank

Run 1 (*modified-tsr*) follows a completely unsupervised setting, where we applied a modified variant of our TextSentenceRank algorithm to the RP. The idea here

---

[4] Here, we restrict the set of relevant tokens to adjectives, nouns, and proper nouns. This information is obtained through part-of-speech tagging.

4   Stefan Klampfl, Andi Rexha, and Roman Kern

was to use a specific weighting of the underlying graph that takes into account the information provided by the CP, in particular, the citing sentence. More precisely, the weight of an edge adjacent to a node corresponding to sentence S is modified by

$$w_{\text{new}} = w_{\text{old}} * [1 + \text{sim}(S, C)], \tag{2}$$

where $\text{sim}(S, C)$ is a similarity measure between sentence S of the RP and citing sentence C of the CP.

In our approach we used the Jaccard similarity [4] on the sets of tokens contained in the respective sentences. Different similarity measures are possible, e.g., a measure capturing the semantic similarity of words in the sentences, but were not applied in the scope of this task. From the resulting list of the most relevant sentences in the RP, we selected the one with the largest similarity to the citing sentence in the CP.

2.3   Run 2: TextSentenceRank and Sentence Classification

In Run 2 (*tsr-sent-class*) we employed a supervised classification setting following an unsupervised preprocessing. First, we pre-selected candidate sentences from the RP through the original version of TextSentenceRank. This selection is thus independent from the CP and consists of potential text spans for being cited. We then selected the corresponding candidate through supervised classification that takes into account the information from the citing sentence in the CP.

We used a Random Forest classifier [3], an ensemble method based on decision trees, with the following features:

- **Section features:** title and number of the section enclosing the candidate sentence,
- **Sentence position features:** relative positions of the candidate sentence within the RP and within the enclosing section,
- **Discriminative term features:** information about tokens shared between the candidate sentence in the RP and the citing sentence in the CP.

This classifier is a binary classifier that decides for each candidate sentence in the RP whether it is an actual referenced text span, based on information from the citing sentence. For training the classifier we used the information provided by the training set. Because of the unbalanced nature of positive and negative training examples we used TextSentenceRank also to pre-select the sentences for training.

2.4   Run 3: Section classification and TextSentenceRank

In Run 3 (*sect-class-tsr*), we took a dual approach to Run 2. Instead of applying an unsupervised preprocessing followed by a supervised classification, we first used supervised learning to identify the relevant sub-part of the RP that corresponds to the citing sentence in the CP. This sub-part can in principle be of any granularity, but as sections are annotated in the provided dataset, we chose the granularity of sections. Once the relevant section has been found, we used the original version of TextSentenceRank on this sub-part, independent from the CP, to identify referenced text spans.

Again, we used a Random Forest classifier, now with these features:

- **Section features:** title and number of the section enclosing the candidate sentence,
- **Tf-Idf features:** information about the frequency of tokens from the citing sentence within the section, normalized by the inverse frequency across all the sections of the RP. This feature is motivated by the standard Tf-Idf measure [8], applied to the sections of the RP. It emphasizes sections that exclusively share tokens with the citing sentence.

This classifier is a binary classifier that decides for each candidate section in the RP whether it is a section containing a referenced text span, based on information from the citing sentence. The cited text span is then selected through the original version of TextSentenceRank, applied to the sub-document spanning the selected section, independently from the CP.

3   Task 1B: Identification of the Discourse Facet

The discourse facet takes the following values in the training set: *Implication, Method, Aim, Results,* and *Hypothesis.* We used a Random Forest classifier with section features, sentence position features, and discriminative term features to distinguish between these classes. That is, we took into account information from both the citing sentence as well es from the extracted text span in the reference document to determine the discourse facet. The same model, which was previously trained on the training set, was applied in all three runs.

4   Evaluation

In our evaluation, we first determine the isolated performance of individual components that we used in our approaches. Then we present our results for the overall task. We performed these evaluations on both the provided development set and the training set, as the results on the test corpus have not yet been made available.

4.1   Performance of individual classifiers

In our contribution we used three different classifiers, which we evaluate separately in this section. For the full system runs we trained the classifier on the training set, and submitted the results produced by applying the trained classifiers on the test set. Here, we evaluate the classifiers on both the development set and on the training set using 10-fold cross validation.

In Run 2 of Task 1A (*tsr-sent-class*) we used a binary classifier that decides for each candidate sentence whether it serves as a referenced text span for a given

6   Stefan Klampfl, Andi Rexha, and Roman Kern

Table 1. Performance of the sentence classifier on the development set and on the training set, evaluated by 10-fold cross validation. Precision, recall, and F1 values are given with respect to the positive class. Accuracy is the amount of correctly classified instances. The numbers in brackets denote the total number of instances for the respective scenario.

	Precision	Recall	F1	Accuracy
development set (2496)	0.803	0.221	0.346	0.926
training set (1338)	0.843	0.291	0.432	0.916

Table 2. Performance of the section classifier on the development set and on the training set, evaluated by 10-fold cross validation. Precision, recall, and F1 values are given with respect to the positive class. Accuracy is the amount of correctly classified instances. The numbers in brackets denote the total number of instances for the respective scenario.

	Precision	Recall	F1	Accuracy
development set (1093)	0.284	0.275	0.279	0.821
training set (561)	0.500	0.487	0.494	0.861

citing sentence. Table 1 shows the cross-validation performance of this sentence classifier on both the development set and on the training set. Since it is a binary classifier, we report here the precision, recall, and F1 values with respect to the positive class, i.e., whether the sentence is classified as a referenced text span. A reasonable precision is achieved, which means that there are relatively few false positives, however, at the expense of low recall, indicating that many true positives are missed. Even though we pre-filtered the negative instances with TextSentenceRank, the classification problem is still quite unbalanced: There are about 10 times as many negative as positive examples. This unbalance might induce a certain bias in the classifier; still, the accuracy, i.e., the fraction of correctly classified instances, across both classes is above 90% for both datasets.

In Run 3 of Task 1A (*sect-class-tsr*) we employed a binary classifier that decides for each section whether it contains a referenced text span corresponding to a given citing sentence. Table 2 shows the cross-validation performance of this section classifier on both the development set and on the training set. Again, we report here the precision, recall, and F1 values with respect to the positive class, i.e., whether the section is classified as containing a referenced text span. It can be seen that the performance is quite lower than for the sentence classifier, but the accuracy is still above 80%. Here the unbalance between positive and negative classes is given by the number of sections in the reference paper (on average about 5 to 6 in the training set).

In Task 1B, for the identification of the discourse facet, we used a multi-label classifier to categorise a referenced text span into one of the following classes:

Table 3. Performance of the discourse facet classifier on the development set and on the training set, evaluated by 10-fold cross validation. Precision, recall, and F1 values are given as micro-averages over the five classes. Accuracy is the amount of correctly classified instances. The numbers in brackets denote the total number of instances for the respective scenario.

	Precision	Recall	F1	Accuracy
development set (584)	0.602	0.707	0.628	0.707
training set (332)	0.698	0.696	0.666	0.696

Table 4. Confusion matrix of the discourse facet classifier on the training set, as well as precision and recall for each label, evaluated by 10-fold cross validation. Column headers denote classifier output, row headers denote true labels created by the human annotators.

	Implication	*Method*	*Aim*	*Results*	*Hypothesis*
Implication	13	14	5	0	0
Method	5	168	7	0	0
Aim	6	53	33	0	0
Results	0	7	0	17	0
Hypothesis	0	4	0	0	0
Precision	0.542	0.683	0.733	1.000	0.000
Recall	0.406	0.933	0.359	0.708	0.000

Implication, *Method*, *Aim*, *Results*, and *Hypothesis*. Table 3 shows the cross-validation performance of this discourse facet classifier on both the development set and on the training set. Precision and recall are given as micro-averages over all labels and lie between 60% and 70%. Classification accuracy is around 70% for both datasets. Table 4 shows the confusion matrix obtained by the classifier on the training set. *Method* is by far the most occurring label in the datasets, and the classifier might have a certain bias of generating this label, but also the quality of retrieving the label *Results* is reasonable. *Hypothesis* is the rarest label and the one with the lowest accuracy.

4.2 Overall task performance

We evaluated all of our three approaches for Task 1A on both the development set and the training set. We compared the extracted reference spans in our system output with the corresponding reference spans provided by the human annotators in terms of overlap and distance. In Table 5 we show for each of the three runs and for each topic in the development set the number of citances for which the extracted reference span lies within 10 sentences of the true reference span and for which both reference spans actually overlap. Table 6 shows the same information for the training set.

8   Stefan Klampfl, Andi Rexha, and Roman Kern

Table 5. Overall task performance on the development set. For each of the three runs and for each topic in the development set we show the number of citances for which the extracted reference span lies within 10 sentences of the true reference span. Numbers in brackets, if available, count citances where the extracted reference span overlaps the true reference span created by human annotators.

Topic	Run 1	Run 2	Run 3
W04-0213	2	1	1
P06-2124	10	0	1
E09-2008	6 (1)	0	3 (1)
W08-2222	2	4	2
C10-1045	5	0	0
W95-0104	2	0	1
C08-1098	1	1	0
D10-1083	1 (1)	0	0
N04-1038	3	0	2
C02-1025	6	3	1
Overall	38 (2)	9	11 (1)

It can be seen that only in few cases a referenced text span is extracted that overlaps the text segment identified by the human annotator. If we allow a certain neighborhood around the true spans, considerably more matches are found. Interestingly, Run 1, the modified TextSentenceRank, achieves the best results, followed by Run 3, the variant with section classification, which slightly outperforms Run 2, the version with sentence classification.

The finding that the modified TextSentenceRank works best suggests that considering the document as a whole might be beneficial for extracting relevant key sentences. The low performance of the classification approaches might be due to a lack of representative features that are relevant for the task at hand. In Run 2 it is possible that the set of sentences provided by the original TextSentenceRank algorithm is already too limited before the sentence classifier can select suitable text spans. The dual approach of Run 3, first selecting a sub-part and then applying TextSentenceRank, works slightly better.

These results also demonstrate the difficulty of this task. It is worth mentioning that all our approaches are solely based on statistics of words and sentences in both the reference document and the citing sentence as well as in their comparison. Currently, we do not incorporate any semantic information, but in principle our approaches can be easily adapted through additional features for classification and a different weighting strategy for TextSentenceRank.

5   Discussion

In this report we have described our contribution to the 2nd Computational Linguistics Scientific Document Summarization Shared Task (CL-SciSumm 2016),

Table 6. Overall task performance on the training set. For each of the three runs and for each topic in the training set we show the number of citances for which the extracted reference span lies within 10 sentences of the true reference span. Numbers in brackets, if available, count citances where the extracted reference span overlaps the true reference span created by human annotators.

Topic	Run 1	Run 2	Run 3
X96-1048	1 (1)	1	0
J00-3003	0	0	0
N01-1011	3 (2)	0	1
E03-1020	5 (1)	2	1 (1)
H89-2014	2	0	0
J98-2005	4	0	1 (1)
P98-1081	4 (1)	0	0
C90-2039	5 (1)	0	0
C94-2154	3 (2)	2	1
H05-1115	0	0	2
Overall	27 (8)	5	6 (2)

which asked participants to identify the relevant text span in a reference paper that corresponds to a citation in another document that cites this paper. We developed three different approaches based on summarisation and classification techniques. They employ both unsupervised and supervised techniques that differ in the way how information from the citing sentence is incorporated into the process. First, we applied a modified version of an unsupervised summarisation technique, TextSentenceRank, to the reference document, which incorporates the similarity of sentences to the citation on a textual level. Second, we employed classification to select from candidates previously extracted through the original TextSentenceRank algorithm. Third, we used unsupervised summarisation of the relevant sub-part of the document that was previously selected in a supervised manner.

We evaluated both the individual classifiers used in our approaches as well as the performance in the overall task. We believe that the performance of our systems could be improved by incorporating different similarity measures, e.g., measures capturing the semantic similarity of citing and cited sentences, not only in the modified weighting of TextSentenceRank, but also into the set of features used for classification. Furthermore, the relative strength of the influence of the citing sentence can be optimised. For example, in the modified TextSentenceRank algorithm there could be a trade-off parameter in equation 2 that weights the relative influences of w_{old} and $\mathrm{sim}(S, C)$. Finally, the inclusion of multiple, non-consecutive sentences in the output would likely include candidate text spans of better quality.

Another aspect that likely influences our system is the fact that the text of the given documents was extracted with OCR methods. These methods sometimes yield noisy and erroneous words, and many of our methods rely on the statistics of terms within and across documents. In our experience, in some cases TextSentenceRank seems to prefer sentences containing such noisy or invalid tokens.

As a contribution to the CL-SciSumm 2016 task our work aimed at facilitating the summarisation of scientific publications. In addition, we hope that our contribution will also provide further insight into the scientific writing habits of researchers, both in terms of how they structure their papers and how they reference the work of others.

Acknowledgements

The Know-Center is funded within the Austrian COMET Program – Competence Centers for Excellent Technologies – under the auspices of the Austrian Federal Ministry of Transport, Innovation and Technology, the Austrian Federal Ministry of Economy, Family and Youth and by the State of Styria. COMET is managed by the Austrian Research Promotion Agency FFG.

References

1. Brin, S., Page, L.: The anatomy of a large-scale hypertextual web search engine. Computer Networks 56(18), 3825–3833 (2012)
2. Cabanac, G., Chandrasekaran, M.K., Frommholz, I., Jaidka, K., Kan, M.Y., Mayr, P., Wolfram, D.: Joint Workshop on Bibliometric-enhanced Information Retrieval and Natural Language Processing for Digital Libraries (BIRNDL 2016)
3. Ho, T.K.: Random decision forests. In: Proceedings of the 3rd International Conference on Document Analysis and Recognition. pp. 278–282. Montreal, QC (1995)
4. Jaccard, P.: The distribution of the flora in the alpine zone. New Phytologist 11, 37–50 (1912)
5. Jaidka, K., Chandrasekaran, M.K., Elizalde, B.F., Jha, R., Jones, C., Kan, M.Y., Khanna, A., Molla-Aliod, D., Radev, D.R., Ronzano, F., et al.: The computational linguistics summarization pilot task. In: Proceedings of TAC. Gaithersburg, USA (2014)
6. Jaidka, K., Chandrasekaran, M.K., Rustagi, S., Kan, M.Y.: Overview of the 2nd Computational Linguistics Scientific Document Summarization Shared Task (CL-SciSumm 2016). In: Proceedings of the Joint Workshop on Bibliometric-enhanced Information Retrieval and Natural Language Processing for Digital Libraries (BIRNDL 2016). Newark, New Jersey, USA (2016), to appear
7. Mihalcea, R., Tarau, P.: Textrank: Bringing order into texts. In: Conference on Empirical Methods in Natural Language Processing. Barcelona, Spain (2004)
8. Salton, G., McGill, M.J.: Introduction to Modern Information Retrieval. McGraw-Hill, Inc., New York, NY, USA (1986)
9. Seifert, C., Ulbrich, E., Kern, R., Granitzer, M.: Text representation for efficient document annotation. Journal of Universal Computer Science 19(3), 383–405 (2013)

PolyU at CL-SciSumm 2016

Ziqiang Cao[1], Wenjie Li[1], and Dapeng Wu[2]

[1] Department of Computing, The Hong Kong Polytechnic University, Hong Kong,
`{cszqcao, cswjli}@comp.polyu.edu.hk`
[2] Department of Electrical & Computer Engineering, University of Florida, USA,
`wu@ece.ufl.edu`

Abstract. This document demonstrates our participant system PolyU on CL-SciSumm 2016. There are three tasks in CL-SciSumm 2016. In Task 1A, we apply SVM Rank to identify the spans of text in the reference paper reflecting the citance. In Task 1B, we use the decision tree to classify the facet that a citance belongs to. Finally, in Task 2, we develop an enhanced Manifold Ranking summarization model.

1 Introduction

The CL-SciSumm Shared Task [2] at BIRNDL 2016 (`http://wing.comp.nus.edu.sg/birndl-jcdl2016/`) focuses on automatic paper summarization in the Computational Linguistics (CL) domain. A document set of CL-SciSumm consists of a Reference Paper (RP) and Citing Papers (CPs) that all contain citations to the RP. In each CP, the text spans (i.e., citances) have been identified that pertain to a particular citation to the RP. Given this dataset, a participant system is expected to handle three tasks. **Task 1A**: For each citance, identify the spans of text (cited text spans) in the RP that most accurately reflect the citance. These are of the granularity of a sentence fragment, a full sentence, or several consecutive sentences (no more than 5). **Task 1B**: For each cited text span, identify what facet of the paper it belongs to, from a predefined set of facets. **Task 2** (optional): Finally, generate a structured summary of the RP from the cited text spans of the RP. The length of the summary should not exceed 250 words.

Our system PolyU implements all the three tasks. For Task 1A, we treat it as a ranking problem modeled by SVM Rank [3]. For Task 1B, since the facet distribution is extremely imbalanced, the Decision Tree Classifier is introduced to naturally conduct the task as hierarchical classification. For the final summarization task, we treat these CPs as queries and each section as a document. The idea behind is that CPs often refer to important sentences and sentences in important sections should also be important. Then we improve the widely-used query-focused summarization model Manifold Ranking [4] to generate summaries. Manifold Ranking can naturally make full use of both the relationships among sentences in different sections and the relationships between the CPs and the sentences. We introduce an extra parameter in Manifold Ranking to adjust the weights for CPs. The overall performance of PolyU is presented in Table 1.

Task	Performance
1A	Accuracy: 11.8, Recall: 8.7, F1-score: 10.0
1B	Micro-accuracy: 61.9, Macro-accuracy: 21.4
2	ROUGE-1: 49.5, ROUGE-2: 15.4

Table 1. Overall performance (%) of PolyU.

2 Task 1A

2.1 Problem Transformation

In this task, we need to identify the spans of text (cited text spans) in the RP that most accurately reflect the citation. Since a citation text span can be linked to many sentences in the reference paper, we firstly analyze the corresponding sentence number distribution, as shown in Fig. 1. As can be seen, a large proportion of reference spans contain more than one sentences. Therefore, the most direct approach for this task is to train a ranking model and select a series of top ranked sentences. However, this idea has two disadvantages. On the one hand, the threshold is hard to set due to the serious variation of ranking scores on different document sets. On the other hand, a reference span tends to contain adjacent sentences, which cannot be reflected by the top ranked items. The adjacency property of reference spans is presented in Fig. 2. In this figure, we count the number of reference sentences which fail to be covered by adjacent sentence chunks. We observe that most multi-sentence reference spans are just a pair of adjacent sentences. Meanwhile, when the chunk size ≥ 4, about 90% reference sentences can be covered by sentence chunks, and the uncovered ratio keeps stable.

Therefore, we simplify Task 1A into a ranking problem which just needs to select the first item. Specifically, like n-grams, we put adjacent sentences into n-sentence chunks. According to the data property, we set $n \in [1, \cdots, 4]$. Then, a reference paper is represented by these n-sentence chunks. The actual ranking score of an n-sentence chunk is the ratio of reference sentences it contains. We extract a series of features from (CP, n-sentence chunk) pairs. Finally, we train a ranking model and choose the top ranked n-sentence chunk as the reference span.

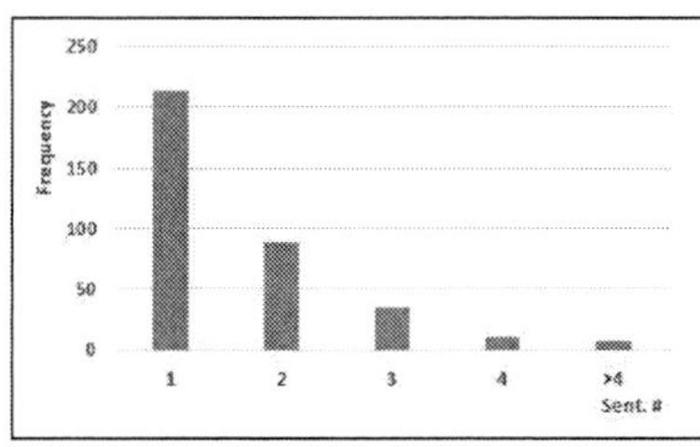

Fig. 1. Reference sentence number distribution on the training set.

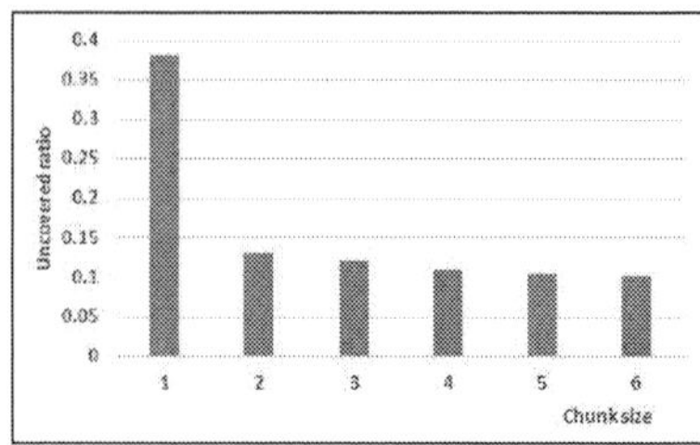

Fig. 2. Numbers of uncovered sentences with the change of chunk sizes.

2.2 Model Description

Since most sentence chunks have no reference sentences, the regression model trained on this dataset tends to predict the zero score. Therefore, we adopt SVM Rank [3] to handle this ranking task. SVM Rank is a popular supervised pair-wise model. It converts a ranking task into a binary classification task, which avoids the problem of data imbalance. The major feature we use is the tf-idf cosine similarity between a citance and a sentence chunk in the reference paper. We also extract some citance-independent features such as the position of the sentence chunk. The motivation behind is that most citances are related to the facet of method. As a result, the reference sentences may have some common characteristics. The whole ranking features are presented in Table 2.

We analyze the model weight for each feature. The feature SIMILARITY holds the highest weight, which accords with common sense. In addition, three position features, i.e., SENT_POSITION, SECTION_POSITION and INNER_POSITION all have relatively large negative weights. It seems sentences in front are more likely to be cited.

Name	Description
SIMILARITY	The tf-idf cosine similarity between a citance and a sentence chunk.
SENT_POSITION	The sentence position, divided by the number of sentences.
SECTION_POSITION	The position of the corresponding section of the sentence chunk, divided by the number of sections
INNER_POSITION	The sentence position in the section, divided by the number of sentences in the section.
NUMBER	Indicate whether there are numbers in the sentence chunk.
NER	Indicate whether there are named entities in the sentence chunk.

Table 2. Ranking features.

3 Task 1B

3.1 Problem Transformation

In this task, we need to identify what facet of the paper a citance belongs to, from a predefined set of facets. In total, there are 5 facets, i.e., Method, Aim, Results, Implication and Hypothesis. Notably, a citance can labeled by multiple facets. Thus, it is a multi-label classification task. However, from the training data, we find more than 90% of citanccs only bclong to onc facet. Therefore, we simply treat this task as the common multi-class classification problem by reserving the first facet for citances with more than one facets.

Afterwards, we analyze the facet distribution on the training set. The result is shown in Fig 3. From this figure, we find the facet distribution is extremely imbalanced. The Method facet takes about 60% proportion of the total data, and there are only 9 instances in the Hypothesis facet. Trained on the extremely biased dataset, many classifiers such as SVM and Naive Bayes tend to classify all the data into the Method facet. Although this practice achieves high overall accuracy, it is not a proper solution. Therefore, we introduce two metrics to measure the performance, i.e., the macro-averaged accuracy (A_M) as well as the micro-averaged accuracy (A_m). Their formulas are as follows:

$$A_m = \frac{\sum_{c \in C} r_c}{\sum_{c \in C} N_c} \tag{1}$$

$$A_M = \frac{1}{|C|} \sum_{c \in C} \frac{r_c}{N_c} \tag{2}$$

where C stands for the class set, r_c is the right number in the Class c, and N_c is the actual number. Just predicting the Method facet, $A_m = 0.59$ and $A_M = 0.2$.

We focus on the increase of the macro-averaged accuracy. To this end, we use the decision tree to conduct hierarchical classification. The most important advantage of the decision tree is that it has the ability to remember patterns of all the facets in the training data. In comparison, SVM and Naive Bayes are likely to merely reserve the patterns of the dominant class.

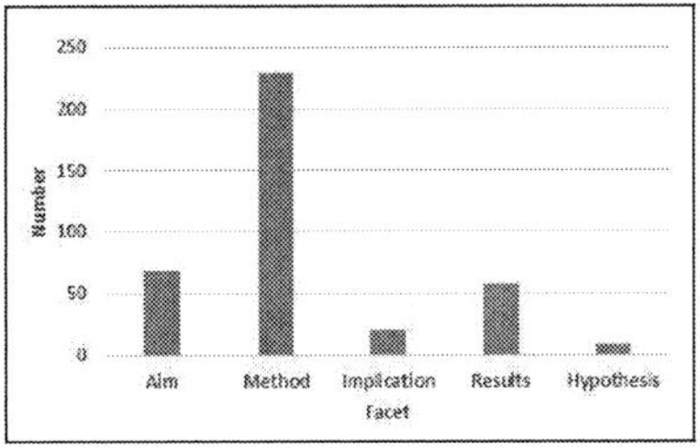

Fig. 3. The distribution of facets.

3.2 Model Description

Since the instances for the Implication and Hypothesis facets are very limited, we only train the classification model on the data of the other three facets. We use the tf-idf vector of the citance as features. Notably, the vocabulary size is too large with respect to the training data. We thereby introduce the χ^2-test to reserve the most significant 125 features. The learned decision tree is displayed in Fig. 4. We can find in the leaf nodes, there is often just one support case. It seems this decision tree is still quite over-fitted. We also consider to add more features such as the position of the citance in the citation paper. However, the result shows these features only make the decision tree more biased to the Method facet.

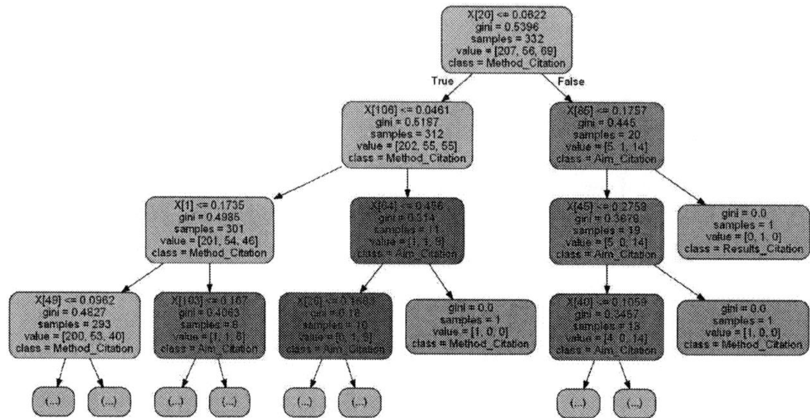

Fig. 4. Decision tree classifier. Each feature $X[.]$ stands for a tf-idf score.

4   Task 2

This task requires to generate a summary for the reference paper with the help of ci-tances. Our summarization system makes full use of the structure information in the corpus. We regard a section of a paper as a document, since sentences in important sections should also be important. Meanwhile, we treat the citance as a query. The idea behind is that sentences relevant to citance may be the focus of the paper. After the above two steps, Task 2 is converted into the query-focused multi-document summarization problem. Then we develop an enhanced version of Manifold Ranking [4] to generate summaries.

4.1   Enhanced Manifold Ranking

Manifold Ranking [4] can naturally make full use of both the relationships among all the sentences in the documents and the relationships between the given query and the sentences. In Manifold Ranking, a document set is represented by a sentence list $D = \{x_1^q, \cdots x_k^q, x_{k+1}^D, \cdots x_n^D\}$, where x_i^q represents a query sentence and x_i^D stands for a document sentence. Then, we compute the similarity matrix $W \in R^{n \times n}$, where W_{ij} is the tf-idf cosine similarity of two sentences. Different from LexRank [1], Manifold Ranking distinguishes the relationships between inter-document and intra-document sentences. Specifically, W can be decomposed as:

$$W = W_{\text{inter}} + W_{\text{intra}} \tag{3}$$

Then, it gives different weights for these two matrices.

$$\widetilde{W} = \lambda_1 W_{\text{inter}} + \lambda_2 W_{\text{intra}} \tag{4}$$

We fix $\lambda_1 = 1$, and change λ_2 in the experiments. If $\lambda_2 < 1$, inter-document links are more important than the intra-document links in the algorithm and vice versa. Note that if $\lambda_2 = 1$, Equation 4 reduces to Equation 3.

Subsequently, We normalize the similarity matrix $\widetilde{W}$ into a probability matrix S.

$$S = G^{-1/2}\widetilde{W}G^{-1/2} \tag{5}$$

where G is the diagonal matrix with (i, i)-element equal to the sum of the i_{th} row of $\widetilde{W}$. With the probability matrix S, we can now apply the random walk algorithm to compute the saliency scores f of the sentences:

$$f(t + 1) = \alpha S f(t) + (1 - \alpha)y, \tag{6}$$

where α is a weight parameter, and y is the prior score distribution. In Manifold Ranking, y is set as follows:

$$y_i = \begin{cases} 1/k, & i \leq k \\ 0, & otherwise \end{cases} \tag{7}$$

It means the query-relevant sentences are most important in the prior.

We improve Manifold Ranking by modifying the prior score distribution to inspect the importance of citances. We introduce an extra parameter $\gamma \in [0, 1]$ to control the weight of citances, and Eq. 7 becomes:

$$y_i = \begin{cases} \gamma/k, & i \leq k \\ \frac{1-\gamma}{n-k}, & otherwise \end{cases} \tag{8}$$

Maniflod Ranking is a special case where $\gamma = 1$.

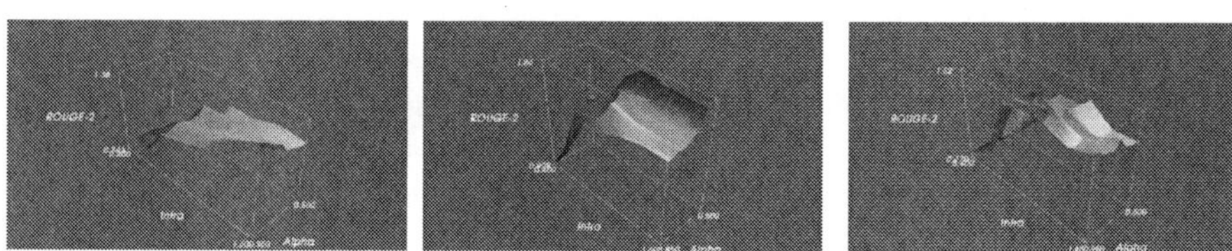

Fig. 5. Grid search with $\gamma = 0, 0.5, 1$ respectively.

4.2 Parameter Selection

There are three parameters in our summarization model, i.e., the intra-document weight λ_2, the random walk weight α and the citance weight γ. We set $\gamma = 0, 0.5, 1$ respectively and conduct grid search on the development set to check the change of performance. The result is shown in Fig 5. As can be seen, $\gamma = 0.5$ shows the highest performance potential. Meanwhile, when $\lambda_2 > 0.6$, the performance is not sensitive to its change. For α, a common value of 0.85 often works well. To sum up, we choose $\gamma = 0.5$, $\lambda_2 = 0.8$ and $\alpha = 0.85$ for the test dataset.

5   Conclusion

This document demonstrates our participant system PolyU on CL-SciSumm 2016. There are three tasks in CL-SciSumm 2016. In Task 1A, we apply SVM Rank to identify the spans of text in the reference paper reflecting the citance. In Task 1B, we use the decision tree to classify the facet that a citance belongs to. Finally, in Task 2, we develop an enhanced Manifold Ranking summarization model.

References

1. Erkan, G., Radev, D.R.: Lexrank: Graph-based lexical centrality as salience in text summarization. Journal of Artificial Intelligence Research pp. 457–479 (2004)
2. Jaidka, K., Chandrasekaran, M.K., Rustagi, S., Kan, M.Y.: Overview of the 2nd computational linguistics scientific document summarization shared task (cl-scisumm 2016). In: Proceedings of the Joint Workshop on Bibliometric-enhanced Information Retrieval and Natural Language Processing for Digital Libraries (BIRNDL 2016) (2016)
3. Joachims, T.: Training linear svms in linear time. In: Proceedings of the 12th ACM SIGKDD international conference on Knowledge discovery and data mining. pp. 217–226. ACM (2006)
4. Wan, X., Yang, J., Xiao, J.: Manifold-ranking based topic-focused multi-document summarization. In: IJCAI. vol. 7, pp. 2903–2908 (2007)

Recognizing reference spans and classifying their discourse facets

Kun Lu

School of Library and Information Studies
University of Oklahoma
kunlu@ou.edu

Jin Mao

School of Information
University of Arizona
danveno@163.com

Gang Li

School of Information Management
Wuhan University
imiswhu@aliyun.com

Jian Xu

School of Information Management
Wuhan University
xukeywhu@163.com

Abstract: In this shared task, we applied "Learning to Rank" algorithm with multiple features, including lexical features, topic features, knowledge-based features and sentence importance, to Task 1A by regarding reference span finding as an information retrieval problem. Task 1B, discourse facet identifying, is treated as a text classification problem by considering features of both citation contexts and cited spans.

Keywords: Learning to rank; Topic model; Facet classification

1 Introduction

The 2nd CL-SciSumm Shared task follows the TAC 2014 Biomedical Summarization Track on scientific paper summarization. An overview of the shared task, including specific details on the dataset, the competitive results and subsequent analyses for each task can be found in the shared task overview paper[1]. In this report, we provide a detailed description of the methods we used for the Task 1A and Task 1B. Our methods are introduced in Section 2 followed by results in Section 3. Some conclusions are presented in the last section.

2 Methods

2.1 Task 1A

We considered Task 1A as an information retrieval problem. A citance (citation context) is regarded as a query and sentences from reference paper (cited spans) are treated as candidate documents. Then, the problem becomes how to rank the sentences of the reference paper (i.e., candidate cited spans in this report) for a given citance. The most relevant sentences of the reference paper to a citation context are selected as the golden sentences of the citation context. We apply "learning to rank" algorithms to address this problem and exploit multiple features. The explored features are as follows:

- **Lexical Features.** Bag of words is a widely used text representation method. By representing citation contexts and candidate cited spans with the bag of words model, the lexical similarities between citation contexts and candidate cited spans can be obtained. We chose four candidate lexical similarity features including Cosine similarity, Jaccard similarity, Dice similarity and LCS (longest common subsequence). When computing cosine similarity, TFIDF term weighing was applied. In the formula below, TF is the number of times a term occurring in a given sentence, while the IDF value of a term is computed from all the 437 papers in the training set (93 papers), development set (155 papers), and test set(229 papers). Thus, $Document\_All\_Number$ is 437, which is the same for all terms. And $Document\_number(Term)$ is the number of the different papers that a term occurs.

$$\text{TFIDF(Term)} = \text{TF(Term)} * \ln \frac{Document_{All_{Number}}}{Document_{number(Term)}} \qquad (1)$$

- **Topic Features.** Bag of words model is insufficient in handling polysemy and synonym problems. Taking topics into account can relieve this problem. Topic modeling method[2] was used to identify latent topics from 10,921 articles of the ACL Anthology Reference Corpus. The topic distributions of both citation contexts and candidate cited spans were predicted through the LDA models. Cosine similarity was then used to measure their topic similarities.
- **Knowledge Based Features.** WordNet[3] was used to compute the concept similarity between citation contexts and candidate cited spans. Lin similarity[4] that measures the similarity of two words was applied. The similarity of two sentences can be compute by cumulating the similarities between their words. We used different combinations of nouns and verbs to calculate similarities: WordNet (N)-only using nouns, WordNet (V)-only using verbs, WordNet (N,V)-using both nouns and verbs, and WordNet (N,Vsep) which is obtained by (WordNet(N)+ WordNet(V))/2.
- **Sentence Importance.** The importance of candidate cited spans in the reference paper is considered as a factor influencing whether they are being cited or not. TextRank[5], which is a widely used unsupervised method to extract the keyword or rank the sentences of a given document, was applied to measure the importance of a sentence in the reference paper. The assumption is that the more important a sentence is in the reference paper, the more likely the sentence belongs to the cited span.

Each pair of a citation context and a candidate sentence from the cited article is an instance. Positive instances (i.e., the candidate cited sentence is one of the gold standard cited sentences) were assigned higher scores than negative instances. The above features were calculated and fed into "learning to rank" methods. For topic similarity, the number of topics varied from 20 to 200 with a step of 20. The features showing high performance were selected as the final set of features. Then, five learning to rank algorithms from RankLib[6], including RankBoost[7], RankNet[8], AdaRank[9], and Coordinate Ascent[10], were compared.

2.2   Task 1B

Task 1B is considered as a text classification problem. The five discourse facets of a sentence in a reference paper are Aim, Method, Result, Implication, and Hypothesis. The features adopted by the classifiers are as follows.

- The text of the reference sentence
- The title of the section that the reference sentence belongs to
- The section type of the section that the reference sentence belongs to
- The text of the citation context
- The title of the section that the citation context belongs to
- The section type of the section that the citation context belongs to

Three classifiers from Weka[11] including Naïve Bayes, Decision Tree and Supporting Vector Machine were applied and compared for Task 1B. The algorithm behind these classifiers are Naive Bayesian classification, C4.5, and Sequential Minimal Optimization. Default parameter settings were used to train the classifiers implemented in Weka.

2.3   Evaluation

2.3.1 Task 1A metrics.

Two groups of precision (P), recall (R) and F_1 measures were used to evaluate the performance in Task 1A. The first group counted the number of sentences returned by our methods that match the gold standard sentences annotated by the task organizers.

$$R = \frac{|G \cap S|}{|G|} \quad P = \frac{|G \cap S|}{|S|} \quad F_1 = \frac{2 * R * P}{(R + P)} \qquad (2)$$

where G indicates the gold standard sentences, S denotes the sentences returned by our methods.
The second group of measures are ROUGE_1[12] (Recall-Oriented Understudy for Gisting Evaluation) measures used as the official comparison measures.

2.3.2 Task 1B metrics.

Precision (P), recall (R) and F_1 measures were calculated to evaluate the performance for each facet. For one facet, a is denoted as the number of correct predictions for this facet, b is the number of wrong predictions for this facet, and c is the number of cited sentences from gold standard sentences for this facet that are not predicted as belonging to this facet.

$$R = \frac{a}{a+c} \quad P = \frac{a}{a+b} \quad F1 = \frac{2*R*P}{(R+P)} \qquad (3)$$

Then, Macro average and Micro average were used to evaluate the system on all facets. Macro average measures are computed as:

$$R_{\text{macro}} = \frac{\Sigma_f^N R_f}{N} \quad P_{macro} = \frac{\Sigma_f^N P_f}{N} \quad F1_{macro} = \frac{2*R_{macro}*P_{macro}}{R_{macro}+P_{macro}} \qquad (4)$$

Micro average measures are computed as:

$$R_{micro} = \frac{\Sigma_f^N a_f}{\Sigma_f^N a_f + \Sigma_f^N c_f} \quad P_{micro} = \frac{\Sigma_f^N a_f}{\Sigma_f^N a_f + \Sigma_f^N b_{f_i}} \quad F1_{micro} = \frac{2*R_{micro}*P_{micro}}{R_{micro}+P_{micro}} \qquad (5)$$

where f is the facet index, N is the number of facets (i.e., 5). A good classifier should have both high Macro and Micro average measures.

3   Results

In this section, the results where the training set is used for training and the development set is used for testing.

3.1   Task 1A results

According to Fig.1, Jaccard similarity and Dice similarity achieved better F_1 measures than Cosine similarity and LCS. Topic similarity feature (indicated as Topic_number in Fig.1) showed slight different performance among different numbers of topics. WordNet based similarity achieved best results when combining the results of standalone nouns similarities and verb similarities. TextRank showed similar results to topic similarity and WordNet based similarity, however, this feature did not improve the performance of learning to rank. Finally, Jaccard similarity, Topic similarity with 200 topics, WordNet (N,Vsep), and TextRank were kept. In the development set, Rank-Net and AdaRank achieved best performance with Overlap/ ROUGE_1 F_1 of 0.057/0.211 (Table 1).

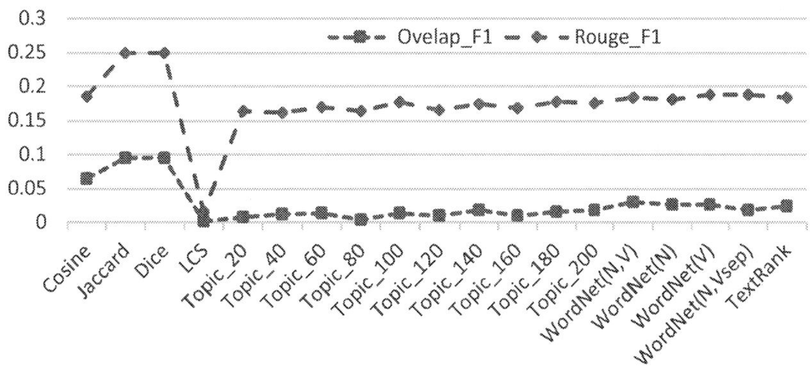

Figure 1. The F_1 values for each ranking feature on development set

Table 1. The performance of different learning to rank algorithms on development set

Learning to rank Algorithms	Overlap			ROUGE_1		
	P	R	F_1	P	R	F_1
RankBoost	0.008	0.015	0.010	0.129	0.171	0.147
RankNet	**0.043**	**0.085**	**0.057**	**0.194**	**0.232**	**0.211**
AdaRank	**0.043**	**0.085**	**0.057**	**0.194**	**0.232**	**0.211**
Coordinate Ascent	0.012	0.024	0.016	0.153	0.190	0.169

3.2 Task 1B results

Table 2 lists results for Task 1B. SVM showed best micro average performance (F_1=0.657), while Naïve Bayes achieved the best macro average performance (F_1=0.269). It's observed that Naïve Bayes showed balanced performance over the five facets. Both Decision Tree and SVM had poor prediction on Aim, Implication and Hypothesis facets.

Table 2. The performance of the three classifiers on development set

Facets	# of Cited Spans	Naïve Bayes			Decision Tree			SVM		
		P	R	F_1	P	R	F_1	P	R	F_1
Aim	29	0.197	0.482	**0.280**	0.023	0.034	0.028	0	0	0
Method	142	0.683	0.578	0.626	0.625	0.634	0.629	0.671	0.950	**0.787**
Result	33	0.407	0.333	0.367	0.615	0.484	**0.542**	0.75	0.272	0.400
Implication	8	0.006	0.015	**0.008**	0	0	0	0	0	0
Hypothesis	7	0	0	0	0	0	0	0	0	0

Micro Avg	-	0.488	0.488	0.488	0.488	0.488	0.488	0.657	0.657	**0.657**
Macro Avg	-	0.259	0.282	**0.269**	0.253	0.230	0.240	0.284	0.244	0.262

4   Final run methods and conclusions

For the last run, we used both training set and development set to train instances. We chose Jaccard, Topic_200, WordNet (N+V) and TextRank as the final ranking features and applied AdaRank learning to rank algorithm on Task 1A. For Task 1B, Naïve Bayes was used as the classifier.

Recognizing the cited spans and determining their discourse facets are very challenging for the summarization of scientific papers. There are some issues to be addressed during our study on the tasks. First, either cited span discovery or discourse facet classification is an unbalanced problem—negative examples are more prevalent than positive examples. That would be our future work. Second, Task 1A involves much more than a similarity problem. This is because the underlying citation intentions are complex. More features that reflect the citation intentions should be explored.

References

[1]Kokil Jaidka, Muthu Kumar Chandrasekaran, Sajal Rustagi, and Min-Yen Kan (2016). Overview of the 2nd Computational Linguistics Scientific Document Summarization Shared Task (CL-SciSumm 2016), To appear in the Proceedings of the Joint Workshop on Bibliometric-enhanced Information Retrieval and Natural Language Processing for Digital Libraries (BIRNDL 2016), Newark, New Jersey, USA.

[2]Blei, D. M. (2012). Probabilistic topic models. Communications of the ACM, 55(4), 77-84.

[3]George A. Miller (1995). WordNet: A Lexical Database for English. Communications of the ACM Vol. 38, No. 11: 39-41.

[4]Lin, D. (1998, July). An information-theoretic definition of similarity. In ICML (Vol. 98, pp. 296-304).

[5]Mihalcea, R., & Tarau, P. (2004, July). TextRank: Bringing order into texts. Association for Computational Linguistics.

[6]Dang, V. The Lemur Project-Wiki-RankLib. Lemur Project,[Online]. Available: https://sourceforge.net/p/lemur/wiki/RankLib.

[7]Freund, Y., Iyer, R., Schapire, R. E., & Singer, Y. (2003). An efficient boosting algorithm for combining preferences. The Journal of machine learning research, 4, 933-969.

[8]Burges, C., Shaked, T., Renshaw, E., Lazier, A., Deeds, M., Hamilton, N., & Hullender, G. (2005, August). Learning to rank using gradient descent. In Proceedings of the 22nd international conference on Machine learning (pp. 89-96). ACM.

[9]Xu, J., & Li, H. (2007, July). Adarank: a boosting algorithm for information retrieval. In Proceedings of the 30th annual international ACM SIGIR conference on Research and development in information retrieval (pp. 391-398). ACM.

[10]Metzler, D., & Croft, W. B. (2007). Linear feature-based models for information retrieval. Information Retrieval, 10(3), 257-274.

145

[11]Hall, M., Frank, E., Holmes, G., Pfahringer, B., Reutemann, P., & Witten, I. H. (2009). The WEKA data mining software: an update. ACM SIGKDD explorations newsletter, 11(1), 10-18.
[12]Lin, C. Y. (2004, July). Rouge: A package for automatic evaluation of summaries. In Text summarization branches out: Proceedings of the ACL-04 workshop (Vol. 8).

RALI System Description for CL-SciSumm 2016 Shared Task

Bruno Malenfant[1] and Guy Lapalme[2]

[1] Université de Montréal, CP 6128, Succ Centre-Ville, Montréal, Québec, Canada, H3C 3J3,
`malenfab@iro.umontreal.ca`
[2] Université de Montréal, CP 6128, Succ Centre-Ville, Montréal, Québec, Canada, H3C 3J3,
`lapalme@iro.umontreal.ca`

Abstract. We present our approach to the CL-SciSumm 2016 shared task. We propose a technique to determine the discourse role of a sentence. We differentiate between words linked to the topic of the paper and the ones that link to the facet of the scientific discourse. Using that information, histograms are built over the training data to infer a facet for each sentence of the paper (*result*, *method*, *aim*, *implication* and *hypothesis*). This helps us identify the sentences best representing a citation of the same facet. We use this information to build a structured summary of the paper as an HTML page.

1   Introduction

One's task in research is to read scientific papers to be able to compare them, to identify new problems, to position a work within the current literature and to elaborate new research propositions [8].

This implies reading many papers before finding the ones we are looking for. With the growing amount of publications, this task is getting harder. It is becoming important to have a fast way of determining the utility of a paper for our needs. A first solution is to use web sites such as *CiteSeer, arXiv, Google Scholar* and *Microsoft Academic Search* that provide cross reference citations to papers. Another approach is automatic summarization of a group of scientific papers dealing with the subject.

This year's CL-SciSumm competition for summarization of computational linguistics papers proposes a community approach to summarization; it is based on the assumption that citances, the set of citation sentences to a reference paper, can be used as a measure of its impact. This task implies identifying the text a citance refers to in the reference paper and a facet (*aim, result, method, implication* and *hypothesis*) for the referred text.

We are building a system that given a topic, generates a survey of the topic from a set of papers. That system uses citations as the primary source of information for building an annotated summary. Our system must be able to identify the purpose/polarity/facet of a citation. to direct the reader towards the more relevant information. The summary is built by selecting sentences from the cited paper and the citations. This process uses a similarity function between sentences. The resulting summaries are presented in HTML format with their annotations and links to the original paper. The only task that is not performed by our system is finding the text referred to by the citation. We intend to use the information already found by our system (facet of citations and sentences) to complete that task.

We had already some experience in dealing with scientific papers and their references, having participated to Task2 of the Semantic Publishing Challenge of ESWC-2014 (Extended Semantic Web Conference) on the extraction and characterization of citations. A short review of previous work follows in Sect. 2. We will summarize the task in Sect. 3 and the techniques for extracting information in Sect. 4. Finally, Sect. 5 will show our results.

2   Previous Work

There has been a growing attention towards the information carried by citations and their surrounding sentences (citances). These contain information useful for rhetorical classification [18], technical surveys [14] and emphasize the impact of papers [12]. Qazvinian [16] and Elkiss [6] showed that citations provide information not present in the abstract.

Since the first works of Luhn [11] and Edmundson [5] many researchers have developed methods for finding the most relevant sentences of papers to produce abstracts and summaries. Many metrics have been introduced to measure the relevance of parts of text, either using special purpose formulas [21] or using learned weights [10]. The hypothesis for CL-SciSumm task is that important sentences can be pointed out by other papers : a citation indicates a paper considered important by the author of the citing paper.

Another domain for study over scientific papers is the classification of their sentences. Teufel [19] identified the rhetorical status of sentences using Bayes classifier.

To find citations inside a paper, we need to analyse the references section. Dominique Besagni et al. [1] developed a method using pattern recognition to extract fields from the references while Brett Powley and Robert Dale [15] looked citations and references simultaneously using informations from one task to help complete the second task.

3   Task Description

For this year competition we were given 30 topics, 10 for training, 10 for tuning and 10 for testing [9]. Each topic is composed of a Reference Paper (RP) and some Citing Papers (CPs). The citing papers contain citations pointing to the RP. An annotation file is given for each topic. That file contains information about each citation, the citation marker and the citance.

There are two mandatory tasks (Task 1A and Task 1B) and an optional task (Task 2)[3].

Task 1A : Find the part of the RP that is indicated with each citance. This will be called the *referenced text*.

---

[3] http://wing.comp.nus.edu.sg/cl-scisumm2016/

Task 1B : Once the referenced text is identified, we need to attribute a facet to it. A facet is one of these : *result, method, aim, implication* and *hypothesis*.

Task 2 : Building a summary for the RP using the referenced text identified in Task 1A.

Both the training and the developing set of topics contain expected results for these tasks. The next section will describe how our system performs on the test set.

4   Our Approach

For the first task, we have to find the referenced text and its facet. We hypothesized that the referenced text should be sentences sharing the same facet as the citance. We use that fact to reduce the set of sentences to choose from for the reference. This is why we execute Task 1B on all the sentences of the RP and all the citances prior to Task 1A. We now present how we determine the facet of a citance, then the facet for sentences in the RP and finally the referenced text.

4.1   Task 1B : Facet Identification

Our goal is to be able to use our system for papers from different domains, without having to train them again. Toward that objective, our system only uses words that are not domain specific. Patrick Drouin [3, 4] compiled such a list of words in his *Transdisciplinary scientific lexicon* (TSL). This lexicon comprises 1627 words such as *acceptance, gather, newly, severe...* We will denote the set of words from the lexicon using $w \in L$.

We trained two systems, one to attribute a facet to sentences in the RP and one to attribute a facet to citances.

We determine the word distribution for each facet using an histogram. We only use words appearing in the TSL. This computation yielded a sum of each words present in all referenced text for each facet. The facet with the highest score is chosen for that sentence.

For training our system, we extract the reference sentences from each annotation with their assigned facet. Each sentence is tokenized using the NLTK library in Python. Only words from the TSL are kept. Our dataset consists of pairs of list of words with a facet : $D = [(\mathrm{ws}_i, f_i)]$.

We build a profile (h_f) for each facet using a histogram. For each word in the lexicon, we compute the number of times it appears in sentence paired with the a specific facet.

$$h_f(w, D) = \sum [\mathrm{cnt}(w, \mathrm{ws}_i) \mid (\mathrm{ws}_i, f) \in D]$$
$$\mathrm{cnt}(w, \mathrm{ws}_i) = \sum [1 \mid w \in \mathrm{ws}_i]$$

When a word appears more then once in a sentence, all its occurrences are counted.

Once the histogram is built, we use it to find the facet of new sentence. First, we extract the words that are part of the lexicon from the sentence, yielding the list of words

p. Then a score s_f for each facet is computed by adding the profile of each word for that facet. The facet that scored the highest value is assigned to the new sentence.

$$s_f(p, D) = \sum_{w \in p} h_f(w, D)$$

Looking closely at the results for the profile, we saw that some words have a negative effect on finding the facet. To find a better sublist of words to use within the TSL, we used a genetic algorithm that uses a population of lists of words.

A genetic algorithm starts with an initial population (set of possible solutions) and tries to find better solutions by applying small changes to existing solutions. In our case, a solution is a subset of words L_i of L. The initial population is built using random subsets.

To build the next generation, we use three different techniques :

1. Adding a random word to an existing solution : $L_i' = L_i + \{w\}$ where $w \in (L - L_i)$.
2. Removing a random word from an existing solution : $L_i' = L_i - \{w\}$ where $w \in L_i$.
3. Combining two subsets of existing solutions : $L_i' = L_j \cup L_k$.

Once enough solutions are built for the new population, each solution is tested using cross-validation with the histogram. The list that performed best in the task is kept for the next generation. We use the same technique over the dataset consisting of the citance texts and their facets.

4.2　Task 1A : Finding the Sentences Referred to by Citances

Having determined the facet of sentences in both the RP and citances, we are now ready to assign referenced text to citances from the CPs. Our hypothesis is that a citance should have the same facet as the text it refers to. We extract Q_f the subset of sentences from the RP that have the same facet f as a citance c_i. To choose the sentence of RP referred to by the citance, we look for the sentence from Q_f that is the most similar with the citance c_i.

$$\text{sim}_{mcs}(P_1, P_2) = \frac{1}{2}\left(\text{hs}(P_1, P_2) + \text{hs}(P_2, P_1)\right) \tag{1}$$

$$\text{hs}(P_i, P_j) = \frac{\sum_{w \in P_i} \text{ms}(w, P_j) \times \text{idf}_w}{\sum_{w \in P_i} \text{idf}_w} \tag{2}$$

$$\text{ms}(w, P_j) = \max_{v \in P_j} \text{sim}_{wup}(w, v) \tag{3}$$

We use the similarity function sim_{mcs} defined by Mihalcea, Corley and Strapparava [13]. This similarity function between sentences P_1 and P_2 (Equation 1) averages two values, the similarity from P_1 to P_2, and the similarity from P_2 to P_1. The similarity from one sentence P_i to the other P_j is computed by first pairing each word from the first sentence $w \in P_i$ with a word in the second one $v \in P_j$. A word is paired with the one that is the most similar to it (Equation 3). For each pair (w, v), the value of the similarity is weighted by the Inverse Document Frequency of the first word idf_w (Equation 2). The average of these weighted similarity values is computed to yield the similarity between P_i and P_j. We use only words that are Noun, Verb, Adjective and Adverb for this comparison. The `POS_tagger` of **NLTK** was used to assert the tag of each word. Since we believe that the domain of the paper is important to compute that similarity, we use all words, not only the ones that are part of the TSL.

Mihalcea et al. [13] reported that within the set of possible metrics to compare words, the one proposed by Zhibiao Wu et Martha Palmer [20] yielded good result (denoted sim_{wup}). This metric is also available with the **NLTK** package. To use that metric, we transform each word into their synonym group synset using **WordNet**. The IDF was computed for each synset. The computation was done over the set of all the documents contained in the ACL Anthology Network[4].

4.3 Task 2 : Summarization

Multiple source summarization adds three problems [17] :

1. Redundancy : a paper will often be cited for the same reason over and over, resulting in many citances having the same subject.
2. Identifying important differences between sources : our goal will be to find those citances/references that bring new information and important information to the summary.
3. Coherence : since sentences come from many sources, we want to ensure that the summary forms an unified whole.

For Task 2, we choose to use the *Maximal Marginal Relevance* (MMR) proposed by Jaime G. Carbonell et Jade Goldstein [2]. Their technique is presented in Equation 4, in which R is the list of possible sentences and V is the summary. They propose to use the title of the research paper as the starting query Q.

$$\arg\max_{s_i \in R \backslash V} \left[\lambda \ \text{sim}_{mcs}(s_i, Q) - (1 - \lambda) \max_{s_j \in V} \text{sim}_{mcs}(s_i, s_j) \right] \qquad (4)$$

At each iteration, their algorithm adds a sentence s_i to V. Sentences are choosen so that they bring new information to the summary (Points 1 and 2) and it must have a certain amount of similarity with the query (Point 2). λ must be adjusted to balance between adding a sentence very similar to the query and a sentence very different from the ones already in the summary V. We use the same metric (sim_{mcs}) as for task 1A to compare sentences.

We divided the summarization process in two steps : adding sentences from the citance ($R = \text{CT}$) and adding sentences from the paper ($R = \text{RP}$). In the first step, the algorithm chooses sentences from the set of citances until it reaches 150 words. For that part, we use $\lambda = 0.3$ to give priority to similarity with the query, trying to remove meaningless citances. Since citances have been identified as bringing new information

---

[4] `http://clair.eecs.umich.edu/aan/index.php`

not present in the original paper, we believe it is important to keep them in the summary. Then, the summary is completed (to 250 words) using sentences choosen from the RP. Here, we use $\lambda = 0.7$. Since sentences are choosen in the RP, most of them are about the same subject, we want to give priority to sentences that are more different.

The summary is built in an XML format. Each sentence is identified with its position (the `id` of the paper it was extracted from, the `sid` and `ssid` attributes inside the XML source files). The citances contain the `id` of the referred paper. This information will enable to point a reader towards the corresponding paper.

To help analyse the summaries, our software builds an HTML page containing the extracted information (see Fig. 1).

5   Evaluation

5.1   Task 1

We present our results for facet attribution to citance and reference text. The set of data we receive is divided in two : the training set contains 197 sentences distributed over the citances and 247 sentences over the reference text; the development set contains 273 sentences distributed over the citances and 330 sentences over the reference text. We first train our system using the training data (**T**) and then we retrained it using both set training and developing set together (**TD**). In each case, we test the result over both sets. We show the result for simple training of the histogram and for the training using the genetic algorithm (**gen_T**) to select the list of words to consider. We also trained our histogram without limiting to the words in the TSL for comparison purpose.

For the genetic algorithm, we let it run over 25 generations. Each generation started with 1 000 lists of words. 9 000 lists are added using the proposed mutations, bringing the number of lists to 10 000.

Table 1. Success rate for attributing facet to citances.

Trained on	Tested on		
	Train	Dev	Train + Dev
T no TSL	47%	61%	59%
T	65%	52%	57%
TD no TSL	56%	61%	59%
TD	61%	57%	58%
gen_T	74%	43%	55%

The result of these experiments are presented in Table 1 and Table 2. We see that, using the training set **T** gives good result on itself but lower result when we apply it on the development set. After training with both set **TD** (Test + Development), the result over the development set raises at the expense of the result for the training set. For citance, the genetic algorithm yields better result over the training set only. It does not help to get better histograms. Considering that fact, we ask ourselves if it is possible to

Table 2. Success rate for attributing facet to references text.

	Tested on		
Trained on	**Train**	**Dev**	**Train + Dev**
T no TSL	60%	60%	60%
T	74%	46%	57%
TD no TSL	60%	61%	61%
TD	70%	59%	64%
gen_T	76%	35%	51%

obtain better results using histograms, or if we have reached the limit of that technique? Limiting our choice of words to the TSL did not give lower results. It is to be tested if the histograms built with the TSL will perform better in another domain than computational linguistics.

Once we had identified the facets, we ran our script for finding the reference text. It was able to reach an F1 score of 0.095 over the training set and 0.052 over the development set (table 3). We reduced the search space for the referred text using the facet of the citance. Since the identification of the facet is not perfect, this reduction might remove a sentence we are looking for. In the future, we have to test our approach with all sentences, instead of the reduced set, to see if this reduction of space causes a problem more than helps the solution.

Table 3. F1 scores for finding the reference text.

	Train	**Dev**
F1	0.095	0.052

5.2   Task 2

Figure 1 shows the HTML interface we have generated for showing the result of our system. It allows for selecting different topics. The top of the page lets us choose between the different topics that were summarised. Each topic will present, on the left side, the text of each CPs and RP. The sentences have been divided and citance identified. The right side contains the different summaries that our software builds (using different values of λ) and the gold standard summary. Each paper links to its pdf version on the ACL Anthology[5].

On the left side of the top part of the figure we see the RP divided in sentences. On the right side, there is a summary built by choosing five sentences from the set of citances using a λ of 0.3. These sentences where selected to be as different as possible by the MMR algorithm. The bottom screen shoot (Fig. 1) presents one of the CP on the left. The citance and citation are colored to be easy to identify. The third sentence from the top was selected by the algorithm for the summaries.

---

[5] http://aclanthology.info/

6   Conclusion

We presented the use of distinguishing between topic and non-topic (TSL) words for determining the facet of sentences in a paper. This technique is useful because it lets our system work on paper in a domain independent way. We obtained good results with a simple histogram. We still have to test our histogram over other domains, to see if they also yield good results. Our experiments with a genetic algorithm to refine the list of used words did not show any improvement.

We presented our interface for browsing the results of our system. That interface presents RP, CPs and summaries with links to the original paper. This interface helps the reader browse through a topic.

References

1. Dominique Besagni, Abdel Belaïd, and Nelly Benet : A Segmentation Method for Bibliographic References by Contextual Tagging of Fields. *ICDAR '03 Proceedings of the Seventh International Conference on Document Analysis and Recognition*, 1:384–388 (2003)
2. Jaime G. Carbonell, and Jade Goldstein : The Use of MMR, Diversity-based Reranking for Reordering Documents and Producing Summaries. *Research and Development in Information Retrieval - SIGIR*, 335–336 (1998)
3. Patrick Drouin : Extracting a Bilingual Transdisciplinary Scientific Lexicon. *Proceedings of eLexicography in the 21st Century : New Challenges, New Applications.* Presses universitaires de Louvain, Louvain-la-Neuve, 7:43–54 (2010)
4. Patrick Drouin : From a Bilingual Transdisciplinary Scientific Lexicon to Bilingual Transdisciplinary Scientific Colloations. *Proceedings of the 14th EURALEX International Congress.* Fryske Akademy, Leeuwarden/Ljouwert, Pays-Bas, 296–305 (2010)
5. Harold P. Edmundson : New Methods in Automatic Extracting. *Journal of the ACM (JACM)*, 16(2):264–285 (1969)
6. Aaron Elkiss, Siwei Shen, Anthony Fader, Günes Erkan, David J. States, and Dragomir R. Radev : Blind Men and Elephants: What Do Citation Summaries Tell Us About a Research Article?. *Journal of the American Society for Information Science and Technology - JASIS*, 59(1):51–62 (2008)
7. C. Lee Giles and Kurt D. Bollacker and Steve Lawrence : CiteSeer: an Automatic Citation Indexing System. *Proceedings of the Third ACM Conference on Digital Libraries*, 89–98 (1998)
8. Kokil Jaidka, Christopher S.G. Khoo, Jin-Cheon Na, and Wee Kim Wee : Deconstructing Human Literature Reviews – A Framework for Multi-Document Summarization. *Proceedings of the 14th European Workshop on Natural Language Generation*, 125–135 (2013)
9. Kokil Jaidka, Muthu Kumar Chandrasekaran, Sajal Rustagi, and Min-Yen Kan : Overview of the 2nd Computational Linguistics Scientific Document Summarization Shared Task (CL-SciSumm 2016). To appear in the *Proceedings of the Joint Workshop on Bibliometric-enhanced Information Retrieval and Natural Language Processing for Digital Libraries (BIRNDL 2016)*, Newark, New Jersey, USA. (2016)
10. Julian Kupiec, Jan O. Pedersen, and Francine Chen : A Trainable Document Summarizer. *Research and Development in Information Retrieval - SIGIR*, 68–73 (1995)
11. Hans P. Luhn : The Automatic Creation of Literature Abstracts. *IBM Journal of Research and Development - IBMRD*, 2(2):159–165 (1958)
12. Qiaozhu Mei, and ChengXiang Zhai : Generating Impact-Based Summaries for Scientific Literature. *Meeting of the Association for Computational Linguistics - ACL*, 816–824 (2008)

13. Rada Mihalcea, Courtney Corley, and Carlo Strapparava : Corpus-based and Knowledge-based Measures of Text Semantic Similarity. *AAAI*, 6:775–780 (2008)
14. Saif Mohammad, Bonnie J. Dorr, Melissa Egan, Ahmed Hassan, Pradeep Muthukrishnan, Vahed Qazvinian, Dragomir R. Radev, and David M. Zajic : Using Citations to Generate Surveys of Scientific Paradigms. *North American Chapter of the Association for Computational Linguistics - NAACL*, 584–592 (2009)
15. Brett Powley, and Robert Dale : Evidence-based Information Extraction for High Accuracy Citation and Author Name Identification. *RIAO '07 Large Scale Semantic Access to Content*, 618–632 (2007)
16. Vahed Qazvinian, Dragomir R. Radev, Saif Mohammad, Bonnie J. Dorr, David M. Zajic, M. Whidby, and T. Moon : Generating Extractive Summaries of Scientific Paradigms. *Journal of Artificial Intelligence Research*, 46:165–201 (2013)
17. Dragomir R. Radev, Eduard Hovy, and Kathleen McKeown : Introduction to the Special Issue on Summarization. *Computational Linguistics - Summarization*, 28(4):399–408 (2002)
18. Advaith Siddharthan, and Simone Teufel : Whose Idea Was This, and Why Does it Matter? Attributing Scientific Work to Citations. *North American Chapter of the Association for Computational Linguistics - NAACL*, 316–323 (2007)
19. Simone Teufel, and Marc Moens : Summarizing Scientific Articles: Experiments with Relevance and Rhetorical Status. *Computational Linguistics - COLI*, 28(4):409–445 (2002)
20. Zhibiao Wu, and Martha Palmer : Verbs Semantics and Lexical Selection. *ACL '94 Proceedings of the 32nd Annual Meeting on Association for Computational Linguistics*, 133–138 (1994)
21. Peter N. Yianilos, and Kirk G. Kanzelberger : The LikeIt Intelligent String Comparison Facility. *NEC Research Institute*. (1997)

Fig. 1. Screen shots of the HTML interface. The top part shows the RP and the corresponding summary. The bottom part shows a CP in which we see sentences from the CP where chosen in the summary.

CIST System for CL-SciSumm 2016 Shared Task

Lei Li, Liyuan Mao, Yazhao Zhang, Junqi Chi, Taiwen Huang, Xiaoyue Cong, Heng Peng

Center for Intelligence Science and Technology (CIST), School of Computer Science and Technology,
Beijing University of Posts and Telecommunications (BUPT), China
leili@bupt.edu.cn, circleyuan@bupt.edu.cn, yazhao@bupt.edu.cn, 709722796@qq.com,
zhidao2010@bupt.edu.cn, cxy0105@bupt.edu.cn, penghengp1@bupt.edu.cn

Abstract. This paper introduces the methods and experiments applied in CIST system participating in the CL-SciSumm 2016 Shared Task at BIRNDL 2016. We have participated in the TAC 2014 Biomedical Summarization Track, so we develop the system based on previous work. This time the domain is Computational Linguistics (CL). The training corpus contains 20 topics from Training-Set-2016 and Development-Set-Apr8 published by CL-SciSumm 2016. As to Task 1A and 1B, we mainly use rule-based methods with various features of lexicons and similarities; meanwhile we also have tried the machine learning method of SVM. As to Task 2, hLDA topic model is adopted for content modeling, which provides us knowledge about sentence clustering (subtopic) and word distributions (abstractiveness) for summarization. We then combine hLDA knowledge with several other classical features using different weights and proportions to evaluate the sentences in the Reference Paper from its cited text spans. Finally we extract the representative sentences to generate a summary within 250 words.

1   Introduction

With the rapid development of Computational Linguistics (CL), the scientific literature of this domain has grown into a rich, complex, and continually expanding resource. Literature surveys and review articles in CL do help readers to gain a gist of the state-of-the-art in research for a topic. However, literature survey writing is labor-intensive and a literature survey is not always available for every topic of interest. What are needed, are resources which can automate the synthesis and updating of text summarization of CL research papers. The CL-SciSumm 2016 (The 2nd Computational Linguistics Scientific Document Summarization Shared Task) has highlighted the challenges and relevance of the scientific summarization problem.

In this paper, we describe our strategies, methods and experiments applied for CL-SciSumm 2016. As to Task 1A, we firstly use different combination methods and strategies based on various feature rules of different lexicons and similarities to identify the spans of text (cited text spans) in the RP (Reference Paper). Then we also have tried the machine learning method of SVM (Support Vector Machine). As to Task 1B, we also use feature rules as a basis. Besides, SVM is used to judge which facet the cited text span belongs to. A voting method is also used to integrate different candidate results. And for Task 2, we firstly adopt hLDA (hierarchical Latent Dirichlet Allocation) topic model for document content modeling. The hLDA tree can provide us good knowledge about latent sentence clustering (subtopic in the document) and word distributions (abstractiveness of words and sentences) for summarization. Then we score the sentences in the RP according to several features including hLDA ones and extract candidate sentences to generate the final summary.

2   Related Work

There are many researches about document summarization [1,2,3,4,5,6,7,8,9,10,11,12,13,14,15,16,17,18,19,20]. LDA has been widely applied [21,22]. Some improvements have been made [23,24,25]. One is to relax its assumption that topic number is known and fixed. [26] provided an elegant solution. [27] extended it to exploit the hierarchical tree structure of topics, hLDA, which is unsupervised method in which topic number could grow with the data set automatically. This could achieve a deeper semantic model similar with human mind and is especially helpful for summarization. [28] provided a multi-document summarization based on supervised hLDA with competitive results.

However, it has the disadvantage of relying on ideal summaries. [29] provided a contrastive theme summarization based on hLDA and SDPPs, which is sensitive to negative correlation.

In recent years, interest about information extraction and retrieval from scientific literature has increased considerably. Some researches [30] have shown that citations may contain information out of the abstracts provided by the authors. However, little work has been done on automatic gist extraction from research papers and their corresponding citation communities.

In order to identify the linkage efficiently between a paper citation and its cited text spans in the RP, we need to catch the deep meaning of natural language sentences. In fact, digging the deep meaning of sentences also has an important sense for information extraction and retrieval. Besides the traditional methods for sentence similarity calculation, recently the open-source tool released by Google -- word2vec [31] has a good performance in word semantic mining. And doc2vec [32] has promoted the information mining to the sentences.

3   Task Description

There are two tasks in the CL-SciSumm 2016. Testing dataset, development dataset and training dataset, each contains 10 topics. Every topic consists of one reference paper (RP), some citing papers (CP) and one annotation file. There are five facets pre-defined, including Aim_Citation, Method_Citation, Results_Citation, Implication_Citation and Hypothesis_Citation. In Task 1, we need to identify the spans of text (cited text spans) in the RP that most accurately reflect the citance (Task 1A), and what facet of the paper that each cited text span belongs to, from the predefined set of five facets (Task 1B). Task 2 demands us to generate a structured summary of the RP from the cited text spans of the RP. The length of the summary should not exceed 250 words. Please refer to [8] for more details.

4   Methods

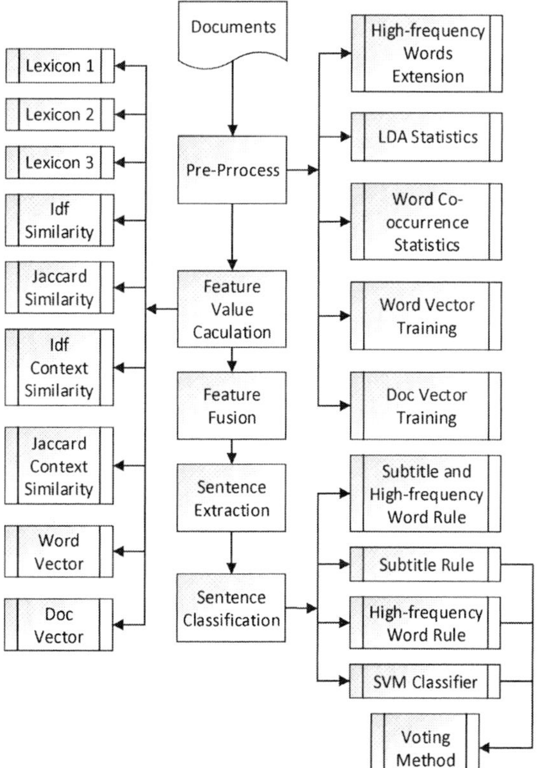

Fig. 1. Framework for Task 1

4.1 Task 1

Our main method is the rule-based method. Fig. 1 shows the framework for Task 1.

Task 1A.

We need to identify the linkage between a paper citation in the CP and its cited text spans in the RP. We think that the linkage is mainly represented by similar meaning between sentences. Hence our work is focused on sentence similarity computing based on various features.

Feature Extraction.

We have two kinds of features, one is from lexicons, and the other is from sentence similarities.

- Three Lexicons:

1. Reference Text high-frequency words (Lexicon 1): We picked up the words with high frequency from reference text in the training corpus artificially, and then expanded them through Wordnet and word vectors.
2. LDA lexicon (Lexicon 2): We used LDA (Latent Dirichlet Allocation) model to train the reference paper and citing papers to get a lexicon of 30 latent topics for files in every topic independently. Table 1 displays the relation of F-measure and the number of latent topics for the training corpus. We can see that the best performance is obtained when the number of latent topics is set to 30.

The number of topics	F-measure
10	0.03924
15	0.0493
20	0.03924
25	0.0503
30	**0.05131**
35	0.04527
40	0.04225
45	0.04024
50	0.03924

Table 1. The performance of LDA

3. Citation Text and Reference Text co-occurrence lexicon (Lexicon 3): We obtained the co-occurrence degree between words by the word frequency statistics of citation text and its reference text from the training corpus.

- Similarity between two sentences:

1. Idf similarity: We add up the idf (inverse document frequency) values of the same words between two sentences.

$$idf_i = log \frac{|D|}{\{j : t_i \in d_j\}} \tag{1}$$

where $|D|$ is the number of sentences, $\{j : t_i \in d_j\}$ is the number of the sentences which contain the word t_i.
2. Jaccard similarity: We use the division between the intersection and the union of the words in two sentences.

$$J = \frac{A \cap B}{A \cup B} \tag{2}$$

where A and B represent two sentences respectively.

- Similarity between two contexts:

The context of a sentence plays an important role in semantic parsing, so we calculate the context similarity.

$$SC_i = \sqrt{d_{i-1} * d_{i+1}} \tag{3}$$

Where SC_i is the context similarity of $sentence_i$, d_{i-1} and d_{i+1} is the imilarity of the sentence before and after it.

We also obtained two kinds of context similarities: Idf context similarity and Jaccard context similarity.

- Two vector similarities:

1. Word vector: We trained every word as a vector with 200 dimensions using Word2Vec. Then a sentence is:

$$W_i = (w_t, w_{t+1}, \cdots, w_{t+k}) \tag{4}$$

where w_t is the word vector and W_i is the vector set to represent a sentence. The vector sets of two sentences W_i and W_j can form a matrix $M_{i,j}$:

$$M_{i,j} = W_i W_j^T = \begin{bmatrix} w_t w_v & \cdots & w_t w_{v+l} \\ \vdots & \ddots & \vdots \\ w_{t+k} w_v & \cdots & w_{t+k} w_{v+l} \end{bmatrix} \tag{5}$$

where (w_t, w_v) is the cosine similarity of w_t and w_v, then the similarity of $sentence_i$ and $sentence_j$ is:

$$Sim_{i,j} = \frac{\sum_{m=i,n=j} max(M_{m,n})}{\sqrt{length_i length_j}} \tag{6}$$

where $length_i$ and $length_j$ represents the length. $max(M_{m,n})$ is the maximum of matrix $M_{m,n}$.

2. Doc vector: We represented every sentence as a vector with 200 dimensions by doc2vec, and used the cosine similarity between vectors to represent the sentence similarity.

We tested the performance of every feature independently for the training corpus as in Table 2. As we can see that Jaccard similarity performs the best.

Feature	F-measure
Lexicon 1	0.01793
Lexicon 2	0.05131
Lexicon 3	0.28437
Idf similarity	0.10589
Jaccard similarity	**0.11167**
Idf context similarity	0.07344
Jaccard context similarity	0.07042
Word vector	0.07771
Doc vector	0.05231

Table 2. The performance of single feature

Methods for linkage.

- SVM Method:

After we have obtained the above features, the first method we thought was to train a classifier based on SVM. But there is a problem of unbalanced data for training. According to our statistics, the number of negative samples is 125 times of the number of positive samples. So we divided the negative samples into 125 groups and train each group with all positive samples. Then using the trained 125 SVM models, we could predict the testing data and get 125 results. Finally, we choose the linkage sentences through a voting system based on these 125 results. When we tried this method on the testing data, unfortunately the performance was not so good as feature rule-based methods. As for the reason, we thought that the number of positive samples was too small, and every training set didn't have enough data to train a good model. To find a better performance, we tried the following methods.

- Voting Method:

Focusing on the F-measure of every feature, we tried different weights and proportions to combine them through experiments, and then got two results through a voting system.

Feature	Weight	Proportion
Idf similarity	1	8
Jaccard similarity	1	12

	1	12
Jaccard context similarity	1	12
Word vector	1	10

Table 3. The parameters of V1.0

Feature	Weight	Proportion
Lexicon 2	0.3	2
Lexicon 3	0.4	2
Idf similarity	1	7
Jaccard similarity	1	3
Idf context similarity	0.5	4
Jaccard context similarity	0.5	8
Word vector	0.5	8
Doc vector	0.3	4

Table 4. The parameters of V2.0

Finally, the text span with the highest-number of votes is chosen as the citation text corresponding sentences in the reference paper. Table 3 and 4 show the two best combinations for the training corpus.

- Jaccard Focused Method:

From Table 2, we found out that Jaccard similarity behaves better than other features obviously. So we chose it as the major feature, and added other features as supplementary in this method. Table 5 shows the parameter setting.

Feature	weight	proportion
Jaccard similarity	10-fold of Jaccard value	7
Idf similarity	0.7	15
Jaccard context similarity	0.7	15
Idf context similarity	0.5	15
Word vector	0.5	25
Lexicon 3	0.2	25

Table 5. The parameters of Jaccard Focused

- Jaccard Cascade Method:

We chose the sentences with top two Jaccard values as the basic answer, then combined other features to find other two sentences with highest values as the improved answer in this method. Table 6 shows the parameter setting.

Feature	weight	proportion
Idf similarity	1.5	16
Jaccard context similarity	1.5	15
Idf context similarity	1	18
Lexicon 3	0.5	15

Table 6. The parameters of Jaccard Cascade

Task 1B.

- Rule-based method

1. Subtitle Rule: First of all, we examine whether the subtitles of reference sentences and cite sentences contains the following facet words: Hypothesis, Implication, Aim, Results and Method. If the subtitle contains any one of these words, it will be directly classified as the corresponding facet. If it contains more than one of these words, it will be classified into all the facets. Else if it contains none of them, we just classify it as the facet of Method.
2. High Frequency Word Rule: According to the High Frequency Word Rule, we firstly count the High Frequency Word of five facets from the Training Set and the Development Set. In order to improve the coverage of sentences, we expanded the High Frequency Word to get some similar words of each facet. We set an appropriate threshold for each facet. If the number of the High Frequency Word of any facet in the sentence is more than the corresponding facet threshold, then we just use the facet whose coverage is the highest as the final class. If some

facets' coverage are same, then we just classify according to the sequence of Hypothesis, Implication, Aim, Results and Method. If all facets have not reached the threshold of each facet, we classify it as the Method.

3. Combine Subtitle and High Frequency Word Rule: We firstly use the Subtitle Rule to classify the testing set. If the results are not in the five facets of Hypothesis, Implication, Aim, Results and Method, then we use the High Frequency Word Rule to get the final facet.

- SVM Classifier

We extract four features of each class. 1) Location of Paragraph: the order number of the paragraph in which the sentence is located. 2) Document Position Ratio: the ratio of sentence Sid to the total sentence number of the corresponding document. 3) Paragraph Position Ratio: the ratio of sentence Ssid to the total sentence number of the corresponding paragraph. 4) Number of Citations or References: the number of Citation Offset or Reference Offset. These features form an 8-dimension vector of a pair of reference sentence and citation sentence. We train SVM to get five classifiers. For the problem of unbalanced training data, we set different weights for different classes. If we cannot get any class of the five facets, then we classify it as Method class.

- Voting Method

We combine the results from Subtitle Rule, High Frequency Word and SVM classifier to generate the final results with most votes.

- Fusion Method

We run the above methods for each run result we obtained in Task 1A and choose a best one as the final result. Then we also tried a fusion method to combine all the run results of the above methods obtained in Task 1A. We counted the number of Method, Results, Aim, Hypothesis and Implication, and set an appropriate threshold for each facet class to get a final result of facet class.

4.2   Task 2

We provide a general overview of our method in Fig. 2.

Pre-processing.
The source documents provided by CL-SciSumm 2016 have some xml-coding errors. Besides, we need specific data format to train our hLDA feature. To obtain relatively a high-quality input dataset, we do pre-processing.

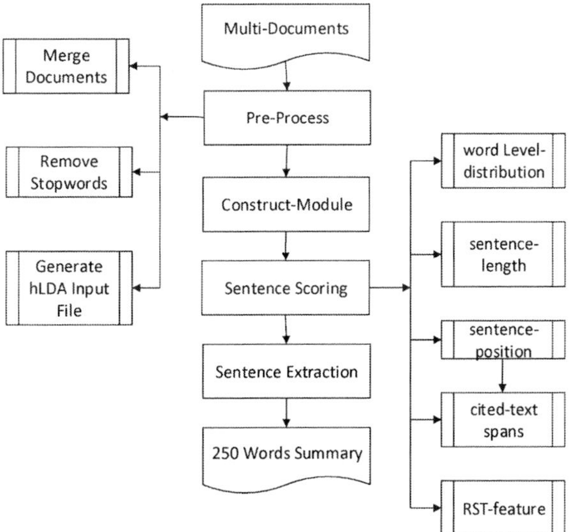

Fig. 2. Overview of our approach to RP summarization

1. Document merging: For each topic, we merge the reference paper and the cited text spans into a big text.
2. Stop words removing: We use the stop-word list to remove stop words. The stop-word list contains punctuation marks and some functional words. At the same time, all capitalized characters are changed to lower case.
3. Input file generation for hLDA: For the selected words, we build a dictionary for each document, which contains words and their corresponding frequency, and the index starts from 1 to word list size. Finally, we generate an input file for hLDA modeling, in which each line represents a sentence presented by word index - frequency pair, such as: [number of words in sentence i] [word-index A : frequency A] [word-index B : frequency B] ...

Feature modeling.

1. hLDA-level distribution feature: To be known as exact description of latent topics over nested Chinese restaurant process, hLDA is one of the non-parametric topic models. Given the input file, unsupervised-hLDA generates tree-like topic structures over documents. Each sentence is assigned to a path starting from the root node to leaf nodes. Sentences sharing the same path are similar with each other and thus constitute a subtopic of the documents. Each node in the tree contains different words, whose distribution is referred to latent-topic. Besides, different level contains different nodes. Each word in a sentence is randomly assigned to the node at different level in the sentence path with some probability, and the probability to different level is the level message we would like to exploit which can represent the abstractiveness of the topic in the document to some extent. Since we have obtained the predefined facet information of cited test spans in Task 1B, we do not use the subtopic knowledge in hLDA here which may not directly match the five facets as defined by CL-SciSumm 2016. [33] investigated the influence of different hyper-parameters in hLDA modeling. Here we just use the result of these research, and set the depth of hierarchal tree to be three. Recently our work has been focused on the research in exploration of hLDA level information. According to recent research, we proposed a new level distribution scores as followed:

$$S_{levels} = \sum_{i=0}^{N}(W_i T_{i-Distribution} + T_{i-NodeFrequency}) \tag{7}$$

where W_i indicates the weight of the node level that word T_i is assigned in, $T_{i-Distribution}$ indicates the score of level distribution of word T_i, $T_{i-NodeFrequency}$ is the frequency of T_i in current node as followed.

$$T_{i-NodeFrequency} = \frac{counts(T_i)}{\sum_{i=0}^{V} counts(T_i)} \tag{8}$$

2. Sentence-length feature: It is a balance between length and sentence meaning. Gaussian Distribution is chosen in order to get a better combination along with the level feature.

$$S_{length} = \frac{1}{\sqrt{2\pi}\sigma} e^{-\frac{(x-\mu)^2}{\sigma^2}} \tag{9}$$

where μ indicates the expectation of word frequency, σ indicates the standard deviation of word frequency.

3. Sentence-position feature: Sentence position is widely used in the summary extraction of news and science paper.

$$S_{position} = 1 - \frac{p_i}{n} \tag{10}$$

where n is the total number of sentences, p_i is the position of i − th sentence. Number i is started from 0.

4. Cited text span: A citation is a summary of other paper authors, and we got all cited text spans of each reference paper from Task 1A. Thus we use it as a weak feature, for the reason that there must be some errors.

$$S_{spans} = sgn(x) = \begin{cases} 1, & sentence\ x\ is\ in\ result\ of\ task\ 1 \\ 0, & others \end{cases} \tag{11}$$

We use the Discourse Facet answer in Task 1B to provide a reference information for sentence extraction.

5. RST-feature: Rhetorical Structure Theory (RST) is the notion of rhetorical relation, a relation existing between two non-overlapping text spans called nucleus (N) and satellite (S). Text coherence in RST is assumed to arise due to a set of constraints and an overall effect that are associated with each relation. The constraints operate on the nucleus, on the satellite, and on the combination of nucleus and satellite. We call each sub-string cut by punctuations as a simple sentence. Using the RST-software we developed ourselves, we can get the RST-score of each simple sentence, then we have RST-score of a sentence as followed.

$$S_{rst} = \sum_{j=1,N} Sims_{rst-j} \tag{12}$$

where $Sims_{rst-j}$ is the RST-score of simple sentences, N is the total number of simple sentences in a sentence.

Structured summary extraction.

With the features above, we combine them to get a better summary result. A simple and efficient way is to combine them by a linear formula as shown below:

$$score_i = \omega_1 S_{level-i} + \omega_2 S_{length-i} + \omega_3 S_{position-i} + \omega_4 S_{spans-i} + \omega_5 S_{rst-i} \tag{13}$$

where ω_j indicates feature weight.

In Task 2, we need to generate a structured summary of the RP from the cited text spans of the RP. The length of the summary should not exceed 250 words. Besides, Task 2 pays more attention to the summary extracted from the third part, so we change the first person of the extracted sentences to third person. In order to extract a high-quality structured summary, we make full use of the prior knowledge that structured summary contains four parts: Introduction, Methods, Results and Conclusion. So we use the Discourse Facet to help extract the summary sentences. We will extract two or three sentences for each part of the summary if exists. Furthermore, we remove redundant candidate sentences. We use the following algorithm 1 to extract summary sentences.

```
for paper in Test-Set:
convert xml formed paper to txt, including title document merging of paper and cited text spans
stop word removing
input file generation for hLDA modeling
calculate scores of five features
while length ≤ 250
    extract sentence i according to feature scoring
    if sentence i is not redundant and length <= 250
    add i to candidate set
    person transformation
```

Algorithm 1 Feature-based summary extraction

To find the best use of hLDA level features, we also proposed two methods to extract level feature sentences. The first one is that, we ignore the clusters of the tree, only use the level feature score to choose best-N sentences. The other one is that each step extracts one sentence from one cluster in the first half of all clusters and adds it to the summary until the summary length is 250. We call the first one as ScoreDesc, the second one as In First Half Path.

5 Experiments

5.1 Task 1

Task 1A.

There are 5 runs that we submitted. From Run1 to Run4, we used the above mentioned methods respectively. Then, we got the performance of training dataset as followed in Table 7. In Run5, we used the SVM Method. And the accuracy we got in training set is 80.59% as a closed testing.

Method	P	R	Fs
Voting 1.0	0.07627	0.18881	0.10865
Voting 2.0	0.08898	0.22028	0.12676
Jaccard Focused	0.09675	0.23951	0.13783
Jaccard Cascade	0.0911	0.22552	0.12978

Table 7. Task 1A results of training dataset

We also have tested our systems on the testing dataset with the golden standard and got the results as in Table 8.

Method	P	R	Fs
Voting 1.0	0.05735	0.16887	0.08562
Voting 2.0	0.05735	0.16887	0.08562
Jaccard Focused	0.05824	0.1715	0.08696

Jaccard Cascade	0.05376	0.15831	0.08027
SVM	0.02222	0.08179	0.03495

Table 8. Task 1A results of testing dataset

From Table 7 and Table 8, we can see that there isn't much difference among the first 4 methods. Although the performance of SVM on training dataset is good, its performance on the testing dataset is very poor. We think that the major reason comes from the shortage of training data. In spite of this, we still set it as one of our system runs. Because we thought that this is an important direction. Later maybe we can improve this method using other strategies like semi-supervised or unsupervised machine learning with more unlabeled data.

After more detailed analysis of the results, we can find two major problems. One is choosing too much sentences, in which the citation text in standard answer contains only one fitful sentence, but we chose more sentences. We got the right answer with the price of more error sentences included. The other is partial answer. For instance, there are 3 sentences in standard answer covering the two classes of features, yet we found only 1 and lost 2 of them with 3 error sentences covering only one class of features. Although there may exist some relevance between the Citation Text and Reference Text in our answers, the standard answers are much better with good precision and complete coverage. Our system cannot achieve this status. We need better methods to locate the best answer accurately and cover all aspects of the citation text.

Task 1B.

We tried all methods in the results from Task 1A, then got the best performances by Voting Method. At last, we submit 6 runs. The first 4 runs are using Voting Method respectively in the results of Task 1A from rule-based methods. We used Fusion Method in Run5. Table 9 shows our experiments of the training data. As for Run6, we used the Voting Method for all SVM results in Task 1A. Table 10 shows their performances on the testing dataset.

Task 1A Method	Best Run	Precision
Voting 1.0	Voting Method	0.6977401
Voting 2.0	Voting Method	0.69491525
Jaccard Focused	Voting Method	0.6920904
Jaccard Cascade	Voting Method	0.7005649
Fusion Method		0.7062146

Table 9. Task 1B results of training dataset

Task 1A Method	Best Run	Precision
Voting 1.0	Voting Method	0.7526881
Voting 2.0	Voting Method	0.7562724
Jaccard Focused	Voting Method	0.7491039
Jaccard Cascade	Voting Method	0.7562724
SVM	Voting Method	0.7598566
Fusion Method		0.7598566

Table 10. Task 1B results of testing dataset

As we can see from Table 9 and Table 10, generally speaking, the best run is Voting Method. Next best is High Frequency Word Rule. The other methods get almost the same precision. The Voting Method is the results combining Subtitle Rule, High Frequency Word Rule and SVM classifier. So it gets the best precision as our anticipation. Although the performance of SVM in Task 1A is poor, using its result for Task 1B is not too bad.

As to the errors, our system may give a wrong decision of the facet, or cover the right answer but with added errors, or cover only part of the answer. The major reason is that the input from Task 1A of the Reference Text in our system has a great difference from that of the standard answer. Our classification methods are based on information contained in Citation Text and Reference Text, thus the quality of the Reference Text can make a great effect on the performance of facet classification.

5.2   Task 2

Our experiment is based on a hypothesis that the training dataset and the testing dataset have similar structures. Thus we can use the parameters learned from the training dataset to the testing dataset evaluation. After adequate experiments of the training dataset, we choose five different parameter values to calculate the testing dataset and get five runs for submission. The Manual ROUGE values of some experiments on the training set are shown in Table 11.

The results show that, definitely the sentence position feature achieves the best run. However, the level feature is the worst. The golden standard summary provided by CL-SciSumm 2016 includes abstract of the reference paper and the summary from the reference span. Sentence position and Cited text spans feature choose sentence from this point, so they get the best precision as our anticipation. Level feature aims to choose sentence from latent topics of the paper. And it is very difficult for unsupervised hLDA to catch correctly the facet information of the sentences just as human pre-defined. So the level feature does not achieve the best result. But, we also did the following experiments to find out the value of cluster message for summary extraction.

We test the different sentence choosing method for level feature using both ScoreDesc Method and In First Half Path Method, Table 12 shows our experiments. From the result we can learn that compared with the ScoreDesc algorithm, the In First Half Path algorithm achieves a better result. Thus we believe that the clusters modeled by unsupervised hLDA could implicate some latent topic messages, although they are not directly matched to the pre-defined five facets, which leads to the poor performance in this pre-defined structured summarization task. But we think that it possibly will work better for other open domains without pre-defined structures.

	ω_1	ω_2	ω_3	ω_4	ω_5	ROUGE-1 F	ROUGE-L F
0	0	1	1	1	0	0.4237	0.3762
1	0	1	1	0	0	0.4628	0.4174
2	1	0	9	0	0	0.3602	0.3202
3	1	0	9	9	0	0.3926	0.3511
4	0.5	1	9	0	0	0.4026	0.3651
5	1	0	0	0	0	0.1770	0.1426
6	0	1	0	0	0	0.3114	0.2588
7	0	0	1	0	0	0.5099	0.4682
8	0	0	0	1	0	0.4449	0.3987
9	0	0	0	0	1	0.2913	0.2399

Table 11. The ROUGE values for training dataset

method	ROUGE-1 F	ROUGE-L F
Score Desc	0.1770	0.1426
In First Half Path	0.2754	0.2447

Table 12. ROUGE values of different sentence choosing method for level feature

Finally, we choose the top five parameters in Table 11 to model the testing data, and got the following answers submitted, detailed in Table 13.

Run	ROUGE-1 F	ROUGE-L F
1	0.5272	0.4881
2	0.4708	0.4238
3	0.4378	0.3931
4	0.4200	0.3685
5	0.3879	0.3451

Table 13. ROUGE values of selected answer for testing data.

6   Conclusion and Future Work

Our system has tried to add some semantic information like word vector, doc vector and word distributions in hLDA tree to improve the citance linkage and summarization performance. Yet the result isn't very satisfied. Our future work is to find some better ways to mine and use more semantic features for citance linkage. As to summarization, we will try to add more predefined semantic features to unsupervised hLDA model and sentences combination and compression for better summary sentences. Furthermore, we will try to find a better method to choose least sentences covering most information.

Acknowledgements

This work was supported by the National Natural Science Foundation of China under Grant 91546121, 61202247, 71231002 and 61472046; EU FP7 IRSES MobileCloud Project (Grant No. 612212); the 111 Project of China under Grant B08004; Engineering Research Center of Information Networks, Ministry of Education; Beijing Institute of Science and Technology Information; CapInfo Company Limited.

References

1. Wan, X., Yang, J., Xiao, J.: Using Cross-Document Random Walks for Topic-Focused Multi-Document. In: IEEE / Wic / ACM International Conference on Web Intelligence, pp. 1012-1018. (2006).
2. García, J., Laurent, F., Gillard, O. F.: Bag-of-senses versus bag-of-words: comparing semantic and lexical approaches on sentence extraction. In: TAC 2008 Workshop - Notebook papers and results. (2008).
3. Bellemare, S., Bergler, S., Witte, R.: ERSS at TAC 2008. In: TAC 2008 Proceedings. (2008).
4. Conroy, J., Schlesinger, J. D.: CLASSY at TAC 2008 Metrics. In: TAC 2008 Proceedings. (2008).
5. Zheng, Y., Takenobu, T.: The TITech Summarization System at TAC-2009. In: TAC 2009 Proceedings. (2009).
6. Annie, L., Ani, N.: Predicting Summary Quality using Limited Human Input. In: TAC 2009 Proceedings. (2009).
7. Darling, W.M.: Multi-document summarization from first principles. In: Proceedings of the third Text Analysis Conference, TAC-2010. NIST (Vol. 150). (2010).
8. Kokil, J., Muthu, K.C., Sajal, R., Min-Yen, K.: Overview of the 2nd Computational Linguistics Scientific Document Summarization Shared Task (CL-SciSumm 2016). In: The Proceedings of the Joint Workshop on Bibliometric-enhanced Information Retrieval and Natural Language Processing for Digital Libraries (BIRNDL 2016), Newark, New Jersey, USA. (2016).
9. Genest, P., Lapalme, G., Québec, M.: Text Generation for Abstractive Summarization. In: TAC 2010 Proceedings. (2010).
10. Jin, F., Huang, M., Zhu, X.: The THU Summarization Systems at TAC 2010. Text Analysis Conference. (2010)
11. Abu-Jbara, A., Radev, D.: Coherent citation-based summarization of scientific papers. In: Meeting of the Association for Computational Linguistics: Human Language Technologies, pp. 500-509. Portland, Oregon (2010).
12. Zhang, R., Ouyang, Y., Li, W., Zhang, R., Ouyang, Y., Li, W.: Guided Summarization with Aspect Recognition. In: TAC 2011 Proceedings. (2011).
13. Marina, L., Natalia, V.: Multilingual Multi-Document Summarization with POLY. In: Proceedings of the MultiLing 2013 Workshop on Multilingual Multi-document Summarization. (2013).
14. Steinberger, J.: The UWB Summariser at Multiling-2013. In: Proceedings of the MultiLing 2013 Workshop on Multilingual Multi-document Summarization. (2013).
15. Ardjomand, N., Mcalister, J.C., Rogers, N.J., Tan, P.H., George, A.J., Larkin, D. F.: Multilingual Summarization: Dimensionality Reduction and a Step Towards Optimal Term Coverage. In: Multiling 2013 Workshop on Multilingual Multi-Document Summarization, pp. 3899-3905. (2013).
16. Anechitei, D.A., Ignat, E.: Multi-lingual summarization system based on analyzing the dis-course structure at MultiLing 2013. In: Proceedings of the MultiLing 2013 Workshop on Multilingual Multi-document Summarization. (2013).
17. El-Haj, M., Rayson, P.: Using a Keyness Metric for Single and Multi Document Summarisation. Multiling 2013 Workshop, ACL. (2013).
18. Fattah, M.A.: A hybrid machine learning model for multi-document summarization. Applied Intelligence, 40(40), 592-600. (2014).
19. Zhang, R., Li, W., Gao, D., Ouyang, Y.: Automatic twitter topic summarization with speech acts. IEEE Transactions on Audio Speech & Language Processing, 21(3), 649-658. (2013).
20. Xu, Y. D., Zhang, X. D., Quan, G. R., Wang, Y. D.: MRS for multi-document summarization by sentence extraction. Telecommunication Systems, 53(1), 91-98. (2013).
21. Arora, R., Ravindran, B.: Latent dirichlet allocation based multi-document summarization. In: The Workshop on Analytics for Noisy Unstructured Text Data, pp. 91-97. ACM. (2008)
22. Krestel, R., Fankhauser, P., Nejdl, W.: Latent dirichlet allocation for tag recommendation. In: ACM Conference on Recommender Systems, pp. 61-68. (2009).
23. Griffiths, T.L., Steyvers, M., Blei, D.M., Tenenbaum, J.B.: Integrating topics and syntax. In: Advances in Neural Information Processing Systems, 17, 537--544. (2010).
24. Blei, D.M., Lafferty, J. D.: Dynamic topic models. In: Proceedings of the 23rd international conference on Machine learning, pp. 113--120. (2006).
25. Wang, C., Blei, D.M.: Decoupling Sparsity and Smoothness in the Discrete Hierarchical Dirichlet Process. Advances in Neural Information Processing Systems 22. In: Conference on Neural Information Processing Systems 2009. Proceedings of A Meeting Held 7-10 December 2009, Vancouver, British Columbia, Canada, pp. 1982-1989. (2009).

26. Teh, Y.W., Jordan, M.I., Beal, M.J., Blei, D.M.: Hierarchical dirichlet processes. Journal of the American statistical association. (2012).
27. Blei, D.M., Griffiths, T.L., Jordan, M.I.: The nested Chinese restaurant process and bayesian nonparametric inference of topic hierarchies. Journal of the ACM, 57(2), 87-103. (2010).
28. Celikyilmaz, A., Hakkani-Tur, D.: A Hybrid Hierarchical Model for Multi-Document Summarization. ACL 2010, Proceedings of the, Meeting of the Association for Computational Linguistics, July 11-16, 2010, Uppsala, Sweden, pp. 815-824. (2010).
29. Ren, Z., De Rijke, M.: Summarizing Contrastive Themes via Hierarchical Non-Parametric Processes. International ACM SIGIR Conference on Research and Development in Information Retrieval, pp. 93-102. ACM. (2015).
30. Elkiss, A., Shen, S., Fader, A., Güne&#x f; Erkan, States, D., Radev, D.: Blind men and elephants: what do citation summaries tell us about a research article?. Journal of the American Society for Information Science & Technology, 59(1), 51-62. (2008).
31. Mikolov, T., Chen, K., Corrado, G., Dean, J.: Efficient estimation of word representations in vector space. Computer Science. (2013).
32. Le, Q. V., Mikolov, T.: Distributed representations of sentences and documents. Computer Science, 4, 1188-1196. (2014).
33. Heng, W., Yu, J., Li, L., Liu, Y.: Research on Key Factors in Multi-document Topic Modelling Application with HLDA. Journal of Chinese Information Processing, 27(6): 117–127. (2013).

NEAL: A Neurally Enhanced Approach to Linking Citation and Reference

Tadashi Nomoto

[1] National Institute of Japanese Literature
[2] The Graduate University of Advanced Studies (SOKENDAI)
nomoto@acm.org

Abstract. As a way to tackle Task 1A in CL-SciSumm 2016, we introduce a composite model consisting of TFIDF and Neural Network (NN), the latter being a adaptation of the embedding model originally proposed for the Q/A domain [2, 7]. We discuss an experiment using a development data, results thereof, and some remaining issues.

1 Introduction

This paper provides an overview of our efforts to tackle Task 1A at CL-SciSumm 2016, whose stated goal is to locate part of a reference paper (RP) most relevant to a given citation made by a citing paper (CP). To give an idea of what it is about, consider Figure 1.

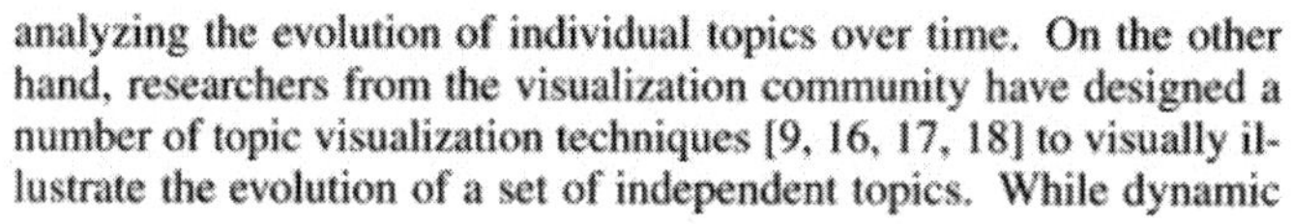

> analyzing the evolution of individual topics over time. On the other hand, researchers from the visualization community have designed a number of topic visualization techniques [9, 16, 17, 18] to visually illustrate the evolution of a set of independent topics. While dynamic

Fig. 1. An example of citation in a scientific publication [3].

In it, you have a sentence that reads:

> On the other hand, researchers from the visualization community have designed to a number of topic visualization techniques [9,16,17,18] ...

Your job is to find passages in the relevant literature (what the authors call 9, 16, 17, and 18), which are most pertinent to the sentence in question. (We denote a passage in referred-to papers linked with a citation by a *citation target* or simply *target*, below and throughout the paper.)

As a way to solve the task, we work with a hybrid of two models: one that is based on TFIDF and another on a single layer Neural Network (NN). Formally, the present approach looks like the following.

$$\sigma(d, r) = \lambda h(d, r) + (1 - \lambda)t(d, r) \tag{1}$$

where h represents a neural network and t a TFIDF based model; d is a citation instance and r a sentence in RP.[3] For a given citation instance d, we rank every sentence r in RP in accordance with σ (while dismissing those with two or less words) and select *two* highest ranked sentences as a target for d. We then remove redundancies in the output with an MMR-like measure: we take a candidate sentence off the output if its similarity with those preceding it exceeds a certain threshold (γ). Thus, the number of the output sentences will be further cut down to one in case they are found to contain redundancies. In the final run, we set γ to 0.24 and λ to 0.1. We call the current setup as 'a neurally enhanced approach to linking citation and reference,' or NEAL for short. Our adding the TFIDF component to NN in σ is meant to compensate for the latter's inability to handle exact word matches effectively due to the low dimensionality of hidden layers into which word features are mapped [9].

One significant consequence of using NN is that it will relieve us from the drudgery of contriving every feature that one needs to train a classifier on: NN learns by itself whatever feature it finds necessary to satisfy an objective function.

In what follows, we discuss the NN portion of σ, which is basically an adaptation of the neural embedding models [2, 1, 7, 8] to the current task. We built the TFIDF part based on statistics collected from the final test data that CL-SciSumm 2016 released.

2 Predicting Similarity with Neural Network

The job of NN is to provides a scoring function h that favors a true target over a false one: that is, to build a function that ensures that $h(d, r^+) > h(d, r^-)$, where r^+ denotes a true target (a sentence humans judged as a target) and r^- a false target (i.e., a sentence not selected as a target). We define h by:

$$h(d, r) = \mathbf{G}(d)^\top \mathbf{F}(r), \tag{2}$$

where $\mathbf{G}(d)$ denotes a vector derived from d and $\mathbf{F}(r)$ a vector from r, through word embedding. In order for d's similarity with its true target (r^+) to be always higher than that with a false target (r^-) [2, 7], we require the following constraint hold for $\mathbf{G}(d)$ and $\mathbf{F}(r)$:

$$\forall_{i,j} \ \mathbf{G}(d_i)^\top \mathbf{F}(r_j^+) > 0.1 + \mathbf{G}(d_i)^\top \mathbf{F}(r_j^-),^4$$

which is tantamount to:

$$\text{minimize:} [0.1 - \mathbf{G}(d_i)^\top \mathbf{F}(r_j^+) + \mathbf{G}(d_i)^\top \mathbf{F}(r_j^-)]_+,$$

Figure 2 gives a general picture of how we arrive at $\mathbf{G}(d)^\top \mathbf{F}(r)$. We start at the bottom, with inputs that represent d and r. We initially translate every word in a citation instance and target into word indices ranging from 0 to 15,456, which will be assembled into a binary vector, where the presence or absence of word is marked with 1 or 0 at an

---

[3] t is defined as: $t(d, r) = \dfrac{\mathbf{d} \cdot \mathbf{r}}{\|\mathbf{d}\| \, \|\mathbf{r}\|}$, where $\mathbf{d}$ and $\mathbf{r}$ are a vector of TFIDF weights representing d and r, respectively.

[4] '0.1' represents a margin we have taken from [2].

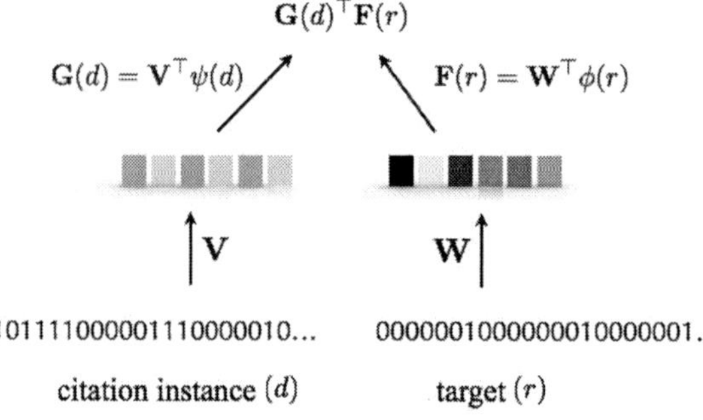

Fig. 2. Predicting Citation/Target Similarity Through Embedding

index assigned to it: thus having a 1 at the i-th unit means that a relevant input sentence contains a word indexed with i. We denote a binary vector for d so derived by $\psi(d)$ and that for r by $\phi(r)$. $[x]_+$ is a positive part of x.

We project $\psi(d)$ and $\phi(r)$ into two hidden layers, $\mathbf{V}$ and $\mathbf{W}$, through word embedding. $\mathbf{V}$ is an $N_v \times K$ matrix ($\in \mathbb{R}^{N_v \times K}$) and $\mathbf{W}$ an $N_e \times K$ matrix ($\in \mathbb{R}^{N_e \times K}$), with N_v, N_e, and K indicating lengths of $\psi(d)$, $\phi(r)$ and a hidden layer, respectively. (In the test run, we set $K = 30$ and $N_v = N_e = 15,457$.) Now we let

$$\mathbf{G}(d) = \mathbf{V}^{\top}\psi(d),$$

and

$$\mathbf{F}(r) = \mathbf{W}^{\top}\phi(r).$$

To determine values in $\mathbf{V}$ and $\mathbf{W}$, we launch an iterative training process. Suppose that we have the training data consisting of triples,

$$D = \{(d_i, r_i^+, S_i^-)\}_{i=1\ldots m}$$

with d_i representing a citing instance, r_i^+ a true target and $S_i^- = \{r_{i1}^-, \ldots, r_{in}^-\}$ indicating a set of false targets for d_i. For each $(d_i, r_i^+, S_i^-) \in D$, we do the following.

1. For each $r_i^- \in S_i^-$, perform a stochastic gradient descent (SGD) to minimize:

$$[0.1 - \mathbf{G}(d_i)^{\top}\mathbf{F}(r_i^+) + \mathbf{G}(d_i)^{\top}\mathbf{F}(r_i^-)]_+$$

2. Ensure that columns of $\mathbf{W}$ and $\mathbf{V}$ are all normalized.

We developed training data from the 'Development-Set-Apr8' dataset (henceforth, DSA) [5], which produced 4,608 training instances. We trained the model over 10 epochs, meaning that it went through 46,080 training instances. We performed SGD using an optimization algorithm known as AdaGrad-RDA, a regularized version of AdaGrad [4].[5]

---

[5] [6] developed a variant of LSTM to address an essentially same problem as discussed here, which could serve as a possible replacement of the embedding model the present model employs.

3 Evaluation

Prior to the actual run, we conducted an experiment using DSA to see how well NEAL works. The dataset comes with ten topic clusters, each of which consists of one reference paper and a number of papers that contain citations to that paper. Following a leave-one-out cross validation scheme, we split DSA into two blocks, one containing nine topic (RP) clusters and the other one. We used the former for training NEAL (or h, to be precise), and tested it out on the remaining block. The performance was measured by ROUGE-LCS, which produces the normalized length of a longest, possibly discontiguous, string of words shared by predicted and true targets. Figure 3 illustrates a citation and a corresponding target (made available by CL-SciSumm 2016 as part of gold standard data). The area shaded in green represents a citation in CP and one in yellow a target in RP. A citation and a target can span an arbitrary number of sentences.

```
Citance Number: 2 | Reference Article:  C02-1025.txt | Citing Article:  C10-2167.txt |
Citation Marker Offset:  ['65'] | Citation Marker:  Chieu et al., 2002 | Citation Offset:
['65'] | Citation Text:  <S sid ="65" ssid = "25">In statistical methods, the most popular
models are Hidden Markov Models (HMM) (Rabiner, 1989), Maximum Entropy Models (ME) (Chieu
et al., 2002) and Conditional Random Fields (CRF) (Lafferty et al., 2001).</S> | Reference
Offset:  ['4'] | Reference Text:  <S sid ="4" ssid = "4">In this paper, we show that the
maximum entropy framework is able to make use of global information directly, and achieves
performance that is comparable to the best previous machine learning-based NERs on MUC6
and MUC7 test data.</S> | Discourse Facet:  Results_Citation | Annotator:
```

Fig. 3. Citation and Target

Table 1. Dry-Run Test Set (DSA)

RP	#CP	$|D|$	$|E|$	$|T|$	RP	#CP	$|D|$	$|E|$	$|T|$
C02-1025	18	4,142	8,284	23	N04-1038	20	4,190	8,340	24
C08-1098	22	3,824	7,648	29	P06-2124	12	4,367	8,734	18
C10-1045	13	3,621	7,242	33	W04-0213	13	4,327	8,654	18
D10-1083	11	4,329	8,658	18	W08-2222	9	4,519	9,038	9
E09-2008	10	4,526	9,052	8	W95-0104	25	3,413	6,826	39

Some statistics on DSA are shown in Table 1. RP refers to a reference paper, #CP the count of relevant citing papers, $|D|$ the the number of instances used for training. $|E|$ indicates how many instances are processed over the entire span of epochs, and $|T|$ the number of citation-target pairs we used to test NEAL. Term and document frequencies (to be used for $t(\cdot, \cdot)$ in σ) were collected from DSA. K, N_v and N_e – parameters that define the shape of NN – were set to 30, 15,457, and 15,457 (we also used the settings for the final run).

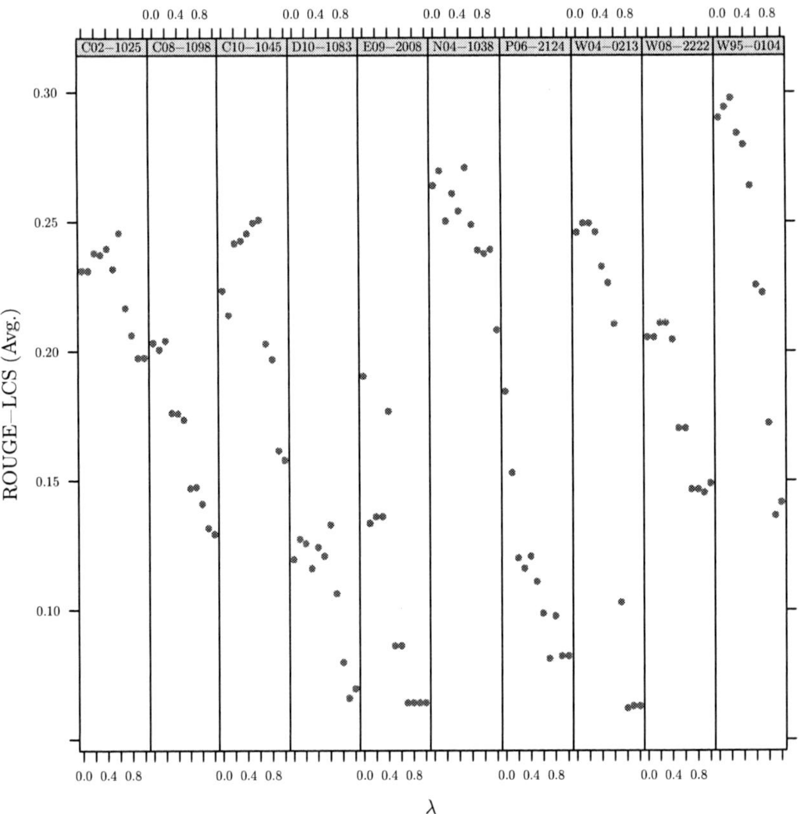

Fig. 4. Plot of Performance vs. λ for DSA. The title of each strip (e.g. C02-1025) represents a designator for a given reference paper, which has 9 to 25 citing papers (Table 1).

The test proceeded as follows. For a given pair c and t of citation and target, we rank each sentence r in RP in accordance to $\sigma(c, r)$ and select top one or two candidates as a possible target (call it g). We then determine ROUGE-LCS for g and its true target t, average scores over a entire set of citation-target pairs that belong to a particular topic cluster. Our computation of ROUGE-LCS, however, did not include tokens with less than 5 characters and those with more than 9 characters, as they were often found to be garbled and unintelligible. We also chose not to use stemming or filter out stop words.

Figure 4 shows by cluster performance of NEAL. The horizontal axis denotes the value of λ and the vertical axis ROUGE-LCS scores. That λ affects the overall performance is clearly seen. Note that NEAL reduces to TFIDF at $\lambda = 0$, and turns into a full-fledged NN at $\lambda = 1$. Thus if NEAL's performance peaks at $\lambda > 0$, it will mean that NN-enabled NEAL performs better than TFIDF, or else is just as good as the latter. We observe in Figure 4 a general tendency for the performance to climb highest somewhere between 0 and 1, suggesting the superiority of NN over TFIDF, although there are notable exceptions at E09-2208 and P06-2124 where the score peaks at $\lambda = 0$.

Table 2. Peak Performance (PP) and λ

RP	PP	λ	RP	PP	λ
C02-1025	0.2457	0.6	N04-1038	0.2710	0.5
C08-1098	0.2040	0.2	P06-2124	0.1845	0.0
C10-1045	0.2507	0.6	W04-0213	0.2494	0.2
D10-1083	0.1329	0.6	W08-2222	0.2109	0.3
E09-2008	0.1904	0.0	W95-0104	0.2977	0.2

Table 2 lists values of λ at which we had peak performance for each of the topic clusters. 8 out of 10 clusters had peak performance at $\lambda > 0$, demonstrating that enabling NN generally leads to a gain in performance.

4 Final Remarks

We have presented what we call a 'neurally enhanced approach to linking citation and reference' or NEAL, describing in some detail what machinery is involved and what we found in an experiment with the development data. The results appear to suggest a moderate impact of the neural network (NN) on the overall performance. But NEAL's performance against TFIDF is far from impressive. We suspect that its somewhat lackluster performance may have been caused by our inability to clearly demarcate true and false targets: there are some words that appear both in true and false targets, which could easily derail the classifier.

Moreover, one could argue that the results of our experiment with DSA substantiated a concern that [9] expressed about NN's handling of word matches: at $\lambda = 1$ when NN was decoupled from TFIDF completely, its performance plummeted to the ground.

As a way out, [9] suggests that we use the following instead of Equation (2).

$$h(d, r) = \mathbf{G}(d)^\top \mathbf{F}'(r, d)$$

$\mathbf{F}'$ is an $\mathbf{F}$ conditioned on d, where you turn off all the words in $\phi(r)$ that are not found in $\psi(d)$. What makes the idea interesting is that it points to a possibility of embedding t into h by slightly modifying the way we build $\phi(r)$ and $\psi(d)$. While it is not clear at the moment how it plays out, we believe that the idea is definitely worth a try, and something we like to explore in the future work.

References

1. Bordes, A., Usunier, N., Weston, J., Yakhnenko, O.: Translating Embeddings for Modeling Multi-relational Data. N pp. 1–9 (2013)
2. Bordes, A., Weston, J., Usunier, N.: Supervised Embedding Models. In: ECML PKDD 2014 (2014)
3. Cui, W., Liu, S., Tan, L., Shi, C., Song, Y., Gao, Z., Tong, X., Qu, H.: Textflow: Towards better understanding of evolving topics in text. IEEE Transactions on Visualization and Computer Graphics 17(12), 2412–2421 (2011)
4. Duchi, J.: Adaptive Subgradient Methods for Online Learning and Stochastic Optimization . Journal of Machine Learning Research 12, 2121–2159 (2011)
5. Jaidka, K., Chandrasekaran, M.K., Rustagi, S., Kan, M.Y.: Overview of the 2nd computational linguistics scientific document summarization shared task (cl-scisumm 2016). In: The Proceedings of the Joint Workshop on Bibliometric-enhanced Information Retrieval and Natural Language Processing for Digital Libraries (BIRNDL 2016). Newark, New Jersey, USA (2016)
6. Palangi, H., Deng, L., Shen, Y., Gao, J., He, X., Chen, J., Song, X., Ward, R.: Deep Sentence Embedding Using the Long Short-Term Memory Networks. In: Proceedings of the 31st International Conference on Machine Learning, Lille, France, 2015. JMLR: W&CP volume 37. (2015), http://arxiv.org/abs/1502.06922
7. Weston, J., Bengio, S., Usunier, N.: Large scale image annotation: Learning to rank with joint word-image embeddings. Machine Learning 81, 21–35 (2010)
8. Weston, J., Bordes, A., Yakhnenko, O., Usunier, N.: Connecting Language and Knowledge Bases with Embedding Models for Relation Extraction. Empirical Methods in Natural Language Processing (October), 1366–1371 (2013), http://aclweb.org/anthology/D/D13/D13-1136.pdf
9. Weston, J., Chopra, S., Bordes, A.: Memory Networks. International Conference on Learning Representations pp. 1–14 (2015), http://arxiv.org/abs/1410.3916

Trainable Citation-enhanced Summarization of Scientific Articles

Horacio Saggion, Ahmed AbuRa'ed, Francesco Ronzano

TALN - DTIC
Universitat Pompeu Fabra
Barcelona, Spain
horacio.saggion@upf.edu,ahmed.aburaed@upf.edu,francesco.ronzano@upf.edu

Abstract. In order to cope with the growing number of relevant scientific publications to consider at a given time, automatic text summarization is a useful technique. However, summarizing scientific papers poses important challenges for the natural language processing community. In recent years a number of evaluation challenges have been proposed to address the problem of summarizing a scientific paper taking advantage of its citation network (i.e., the papers that cite the given paper). Here, we present our trainable technology to address a number of challenges in the context of the 2nd Computational Linguistics Scientific Document Summarization Shared Task.

1 Introduction

During the last decade the amount of scientific information available on-line increased at an unprecedented rate with recent estimates reporting a new paper published every 20 seconds [17]. In this scenario of scientific information overload, researchers are overwhelmed by an enormous and continuously growing number of articles to consider in their research work: from the exploration of advances in specific topics, to peer reviewing, writing and evaluation. In order to cope with the growing number of relevant publications to consider at a given time, automatic text summarization is a useful technique [23]. However, generic text summarization techniques may not work well in specialized genres such as the scientific genre and domain specific techniques may be needed [25, 26]. Scientific publications are characterized by several structural, linguistic and semantic peculiarities. Articles include common structural elements (title, authors, abstract, sections, figures, tables, citations, bibliography) that often require specific text processing tools. Additionally, scientific documents have specific discourse structure [27, 12]. Another important aspect of scientific papers is their network of citations that identifies links among research works, making them also particularly interesting from the social viewpoint. Although citation counts had been used to assess some aspects of research output for a long time, citation semantics has started to be exploited in several context including opinion mining [28, 1] and scientific text summarization [18, 2].

Considering the urgent need for new, automated approaches to browse and aggregate scientific information, in recent years a number of natural language processing challenges have been proposed: the Biomedical Summarization Task (BioSumm2014) carried out in the context of the Text Analysis Conferences[1] provided a forum for researchers interested in exploring the summarization of clusters of documents where one of the documents is a *reference paper* and the rest of the documents in the cluster are *citing papers* which cite the reference paper. In particular, the BioSumm2014 evaluation released a dataset consisting of 20 collections of annotated papers (i.e., clusters), each one including a reference article and 10 citing articles. Similarly, a pilot task on summarization of Computational Linguistic papers was proposed in 2014 [8]. Unfortunately, none of the evaluation contests provided with official evaluation results.

In this paper, we report our efforts to develop a system to participate in the CL-SciSumm 2016 evaluation [9] which is a renewed effort to address the challenges proposed in 2014. In a nutshell, participants were given a set of clusters, each one composed of n documents where one is a reference paper (RP) and the n-1 remaining documents are referred to as citing papers (CPs) since they cite the reference paper. Participants have to develop automatic procedures to perform the following tasks:

- **Task 1A**: For each citance (i.e., a reference to the RP), identify the spans of text (cited text spans) in the RP that most accurately reflect the citance.
- **Task 1B**: For each cited text span, identify what **facet** of the paper it belongs to, from a predefined set of facets, namely: Aim, Hypothesis, Implication, Results or Method.
- **Task 2**: Finally, an optional task consists on generating a structured (of up to 250 words) summary of the RP from the cited text spans of the RP.

In the rest of this paper we first present related work on summarization of research articles to then explain how we have addressed the different summarization tasks.

2 Related work

Although research in summarization can be traced back to the 50s [14] and although a number of important discoveries have been produced in this area, automatic text summarization still faces many challenges given its inherent complexity. Scientific text summarization is of paramount importance and scientific texts were automatic summarization's first application domain [14, 5]. Several methods and techniques have been already reported in the literature to produce text summaries by automatic means [23]. Summarization of scientific documents has been addressed from different angles: in [26] summarization is treated as

---

[1] `http://www.nist.gov/tac/2014/`
`BiomedSumm/`

a rhetorical classification task where each sentence in an input text is classified as belonging to specific rhetorical categories (background, objective, etc.). Although the approach is interesting from the point of view of document interpretation, it is not a proper summarization task since no summary of the input is produced. [25] addressed the summarization problem as one of information extraction and text generation: the idea behind the approach is that a number of important concepts and relations should be extracted from text in order to create a summary independently of the particular scientific domain of the text. In recent years new generations of scientific summarization approaches have emerged which take advantage of the citations that a research paper has in order to extract and summarize its main contributions [19]. Methods to improve the coherence of the generated citation summaries use sentence classification to decide what type of information a sentence is conveying [1].

3 Transforming the Source Documents into GATE Language Resources

CL-SciSumm 2016 Challenge organizers have provided training data structured in clusters of reference and citing papers together with manual annotations indicating for each citance to the reference paper, the facet of this citance and the text span(s) in the reference paper that best represent the citance. In order to properly analize the provided training and testing documents, we transformed the provided clusters into GATE documents. Given the manual annotations provided in text files, we automatically annotated the training set by creating in the reference paper a *References Annotation* set which contains the annotations corresponding to the text spans being cited by each citing paper. On the other hand, an *Annotation set* for the citances in each of the citing papers was also created. The link between citing paper annotations and reference paper annotations is implemented through a unique identifier (a concatenation of citance number, reference paper, citing paper, and annotator).

Such annotations are helpful in order to retrieve the necessary information from the documents. In this way, in each citing paper we are able to identify for each sentence that belongs to a citance, which are the sentences of the corresponding reference paper that most accurately reflect the citance. Thanks to this information, we can build pairs of matching sentences (Citing Paper Sentence, Reference Paper Sentence) and associate to each pair the facet that each annotator considers the citation is referring to (see Task 1B).

An example of the representation can be seen in Figure 1 where it is shown a reference paper (on the left side of the Figure) annotated with information from the citing papers (on the right side of the Figure).

3.1 Text Processing

Each document was annotated using processing resources from the GATE system [15] and the SUMMA library [22]. Additionally, and in order to further

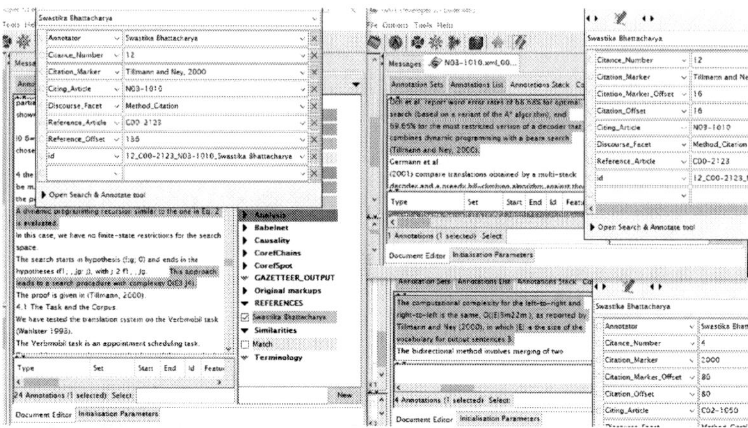

Fig. 1. GATE GUI represenation of the annotations of a reference paper (left side) and two citing papers from the same cluster (right side).

enrich the documents, some components from the freely-available Dr Inventor library[2] (DRI Framework) were used [21]. The GATE system was used to tokenize, sentence split, part of speech tag, and lemmatize each document. The SUMMA library was used to produce normalized term vectors for each document (see Section 5). Although the Dr Inventor's library produces very rich information, for the experiments we present here we rely only on its rhetorical sentence classification capabilities. The DRI Framework classify each sentence of a paper as belonging to a rethorical category of scientific discourse among: Approach, Background, Challenge, Outcome and FutureWork. In particular, the framework computes for each sentence the probability the sentece has to belong to each rhetorical category. See [6] for details about the corpus used for training the classifier. For each sentence in the reference paper, we computed the cosine similarity between its sentence vector (see Section 5) and the vectors corresponding to the sentences citing the reference paper in the citing articles. These values were stored in the reference paper for further processing.

4 Method

In order to identify reference paper text spans for each citance (Task 1A), we modeled pairs of reference and citance sentences as a feature vector. Then, we used such pair representation to enable the training of distinct binary classification algorithms tailored to determine whether they are a match.

On the other hand we used the same representation of pairs of sentences for identifying to what facet of the reference paper a cited text span belongs to

---

[2] http://backingdata.org/dri/library/

(Task 1B): we classified each pair of sentences in one out of 5 predefined facets Aim, Hypothesis, Implication, Results or Method.

To this end, we relied on the Weka machine learning framework [29]. We evaluated the performance of six classification algorithms: SMO, Naive Bayes, J48, Lazy IBK, Decision table and Random Forest for both tasks. We performed 10-fold cross validation experiments with the training data in order to decide which algorithm to use during testing.

In the remainder of this Section, we describe the set of sentence pair features we used, and motivate their relevance with respect to the characterization of sentences similarity. When presenting the features, we group subsets of related features in the same subsection (Position features, Similarity features, etc.).

4.1 Position Features

We exploited the following set of position related features for both Task 1A (text spans for citance sentence) and 1B (the facet such text span belongs to):

- *Sentence position* (**sentence_position**): the normalized position of the sentence in the reference paper.
- *Sentence section position* (**sentence_section_position**): the normalized position of the sentence in the section of the reference paper.
- *Facet position* (**facet_aim, facet_hypothesis, facet_implication, facet_method** and **facet_result**): five features were generated to indicate which facet a cited text span belongs to. Binary values were calculated by analyzing the reference paper sentence's section title and looking for any words which could indicate the feature facet: aim, hypothesis, implication, method or result. The value of the feature is 1 for section titles containing a word that indicate such facet and 0 otherwise.

4.2 WordNet Semantic Similarity Measures features

The following set of Semantic Similarity features were exploited for task 1A (text spans for citance sentence) only with the exception of the cosine similarity which was used for both task 1A and task 1B. We used WS4J (WordNet Similarity for Java) library which includes several semantic relatedness algorithms that rely on WordNet 3.0. Given a pair of sentences (reference and citance), we retrieve all the synsets associated to nouns and verbs in each one of them. Then, by considering all the pairs of synsets belonging to different sentences, we compute similarity values between citance sentence and reference sentence as follows[3]:

- *Path similarity* [7] (**path_similarity**): The shorter the path between two words/senses in WordNet, the more similar they are.

---

[3] We calculated similarity values between each token in the citance sentence and each and every token in the reference sentence. Finally averaging all the similaries for the given sentence pair.

- *JCN similarity* [10] (**jiangconrath_similarity**): the conditional probability of encountering an instance of a child-synset given an instance of a parent synset.
- *LCH similarity* [11] (**lch_similarity**): the length of the shortest path between two synsets for their measure of similarity.
- *LESK similarity* [3] (**lesk_similarity**): Similarity of two concepts is defined as a function of the overlap between the corresponding definitions (i.e., their WordNet glosses).
- *LIN similarity* [13] (**lin_similarity**): The Similarity between A and B is measured by the ratio between the amount of information needed to state the commonality of A and B and the information needed to fully describe what A and B are.
- *RESNIK similarity* [20] (**resnik_similarity**): The probability of encountering an instance of concept c in a large corpus.
- *WUP similarity* [30] (**wup_similarity**): The depths of the two synsets in the WordNet taxonomies, along with the depth of the lowest common subsumer.
- *Cosine similarity* (**cosine_similarity**): The cosine similarity between the normalized vectors of the two sentences in the instance pair (this computation is different from the other similarity features).

4.3 Rhetorical Category Probability Features

We exploited the following set of rhetorical features for both task 1A (text spans for citance sentence) and 1B (the facet which the text span belongs to):

- *Rhetorical Category Probability* (**probability_approach, probability_background, probability_challenge, probability_future_work** and **probability_outcome**): five features were exploited to represent the probability of the reference text span to belong to such facet (from the Dr Inventor corpus and computed from the Dr Inventor library).

We also added both the reference sentence string and the citance sentence string to the set of features and then converted them to word vectors by using WEKA (i.e., bag-of-words).

4.4 Matching Citations to Reference Papers

The training data was prepared as follows: positive instances of the problem were the pairs of sentences from the citance which where matched with cited text spans from the references (according to information given in the gold annotations). Negative instances, instead, were pairs of sentences from citances to identified cited text spans which were not annotated as matches by the annotators (complementary information). As a consequence we casted the Task 1A as a binary classification problem where we decide for each pairs of citance sentence and reference paper sentence whether they match or not, or in other words whether the reference paper sentence reflects the reason of that specific

Class	Precision	Recall	F-Measure
Sent. Match	0.674	0.293	0.408
Sent. NoMatch	0.916	0.982	0.948
Averages	0.888	0.904	0.886

Table 1. J48 performance on testing data (10-fold cross validation) for the citance/reference matching problem (Task 1A). Last row of the table contains weighted average values.

citations. These procedure, which was decided upon to reduce the number of negative cases, produced 3,786 instances unevenly distributed (3,356 no matches vs 430 matches). After testing several algorithms from WEKA, we opted for the J48 implementation of decision threes. Ten fold cross-validation results are presented in Table 1.

4.5 Citation Purpose Identification

The training data was prepared as follows: similarly to the previous task, pairs of citing sentences and matched cited sentences (according to the gold annotations) were used to create instances. The facet of each instance was also given by the gold standard. This procedure produced just 432 instances with the following distribution: Aim (72), Implication (26), Result (76), Hypothesis (1), Method (257). After testing several algorithms from WEKA, we opted for the Support Vector Machines (SMO) implementation provided by the tool. We used polynomial Kernels and performed no parameter optimization due to time constraints. Ten fold cross-validation results are presented in Table 2.

Class	Precision	Recall	F-Measure
Aim	0.886	0.861	0.873
Implication	0.875	0.808	0.84
Results	0.971	0.895	0.932
Hypothesis	0.0	0.0	0.0
Method	0.929	0.969	0.949
Averages	0.924	0.926	0.924

Table 2. SMO performance on testing data (10-fold cross validation) for the facet identification problem (Task 1B). Last row of the table contains weighted average values.

5 Summarizing Scientific Articles

In order to summarize the reference paper by taking into account how it is mentioned in the citing papers, we combined information from the reference and citing papers. We have implemented, using the resources of the freely available text summarization library SUMMA [22, 24], a series of sentence relevance features, all numeric, which are used to train a linear regression model following the methodology that was already used in [4].

In addition to rich set of features provided by the DRI Framework, document processing for summarization is carried out with SUMMA on reference and citing papers. More specifically, the following computations with the library are carried out to enable the summarization of scientific documents:

- Each token (i.e., lemma) is weighted by its term frequency* inverted document frequency, where inverted document values are computed from training data previously analysed (test documents in the CL-SciSumm 2016 dataset);
- For each sentence a vector of terms and normalized weights is created using the previously computed weights;
- For the title, a single vector of terms and normalized weights is also created (*title vector*);
- Using the normalized sentence term vectors in the whole document a centroid vector of terms is computed (*document centroid*);
- Using the normalized sentence term vectors of the abstracts a centroid vector of terms is computed (*abstract centroid*);
- All vectors corresponding to sentences citing the reference paper (from all citing papers) are used to create a centroid (*citances vector*).

The following is the set of sentence relevance features we have used for training a linear regression summarization system. Note that all text-based similarities we mention are the result of comparing two vectors using the cosine similarity function implemented in SUMMA. The reference paper features are as follows:

- *Sentence Abstract Similarity (**abs_sim**)*: the similarity of a sentence to the author abstract;
- *Sentence Centroid Similarity (**centroid_sim**)*: the similarity of a sentence to the document centroid (e.g., the average of all sentence vectors in the document);
- *First Sentence Similarity (**firt_sim**)*: the similarity of a sentence to the title vector;
- *Position Score (**position_score**)*: the SUMMA implementation of the position method where sentences at the beginning of the document have high scores and sentence at the end of the document have low scores;
- *Position in Section Score (**in_sec**)*: an score representing the position of the sentence in the section of the document. Sentences in first section get higher scores, sentences in last section get low scores;
- *Sentence Position in Section Score (**in_sec_sent**)*: a position method applied to sentences in each section of the document (sentence at the beginning of the section get higher scores and sentences at the end of the section get lower scores);
- *Normalised Cue-phrase Score(**norm_cue**)*: we produce a normalized score for each sentence which is the total number of cue-words in the sentence

divided by the total number of cue-words in the document. We have relied on [26] formulaic expressions to implement our cue-phrase gazetteer lookup procedure;

- *TextRank Normalized Score (**textrank_score**)*: the SUMMA implementation of the TextRank algorithm [16] but with a normalization procedure which yields values for sentences between 0 and 1.

The cluster-based features are as follows:

- *Citing Paper Maximum Similarity (**cps_max**)*: each reference paper sentence vector is compared (using cosine) to each citance vector in each citing paper to obtain the maximum possible cosine similarity;
- *Citing Paper Average Similarity (**cps_avg**)*: the average cosine similarity between a reference paper vector and all citance vectors in the cluster is produced;
- *Citing Paper Citances Similarity (**cps_sim**)*: the similary of the sentence vector to the centroid of the citance vectors.

The approach taken to score sentence is to produce a cumulative score of the weighted values of summarization features $f_1, ... f_n$ using the following formula:

$$score(S) = \sum_{i=0}^{n} w_i * f_i \qquad (1)$$

with S as the sentence to score, f_i as the value of feature i and w_i as the weight assigned to feature i. As we stated before, the weights of each features in the formula are learned from training data. We fit a linear regression model using the 10 testing documents from the provided annotated document for a total of 2,585 instances. The target numerical value to learn is computed from two sources (giving rise to two different systems): On the one hand, we compute the similarity of each reference paper sentence (i.e. vector) to the combined vectors of texts fragments identified as the annotators as cited text spans; on the other hand, we compute the similarity of each reference paper sentence (i.e. vector) to a vector of the community-based summary provided for training by the organizers. Table 3 shows the weights of the features learnt by the linear regression implementation from WEKA [29].

6   The Final System

The final system was assembled as follows. Given a cluster of documents with reference and citing papers, the following pipeline was applied for tasks 1A and 1B.

1. The documents were annotated with the citance information (no matched reference sentences were annotated);
2. All the document processing algorithms were applied to reference and citing papers as described in Section 3.1 and the features computed;

Feature	Citance Relevance	Community Relevance
abs_sim	0.0843	-0.0751
centroid_sim	0.7231	0.5795
cps_avg	0.0	0.3984
cps_max	0.1111	0.0
cps_sim	0.27	0.2806
first_sim	-0.0359	0.1801
in_sec	0.0	-0.0287
norm_cue	0.0921	0.1497
position_score	0.0483	0.0611
textrank_norm	-0.1622	-0.2251
Corr.	0.88	0.78

Table 3. Linear regression learnt weights for two conditions: relevance to cited text spans and relevance to a community-based summary. Last row indicates correlation cohefficient of the model (in 10-fold cross-validation).

3. Instances were created using a citance sentence from each citing paper and each sentence from the reference paper;
4. The instances were sent to the matching classifier which returned a match/no match class and a confidence value;
5. The matched instances according to the previous steps were sent to the facet classifier to obtain the predicted citation facet.

Two runs were produced for tasks 1A and 1B. In one run, all matched sentences for a given citance were returned. In a second run, only top matches (with higher confidence) were returned. In order to produce the summaries for each cluster, summarization features were computed using the procedure described in Section 5, and SUMMA was exploited to score and extract top scored sentences based on formula (1). Two 250-word text summaries were produced per cluster using the models described in Section 5.

7 Outlook

In this paper, we have presented the techniques used to participate in the Computational Linguistics Summarization challenge. We have relied on competitive text processing and summarization tools to compute features to create rich document representations for dealing with the proposed tasks. Our approach is supervised combining evidence from several sources. Due to time limitations we could not carry out an exhaustive performance and feature analysis on test/development data, which we intend to carry out as future work. We look forward to know the official results of the evaluation so as to better understand the pros and cons of our approach.

Acknowledgements

This work is (partly) supported by the Spanish Ministry of Economy and Competitiveness under the Maria de Maeztu Units of Excellence Programme (MDM-

2015-0502), the TUNER project (TIN2015-65308-C5-5-R, MINECO/FEDER, UE) and the European Project Dr. Inventor (FP7-ICT-2013.8.1 - Grant no: 611383).

References

1. Abu-Jbara, A., Ezra, J., Radev, D.R.: Purpose and polarity of citation: Towards nlp-based bibliometrics. In: HLT-NAACL. pp. 596–606 (2013)
2. Abu-Jbara, A., Radev, D.: Coherent citation-based summarization of scientific papers. In: Proceedings of the 49th Annual Meeting of the Association for Computational Linguistics: Human Language Technologies - Volume 1. pp. 500–509. HLT '11, Association for Computational Linguistics, Stroudsburg, PA, USA (2011)
3. Banerjee, S., Pedersen, T.: An adapted lesk algorithm for word sense disambiguation using wordnet. In: Computational linguistics and intelligent text processing, pp. 136–145. Springer (2002)
4. Brügmann, S., Bouayad-Aghab, N., Burga, A., Carrascosa, S., Ciaramella, A., Ciaramella, M., Codina-Filba, J., Escorsa, E., Judea, A., Mille, S., Müller, A., Saggion, H., Ziering, P., Schütze, H., Wanner, L.: Towards content-oriented patent document processing: Intelligent patent analysis and summarization. World Patent Information 40, 30–42 (2015)
5. Edmundson, H.P.: New methods in automatic extracting. J. ACM 16(2), 264–285 (Apr 1969)
6. Fisas, B., Ronzano, F., Saggion, H.: A Multi-Layered Annotated Corpus of Scientific Papers. In: Calzolari, N., Choukri, K., Declerck, T., Grobelnik, M., Maegaard, B., Mariani, J., Moreno, A., Odijk, J., Piperidis, S. (eds.) Proceedings of the Tenth International Conference on Language Resources and Evaluation (LREC 2016). European Language Resources Association (ELRA), Paris, France (may 2016)
7. Hirst, G., St-Onge, D.: Lexical chains as representations of context for the detection and correction of malapropisms. WordNet: An electronic lexical database 305, 305–332 (1998)
8. Jaidka, K., Chandrasekaran, M.K., Elizalde, B.F., Jha, R., Jones, C., Kan, M.Y., Khanna, A., Molla-Aliod, D., Radev, D.R., Ronzano, F., Saggion, H.: The computational linguistics summarization pilot task. In: Proceedings of TAC 2014 (2014)
9. Jaidka, K., Chandrasekaran, M.K., Rustagi, S., Kan, M.Y.: Overview of the 2nd Computational Linguistics Scientific Document Summarization Shared Task (CL-SciSumm 2016). In: To appear in the Proceedings of the Joint Workshop on Bibliometric-enhanced Information Retrieval and Natural Language Processing for Digital Libraries (BIRNDL 2016) (2016)
10. Jiang, J.J., Conrath, D.W.: Semantic similarity based on corpus statistics and lexical taxonomy. arXiv preprint cmp-lg/9709008 (1997)
11. Leacock, C., Chodorow, M.: Combining local context and wordnet similarity for word sense identification. WordNet: An electronic lexical database 49(2), 265–283 (1998)
12. Liakata, M., Teufel, S., Siddharthan, A., Batchelor, C.R., et al.: Corpora for the conceptualisation and zoning of scientific papers. In: LREC (2010)
13. Lin, D.: An information-theoretic definition of similarity. In: ICML. vol. 98, pp. 296–304 (1998)
14. Luhn, H.P.: The automatic creation of literature abstracts. IBM J. Res. Dev. 2(2), 159–165 (Apr 1958)

15. Maynard, D., Tablan, V., Cunningham, H., Ursu, C., Saggion, H., Bontcheva, K., Wilks, Y.: Architectural Elements of Language Engineering Robustness. Journal of Natural Language Engineering – Special Issue on Robust Methods in Analysis of Natural Language Data 8(2/3), 257–274 (2002)
16. Mihalcea, R., Tarau, P.: TextRank: Bringing order into texts. In: Proceedings of EMNLP-04and the 2004 Conference on Empirical Methods in Natural Language Processing (July 2004)
17. Munroe, R.: The rise of open access. Science 342(6154), 58–59 (2013), `https://www.sciencemag.org/content/342/6154/58.full`
18. Qazvinian, V., Radev, D.R.: Identifying non-explicit citing sentences for citation-based summarization. In: ACL 2010, Proceedings of the 48th Annual Meeting of the Association for Computational Linguistics, July 11-16, 2010, Uppsala, Sweden. pp. 555–564 (2010)
19. Qazvinian, V., Radev, D.R.: Identifying non-explicit citing sentences for citation-based summarization. In: Proceedings of the 48th annual meeting of the association for computational linguistics. pp. 555–564. Association for Computational Linguistics (2010)
20. Resnik, P.: Using information content to evaluate semantic similarity in a taxonomy. arxiv preprint cmplg/9511007 (1995)
21. Ronzano, F., Saggion, H.: Dr. inventor framework: Extracting structured information from scientific publications. In: Discovery Science - 18th International Conference, DS 2015, Banff, AB, Canada, October 4-6, 2015, Proceedings. pp. 209–220 (2015)
22. Saggion, H.: SUMMA: A Robust and Adaptable Summarization Tool. Traitement Automatique des Langues 49(2), 103–125 (2008)
23. Saggion, H., Poibeau, T.: Automatic text summarization: Past, present andfuture. In: Poibeau, T., Saggion, H., Piskorski, J., Yangarber, R. (eds.) Multi-source, Multilingual Information Extraction and Summarization. Springer Verlag, Berlin (2013)
24. Saggion, H.: Creating summarization systems with SUMMA. In: Proceedings of the Ninth International Conference on Language Resources and Evaluation (LREC-2014), Reykjavik, Iceland, May 26-31, 2014. pp. 4157–4163 (2014)
25. Saggion, H., Lapalme, G.: Generating indicative-informative summaries with sumum. Comput. Linguist. 28(4), 497–526 (Dec 2002)
26. Teufel, S., Moens, M.: Summarizing scientific articles: Experiments with relevance and rhetorical status. Comput. Linguist. 28(4), 409–445 (Dec 2002)
27. Teufel, S., Siddharthan, A., Batchelor, C.: Towards discipline-independent argumentative zoning: evidence from chemistry and computational linguistics. In: Proceedings of the 2009 Conference on Empirical Methods in Natural Language Processing: Volume 3-Volume 3. pp. 1493–1502. Association for Computational Linguistics (2009)
28. Teufel, S., Siddharthan, A., Tidhar, D.: Automatic classification of citation function. In: Proceedings of the 2006 conference on empirical methods in natural language processing. pp. 103–110. Association for Computational Linguistics (2006)
29. Witten, I.H., Frank, E., Hall, M.A.: Data Mining: Practical Machine Learning Tools and Techniques. Morgan Kaufmann Publishers Inc., San Francisco, CA, USA, 3rd edn. (2011)
30. Wu, Z., Palmer, M.: Verbs semantics and lexical selection. In: Proceedings of the 32nd annual meeting on Association for Computational Linguistics. pp. 133–138. Association for Computational Linguistics (1994)

Association for Computational Linguistics
209 N. Eighth Street
Stroudsburg, Pennsylvania 18360

ISBN 978-1-5108-2511-6